Mr. *and* Mrs. Grassroots:

How Barack Obama, Two Bookstore Owners, and 300 Volunteers Did It

By John Presta

To Barb,

To another Obama
fan, thanks,

John Presta

Mr. and Mrs. Grassroots: How Barack Obama, Two Bookstore Owners, and 300 Volunteers Did It

Published by
The Elevator Group
Paoli, Pennsylvania

Copyright © 2010 by John Presta

Library of Congress Control Number: 2009941893

Limited Edition Hardcover: ISBN 978-0-9819719-2-6
Trade Paperback: ISBN 978-0-9819719-6-4

First Edition Printing January 2010

Jacket and interior design by Stephanie Vance-Patience.
Published in the United States by The Elevator Group.

Photo credits: John and Michelle Presta and friends, unless otherwise noted.

This book was printed in the United States.

To order additional copies of this book, contact:
The Elevator Group
PO Box 207
Paoli, PA 19301
www.TheElevatorGroup.com
610-296-4966 (p) • 610-644-4436 (f)
info@TheElevatorGroup.com

Dedication

This is dedicated to the one I love, my wife,
my love, and my life, Michelle,
who blessed my life with purpose,
direction, and fun.
— *John Presta*

Prologue

This book was a long, difficult road, but it was a worthwhile journey.

One thing I would like to clear up is any implication that without Michelle and me, Barack Obama would have been nowhere. We were one element and one story in his meteoric rise. We were not "the" most important element in his rise and not the only one.

Michelle and I were one of many, many people and one of many, many factors.

We were one element, but the most unlikely of all the stories that will be written over the next several hundred years about Barack Obama. Moreover, it was a story that needed telling because it is American History, and I tell it with great pride and joy.

⌒

With apologies to Barack Obama, I am paraphrasing his victory speech in Iowa 2008 to reflect my feelings on this book being published.

⌒

They said this day would never come that this book would be published.

They said our sights in composing this book were set too high and that this book would only appeal to a regional audience and not a national audience. And they were right. It appeals to an international audience, too.

They said that this material is inextricably personal and focused on the author's struggles, not Mr. Obama's.

They said that this book would not resonate with readers outside of Chicago or those who have first-hand experience running a small business like us. But on this great day, at this defining moment in American history and in the history of American book publishing, this publisher has done what the cynics said we could not do.

They said we could not get it published.

They said, "Oh no you can't." And we said, "Oh Yes We Can."

They said that it would not sell. That is a question I cannot answer at this time, but to all the doubters I say, "Together We Can," and I say, "Of Course We Can" and, come to think of it, I resoundingly say, "Yes We Can."

— John Presta

Table of Contents

CHAPTER ONE

The Introduction to Barack Obama: 'The First Time Ever I Saw His Face'

~

My name is John Presta, and I have been a volunteer for Barack Obama for the past ten years, since the year 2000. I reside in Chicago. The 2008 Presidential campaign was my fifth Obama campaign. We were four for five. In baseball, I would be batting .800. Not bad. But that one defeat in 2000, when Obama ran for the 1st Congressional District seat in the U.S. House of Representatives, always stuck in my craw. I sometimes think that was the motivation for all of the work that I've done for him since. I did not ever want to feel that way again.

The moment I first saw Barack Obama is frozen in time. I even remember the exact date and the exact time. The date was March 7, 2000, and the time was 6:45 pm. I was standing at the doorway of Bethany Union Church, surrounded by 600 of my closest friends, and I was nervous.

I was not nervous because I was about to meet a future President of the United States. Who could know? No, I was nervous because I was caught up in the moment. I had organized an event with my wife Michelle and our friend Susan Burnet, the East Beverly Association, the Beverly Improvement Association, the League of Women Voters, and the Citizens Information Service. If I had an inkling of the historical significance of all this, I would have really been nervous.

That was not it. It was the excitement of the evening. The months of planning leading to this evening. And what a crowd.

I vividly recall looking behind me, and I recognized Dan Shomon, Barack Obama's campaign manager in 2000. Dan Shomon was standing next to a rather striking figure that was handsome, well-dressed, smiling, shaking hands with all of those around him. A man who looked you in the eye. A man who was comfortable in his own skin. It was one of those quick glances. I waved rather quickly at Dan, and I remember he called me over. I did not have much time, but I quickly ran over to him. It took me a couple of minutes, but I made my way through the crowd to him.

"John Presta, I want you to meet Barack Obama," Dan said.

"A pleasure to meet you," I said.

And as was always his charming style, Obama said, "The pleasure is mine. I have heard so much about you, your wife and your bookstore." I recall that he looked me straight in the eye. He has that special talent of making you feel you are the only person in the room. That is a gift. Obama is a "What You See is What You Get" politician or, in the current vernacular, WYSIWYG.

I thanked him and led him to the front tables where he would be seated with the other three candidates running for the 1st Congressional District seat.

We saw him again at the St. Patrick's Southside Irish parade on Sunday, March 12th, when he marched with then State Representative Tom Dart and a contingent of southside politicians. We have a photo where he spotted Michelle and me in the crowd, pointed at us, and then hugged us both.

We saw him again the next day, on Monday, March 13th, six days after the forum, at Café Luna in our community, at what was billed as a "Meet and Greet." There was no donation required. A number of elected officials were there, and, frankly, the elected officials outnumbered the "regular folk" like us. It was that evening that I became convinced he would become President of the United States one day. So did Michelle.

Obama had that special something. I saw it as a seven year old when John F. Kennedy was elected as President of the United States in 1960. He was electrifying. He was youthful and energetic and inspiring. JFK got me excited about politics and government. Obama inspired me that evening much like JFK inspired me many years earlier. JFK had this 'indomitable spirit.' As I discovered, so did Obama.

How It All Began

Our story starts in late 1999 when, through a series of interesting circumstances, Michelle and I met Dan Shomon, who managed Obama's campaign for Illinois Senate and was then managing Obama's campaign for the 1st Congressional District in the U.S. House of Representatives. We got involved with Obama's campaign against an "entrenched" Democratic incumbent Congressman, Bobby Rush. We got involved through our community bookstore, Reading on Walden on Walden Parkway, in the heart of Chicago's Beverly community on the southwest side of Chicago.

Bookstores were an important part of Barack Obama's life, such as the bookstore that Michelle and I owned. We were a small bookstore, and when I tell people that we were small, they invariably ask, "What do you mean small? Like two or three thousand square feet?"

"No, small. Really small," I would say. The space that we rented was less than 800 square feet. Less than half of that space was selling space. Less than 400 square feet of selling space, but we packed them in: books, magazines, sidelines, enthusiasm, and excitement. I suppose we symbolically packed them in, too. We generally stocked more books than stores five times our size. A customer and friend, Stan Plona, who was a publisher's representative for the University of California/Princeton Fulfillment Services, Inc. for many years, told us about a new store that opened in The Plaza in Evergreen Park. He told us, "They have a nice store, but you definitely have more books and more of the right books. Kind of a cold reception there, not like you guys. You are warmer and friendlier."

We were an ordinary bookstore, run by ordinary people, that made extraordinary achievements. We believed in ourselves, and we believed that books are not luxuries, but essentials. We believed that books have transformative value and that books teach valuable lessons about life, such as being in physical health, spiritual health, and financial health, and how those three are intertwined. Physical health leads to spiritual health and can often lead to financial rewards.

Our bookstore was a tremendous community resource. We would get streams of telephone calls asking questions about books, the community, events and anything else that might be on their minds, or just what is going on. We would also be "directory assistance."

"What's the phone number of that flower shop next to you?"

Sometimes we would get telephone calls about safety issues. "Is this community still safe?" "Have you heard about this incident?" Or we would receive questions about a rumor circulating in the community.

Michelle and I have had an impact on the lives of so many people during our time on Walden Parkway. We were involved with Mayor Daley's Chicago Alternative Policing Strategy, known as the CAPS program, from its inception in 1992. We led marches against crime and drugs in the community with our neighbors and friends. We helped to organize the successful Beverly Hills/Morgan Park Garden Walk, sponsored by the East Beverly Association. We sponsored our Book Discussion Group at the local library. We sponsored exciting author events. We were the first 'Obama for Illinois' volunteer group, and we were a model for grassroots volunteerism that helped to elect Barack Obama to the United States Senate. We were known throughout the community as the Beverly Area 'Obama for Illinois' volunteers. The Obama for Illinois website listed us as a place to pick up yard signs and obtain campaign materials.

We paid our bills on time, and Michelle kept a cleanly organized bookstore. Our reputation was that we had the knack to have the "hot book" in stock, and we always seemed to have a sense of when something was hot. We would get several frantic telephone calls, usually from a cell phone.

"You got any '*Marley and Me*[1]' left. You know. The book about the world's worst dog."

"Yes," I would say.

The caller would say, "Great. I have been looking all over. How many you got buddy?"

"How many you want?" I would say.

"Hold me three copies. I'll be there in a half hour."

Our sales per square foot were well above average. Do not ask me what. I know they were good. We only had less than 400 square feet of selling

---

1   Grogan, John. *Marley & Me: Life and Love with the World's Worst Dog.* New York: Morrow, 2005.

space, but we "packed a wallop." We were a small, cozy bookstore, but without the comfortable seating. That would eliminate several hundred books and, at that size, we would have less than 400 square feet of selling space.

We simply took bookselling to a different level because we possessed high energy and a positive spirit. We made "bookselling" fun, and Michelle made bookselling even more fun, not only for me, but also for our customers. Every book that we sold brought us great joy, not only because of the money it brought, but because of the deeper implications that book will have to the customer.

Where will this book take them? *Oh, The Places You'll Go.*[2] The journey and adventure of reading a book is still a thrill for me. Will this book transform this person's life? Will a discovery be made that will allow this person to fulfill a dream or maybe start a dream? Or lead someone to the White House? Wow, the places we'll go.

Powell's Bookstore in the Hyde Park community was a store that Barack Obama frequented. He became friendly with the bookstore owner at Powell's, Brad Jonas. Women and Children First was another bookstore that had significance in his rise. Obama's favorite bookstore to shop and browse was 57th Street Books in Hyde Park. When his book, *The Audacity of Hope: Thoughts on Reclaiming the American Dream,*[3] came out in 2006, he did his first book signing at 57th Street Books to a ticket-only, packed crowd, a scene that was repeated at many more bookstores throughout Chicago and the suburbs.

The Book and The Candidate

The book that bonded us with Barack Obama was *Dreams from My Father: A Story of Race and Inheritance.*[4] I had always believed that the book should and would find an audience. I just did not know when. I believed in the strength of Obama's book. While I believed in the strength of his book, I also believed in the strength of the man. It was

---

2   *Dr. Seuss. Oh, the Places You'll Go.* New York, NY. Random House Children's Books. 1990.
3   Obama, Barack. *The Audacity of Hope: Thoughts on Reclaiming the American Dream.* New York: Crown Publishers, 2006 (hereafter referred to as Obama, *The Audacity of Hope.*)
4   Obama, Barack. *Dreams from My Father: A Story of Race and Inheritance.* New York: Times Books, 1995 (hereafter referred to as Obama, *Dreams from My Father.*)

truly worthy, but it turned out that the book did indeed eventually find its audience through a series of circumstances that are incredible and now part of our American History. In large part, that is the nature of this book. How books connect, transform, and have an 'indomitable spirit.' While my book will focus on Obama's first book, this book will also focus on the importance of books in our everyday lives and why books have transformative value. Another focus of my book is the importance of independent booksellers to a community and the many contributions booksellers have made over the years. To state that independent bookstores are the foundations of their communities is no exaggeration.

I could not separate the book from the man. The book and the man took parallel paths. The book would be down, and the man would be down. The book would be up, and Obama would be up. Then the book would be re-issued, and the book would skyrocket, and so would the man. To this day, the book and the man have never returned to earth. They are in a different orbit.

And with Barack Obama as President of United States, historians will find the connections of a book, two bookstore owners, 300 friends and customers who volunteered to help elect him to the United States Senate. This is the story about how Obama's book and Obama the candidate were both launched onto the national scene in 2004.

A bookstore like Women and Children First in Chicago, owned by Linda Bubon and Ann Christopherson, was at the forefront of a key moment in the campaign for United States Senate when Obama received one of the most important endorsements in December 2003 from Congresswoman Jan Schakowsky. The Evanston Democratic Party, which endorsed Obama, is capable of delivering a large plurality of votes for candidates it gets behind. This endorsement strengthened and encouraged Obama because it meant his support was building slowly but surely.

Another significant bookstore located in Obama's Hyde Park community, Powell's Bookstore, and a bookstore owner, Brad Jonas, played a key role in the promotion and marketing of Barack Obama through the book, *Dreams from My Father*.

Our story is as much about the book, *Dreams from My Father*, as it is about Barack Obama. It is about our never giving up on Obama's book or Obama the candidate. After Dan Shomon told us, "Well, he's an author you know," Shomon ordered 20 copies. Shomon later commented, "I was wondering how many copies I would have to buy to get your support." None. That is not how it worked with us.

Before the election on March 21, 2000, Michelle and I both read the book and liked it. We started to feel a connection and closeness to Obama. I was especially touched about the relationship with his father. I felt empathy toward him.

When Obama lost the race to Congressman Bobby Rush on March 21, 2000, we ordered a dozen copies of *Dreams from My Father* and I asked Shomon to have Obama sign them, and he did. We placed the signed copies on the shelf, and you would have thought that they would have flown out of the store.

But, they did not sell at all. They just sat on the shelf. Michelle removed them, dusted them, and put them back on the shelf. Through the remainder of the year 2000, that is how it went.

And through the year 2001, Michelle removed them, dusted them, and put them back on the shelf.

And through the year 2002, Michelle removed them, dusted them, and put them back on the shelf.

And through the year 2003, Michelle removed them, dusted them, and put them back on the shelf.

Then on March 16, 2004, Barack Obama won the United States Senate Democratic primary. The next day those copies sold. All of them. If we had several hundred more, we would have sold them, too.

We never stopped believing in the book or the candidate.

This is the story of a book that would not die.

This is the story of a candidate that would not die.

The book and the candidate sold slowly, gradually, incrementally and, then all in one swift moment, sold and resonated suddenly.

Such was the rise of the book and of Barack Obama.

Change comes slowly, gradually, incrementally, and suddenly.

Those words, "President Barack Obama," make it a little easier to forget the pain of that defeat back in 2000. Well, a lot easier. I hardly ever think of that time except for the lessons it taught.

And those words. "President Barack Obama." I will simply never grow weary of those words.

Enjoy our story. It is something that Michelle and I, our 300 volunteers and our community will not soon forget.

Change comes slowly, gradually, incrementally, and suddenly.

CHAPTER 2

The Obscure State Senator, Barack Obama

~

In early fall 1999, our bookstore life went on as usual. We attended to our day-to-day business: meeting with publishing house representatives in person and on the telephone, in preparation for the all-important fall season and preparing mass mailings for the Christmas season. Somewhere along the line, we became familiar with this obscure state senator from Hyde Park, Barack Obama. It was more of knowing him through an evolution and not just one big thunderbolt.

Sales volume during the fourth quarter is a significant portion of a bookstore's revenues. That time between Thanksgiving and Christmas Eve is crucial to having a successful year. Every year the trick was to find the hot books and then be sure to have plenty of stock on hand. The "hot book" makes the difference between a modest profit and a modest loss.

That particular year, *Tuesdays with Morrie*[5] by Mitch Albom was number one on the nonfiction bestseller list and had been for nearly two years. This was an unusually long period for a book to remain only in hardcover. The book is a simple story of a sportswriter who visits his college mentor weekly. The college mentor is at death's door. Customers would often ask, "When will it be out in paperback?" and it was not a question that I could answer. As it turned out, the paperback came out in 2002, an unusually long time, but not without precedent.

5   Albom, Mitch. *Tuesdays with Morrie: An Old Man, a Young Man, and Life's Greatest Lesson.* New York: Doubleday, 1997.

Two other significant books were on the bestseller list. They were J.K. Rowling's first two Harry Potter books, *Harry Potter and the Sorcerer's Stone*[6] and *Harry Potter and The Chamber of Secrets*.[7] Both were in hardcover and priced under $20.00. These two books were the start of something big.

Finding the 'Hidden Gems'

As bookstore owners, hidden gems were what Michelle and I sought. As the years went on, we became more adept at finding those books, the hidden gems, and ordering enough of them so that we would meet demand.

In late 1999, it turns out, we found an unexpected "hidden gem," Barack Obama. We just did not know it yet! We had the Harry Potter books on our shelf before they became a phenomenon because for a brief time, the Harry Potter books failed to find their audience. That all changed quickly.

Change comes slowly, gradually, incrementally and suddenly.

We did not always find the hidden gems. Choosing the wrong book, we would find, meant that we would return boxes and boxes of books to the publishing houses, which translated into losses for the retail bookstore and the publishing house. It also meant a demand on our time that was unwelcome. If we spent too much time returning too many books, our attention would be diverted from our true love — chasing the right books for our bookstore and spending time with our booklover friends, our customers.

It did not mean we were afraid to return books. If a book did not sell within 90 days, the bookstore had the option of returning the book to the publisher for credit. With age and maturity, we improved in that vaunted bookselling skill: guessing.

During the many years we operated our bookstore on Walden Parkway, we judged our success neither by the cash register tally at the end of each day nor by the sales figures for the week, month, or quarter. It was an exciting time of our lives. Most days we would share something with our

---

6   Rowling, J. K., and Mary GrandPré. *Harry Potter and the Sorcerer's Stone*. New York: Arthur A. Levine Books, 1998.
7   Rowling, J. K., and Mary GrandPré. *Harry Potter and the Chamber of Secrets*. New York: Arthur A. Levine Books, 1999.

friends, get news about the latest in the lives of our customer's children, get the latest about work being done on our customer's house, or share a joke or a warm story.

Reading on Walden Bookstore was a legend by this time in 1999, as was our involvement in community policing.

Our community involvement began with a local not-for-profit group, the Beverly Area Planning Association (BAPA). The group had recently formed a committee, the BAPA Safety Committee, which organized in a short period of time in response to a brutal murder. The community expressed outrage at the murder of Ruth Ellen Church, 81, a longtime *Chicago Tribune* food editor and wine columnist. Her readers knew her as "Mary Meade." Ruth Ellen Church was discovered in her home after a series of break-ins in a four-block area on the southwest side of Chicago's Beverly community, police reported[8].

Involvement with this small group started with a series of break-ins at our store, which led to our involvement in the community.

"Community Policing," many of our friends and customers would say, was our middle name. Larry Stanton, Executive Director at the time of the Beverly Area Planning Association, called me "Mr. Crime." Before Mayor Richard M. Daley had officially announced and implemented the Community Policing program, we were already taking a proactive approach to solving community crime. We were a precursor to Chicago's implementation of the Community Policing program by organizing a neighborhood watch program, a court watch program, and an innovative graffiti-blaster program, which grew out of our frustration of trying to physically remove graffiti ourselves. The most important element of community policing is the beat meetings. Groups can solve community problems by first identifying problems and then implementing strategies in partnership with police to solve the problem.

"Together we can," was our motto. That was also a motto, we found later, that fit quite nicely into the Obama campaigns.

We had no idea at what was to come, becoming involved with a future President of the United States. The first African-American President. We would have "a ringside seat to American History." This involvement is what

---

8   Jodi Wilmore, "Ex-Tribune food editor killed in her South Side home:" [SOUTH SPORTS FINAL, C Edition]. 21 Aug. 1991, 4. *Chicago Tribune*.

led the Obama campaign to our humble little cozy bookstore.

It is still so hard for us to believe that we would meet Barack Obama and that in eight short years he would become the most powerful and well-known man on the planet. Our little cozy bookstore. Why our store of all the places? Why were we pursued so aggressively? Our initial response to the Obama campaign was lukewarm.

Hunting for hidden gems was something we loved to explore.

Barack Obama.

Barack Obama, the "Hidden Gem"

He was a hidden gem. Little did we know in late 1999 that this hidden gem would transform our lives and our nation in such a positive manner. Little did we know that Barack Obama would walk into our lives and we would forever be identified in our community as the "discoverers of Barack Obama."

We did hear rumors that fall of 1999 that our Congressman, Bobby Rush, would be challenged. Michelle and I were supporters of Bobby Rush. Not the working kind of supporters where we would spend time campaigning for him. He got our vote. Period.

After all, he voted our way on the issues. Why would it matter who took him on? Bobby Rush was the incumbent. Obama believed that Rush was politically weakened by running for mayor against Richard M. Daley in the spring of 1999 mayoral primary and losing.[9]

One reason for Rush's loss was because in early 1999, Chicagoans were generally satisfied with the direction Daley was taking the city. The State Legislature had already granted Daley free reign in the Chicago Public Schools, through what was the Chicago Public School Reform bill. Daley hired his former Budget Director, Paul Vallas, to be his first school CEO. Vallas was just beginning to hit his stride in changing the Chicago Public School System. The previous heads of the school system were typically PhDs in Education who tended to be more theoretical and less pragmatic. Paul Vallas was less theoretical and more pragmatic. Vallas had a background in finance and budgeting. During his tenure, Vallas turned around test scores, increased school

---

9   Rick Pearson, Tribune Political Writer. "2 MAY CHALLENGE RUSH FOR CONGRESSIONAL SEAT :[CHICAGOLAND FINAL Edition]." *Chicago Tribune* [Chicago, Ill.] 1 Aug. 1999, 3.

attendance and made peace with the Chicago Teachers Union — all difficult tasks.

Beautification had started to hit its stride with decorative medians, wrought iron fences, plantings in newly constructed parking lots, miles and miles of new roads and newly paved alleys. Construction was everywhere. Much of it started in 1996, when Chicago hosted the Democratic National Convention and Daley wanted to display the city. Chicago was booming economically. Daley's beautification programs, which included the planting of new trees on city parkways and the decorating of the medians on busy city streets, with colorful floral arrangements were changing the political landscape.

Congressman Rush tried to make safety an issue, but at this point Chicago's community policing program had been receiving national accolades for its participatory style of policing. This especially struck a chord in the African-American community, a place where Congressman Rush envisioned some strength, but where Mayor Daley's Community Policing program was getting praise nationally.

Congressman Rush tried to hammer away at the theme that Chicago's prosperity had not reached the lower classes, but this also failed to resonate with the voters. Neither the voters nor the media took Bobby Rush's candidacy seriously.

Once, a South Side minister claimed the Chicago Fire Department closed his church because he refused to endorse Daley. Rush called a press conference at the church, but the city countered with a long history of building code violations. Rush failed to check his facts, and this incident served to epitomize his failed campaign. In addition, Daley simply responded, "Why would I harass a church and a school as mayor?" Daley said, "All the things I have to do, I am going to harass a church?" [10]

Daley won reelection with more than 70% of the vote, including nearly 50% of the African American vote. Given Chicago's recent history, the African American total against an African American candidate was quite remarkable. Daley's popularity was reaching new heights.

An African-American insurgency candidacy required a bare minimum

---

10 Janita Poe, Tribune Staff Writer. Tribune staff writer Gary Washburn contributed to this report, "RUSH SAYS BASE UNDER FIRE MAYOR ACCUSED OF HARASSING BLACK CHURCHES :[NORTH SPORTS FINAL Edition]. " *Chicago Tribune* [Chicago, IL] 17 Dec. 1998, 3.

of 70% of the African-American vote to make it close, and over 90% to run away with it, assuming a large African-American voter turnout. It was under this cloud that State Senator Barack Obama decided to try to unseat a sitting Democratic Congressman. Rush was weakened politically by the 1999 mayoral primary challenge of Daley, therefore Obama reasoned that Rush was vulnerable and could be defeated. However, Rush was the incumbent, and it is tough to beat one, in spite of the weakening. While this reasoning made logical sense, it really made no political sense.

Chicago Sun Times columnist Steve Neal wrote many flattering pieces about Obama during the Congressional campaign. These pieces started on August 1, 1999. Steve Neal was one of my favorite columnists and, in my view, one of the most astute. Neal was clearly an early Obama fan, and he was not afraid to say it.

Thus were the rumors, fueled in large part by Steve Neal, that Rush would have serious opposition. I am sure I read the Neal columns, but it did not register with me. If an "entrenched incumbent" could be defeated in the Illinois 1st Congressional District, there must be a very good reason. However, Rush himself took out an "entrenched incumbent" in 1992 and defeated then-Congressman Charles Hayes. So it is possible to defeat one. Rush's victory then was an amazing feat, although corruption makes defeating an incumbent much easier. Rush defeated Hayes because he had been involved in the "check overdraft" scandal of the early 1990's.[11] There were no rumors about corruption surrounding Rush, although some voters referred to him as a "Black Panther," which was meant as a derogatory name.

Illinois' 1st Congressional District was traditionally a Democratic "safe" seat. The news that an obscure Illinois State Senator from Hyde Park, Barack Obama, would be taking on Congressman Bobby Rush failed to generate excitement in the District, especially without a taint of scandal or good gossip.

Obama acknowledged that he was "seriously considering" challenging Rush. He said that he expected "to make a final decision with respect to an

---

11   House Ethics Committee revealed that Hayes wrote 716 checks exceeding his account balance in a 39-month period. The Ethics Committee report was revealed prior to the 1992 primary election. Hayes lost to Rush 42 to 39 percent due to the House Ethics revelation. However, in 1993, the Justice Department cleared Hayes of any criminal wrongdoing for bouncing checks while he was a Member of the House.

exploratory committee in the next couple of weeks."[12]

In every campaign where a candidate challenges an incumbent like Rush, the challenger typically charges the incumbent with planting an opponent. State Senator Donne Trotter eventually jumped into the race, and he would be labeled by some Obama supporters as a "plant," although I never heard that charge directly from Dan Shomon or Barack Obama.

Obama's community involvement was striking as Executive Director of the Developing Communities Project that got involved in Altgeld Gardens. He fought the Chicago Housing Authority over the removal of asbestos in their apartments. He was involved in a group around that period called Calumet Community Religious Conference, which assessed the skills of unemployable workers and sought to place them in jobs.[13] Many people were surprised that someone with Obama's background would be working as a community organizer. As with much of his life, Obama took the journey on *The Road Less Traveled*.[14]

~

Obama took a road never traveled before when, two years after he enrolled in Harvard Law School, in February 1990, at age 28, he was elected President of the Harvard Law Review. He was the first African-American ever named to that post.[15]

According to the *Chicago Tribune*, in an article written by Michael J. Ybarra on February 2, 1990, being President of the Harvard Law Review was a forum for judges and scholars. It is also a high-powered springboard for aspiring lawyers. Its presidents usually go on to serve as a clerk for a judge on the U.S. Court of Appeals for a year and then as a clerk for one of the Justices of the United States Supreme Court. But, Obama said that he wanted to get back to community organizing and possibly run for political office. In an interview with Michael Ybarra of the *Chicago Tribune*, Obama brought up the themes that we identify with him, such as fighting for the powerless against the powerful and giving voice to the voiceless.

---

12 Rick Pearson, Tribune Political Writer. "2 MAY CHALLENGE RUSH FOR CONGRES-SIONAL SEAT: [CHICAGOLAND FINAL Edition]." *Chicago Tribune* [Chicago, IL] 1 Aug. 1999, 3.
13 6 SELF-HELP GROUPS GET GRANTS; [NATIONAL, C Edition] *Chicago Tribune*. Chicago, IL: Oct. 28, 1985. Pg. 7.
14 Peck, M. Scott. *The Road Less Traveled: A New Psychology of Love, Traditional Values, and Spiritual Growth*. New York: Simon and Schuster, 1978.
15 Michael J. Ybarra. "Activist in Chicago now heads Harvard Law Review: [NORTH SPORTS FINAL, C Edition]." *Chicago Tribune* [Chicago, IL]. 7 Feb. 1990, 3.

These were themes that would later emerge and that he would amplify.

Obama also interviewed with the *L.A. Times* and discussed his intention of entering public life, which was in line with what he stated many times on the campaign trail. He preferred the pursuit of public life to the pursuit of wealth.

In 1992, Obama directed Illinois Project VOTE!, a statewide voter registration and education campaign. Project VOTE! had the financial backing of Soft Sheen hair-care magnate Edward Gardner.[16] Project VOTE! was a collective of ten church-based community organizations dedicated to African-American voter registration.[17]

Obama is widely given credit for bringing out the vote through Project VOTE! for U.S. Senator Carol Mosley Braun and for helping then Governor Bill Clinton take the electoral votes from Illinois by coordinating the registration of over 150,000 new voters, mostly African-Americans. One of our friends, Harvey Mader, who was born on January 7, 1916, helped Illinois Project VOTE! as a volunteer, and he was impressed with this, fine young man, Barack Obama.

"Oh sure, I remember him well. Focused, organized and driven. Nice man, too. A progressive, too, I think," Mader told us. Mader was one of the first dedicated community activists we met. Voting and voter registration is his passion in life. He advocated for laws that made voting easy and simple. Mader's ultimate goal would have been "same day registration." Mader inspired us for political activism.

Mader met then-Professor Paul Wellstone during the late 1980's at his alma mater, Carleton College. Mader and Wellstone developed a close friendship, and when Wellstone decided to run for United States Senate in Minnesota in 1990, Harvey and his late wife Norma volunteered for Wellstone's successful campaign. Wellstone remained close friends with Harvey and Norma Mader until his untimely death in a plane crash on October 25, 2002.

U.S. Senator Carol Mosley Braun's election in 1992 was a historic event as she became the second African-American Senator since Reconstruction (Senator Brooke, a Republican from Massachusetts was the first).

---

16 Edward Gardner also resides in the Beverly community.
17 Vernon Jarrett. "'Project Vote' Brings Power to the People." Chicago Sun-Times August 11, 1992, FIVE STAR SPORTS FINAL, EDITORIAL: 23.

On February 10, 1993, Barack Obama was named in a *Chicago Tribune* article as one of 25 Chicagoans on the Road to Making a Difference.[18] In mid-1993, he joined the law firm of Davis, Miner, Barnhill & Galland. The firm is one of the best-known and most experienced firms in the country in large-scale voting rights cases. This practice, led by Judson Miner and which includes Jeffrey Cummings, has achieved important victories in race discrimination lawsuits challenging redistricting of Chicago's aldermanic districts and Illinois congressional districts.[19]

Obama also chaired the Chicago Annenberg Challenge as its first chairman and was a member of the board until 2001. The Annenberg Challenge was a $50-million philanthropic effort to reform the city's public schools.[20]

The summer of 1995 saw the release of Obama's book, *Dreams from My Father: A Story of Race and Inheritance.*[21] It received several good reviews, including the *L.A. Times.*[22]

Two small and seemingly minor events set the stage for Obama, unbeknownst to him in how they would affect his life.

1. June 1992: A campaigning Congressman Mel Reynolds, from the Illinois 2nd Congressional District, stops his car to talk to Beverly Heard, 16, and asks for her phone number. Shortly thereafter, she begins working for him, and they start a sexual relationship.

2. June 1994: Beverly Heard, now 18, confides to a next-door neighbor, Chicago police officer Ernest Wilson, that she and Reynolds had sex when she was 16. Police tape two phone calls between Heard and Reynolds where they discuss their sexual relationship and how he can get lewd photos of an underage girl. Heard then disappears to Tennessee, and police — and later, the jury —

---

18 25 Chicagoans on road to making a difference; [NORTH SPORTS FINAL,] Frank James. *Chicago Tribune.* Chicago, Ill.: Feb 10, 1993. Pg. 5.

19 Davis, Miner, Barnhill & Galland is the firm that was involved in the 19th Ward Remap fight, which proposed cutting off the East Beverly area from the 19th Ward.

20 The Chicago Annenberg Challenge gave money to BAPA for the Annenberg program, during Obama's term as Chairman, another involvement in our community where he developed later contacts.

21 Obama, *Dreams from My Father.*

22 MICHAEL HARRIS. "BOOK REVIEW / NONFICTION Man on a Mission Comes to Term With His African Roots DREAMS FROM MY FATHER: A Story of Race and Inheritance by Barack Obama; Times Books $23, 383 pages: [Home Edition]." *Los Angeles Times* (pre-1997 Fulltext) [Los Angeles, Calif.] 7 Aug. 1995, 4.

believe that Reynolds paid her to leave town.[23]

These two incidents eventually cleared the path for Obama to begin his career in politics.

Congressman Mel Reynolds was indicted and convicted of a crime and had to resign his seat. State Senator Alice Palmer, a respected South Side lawmaker, decided to run for the seat vacated by Reynolds. She was sure that she would breeze to victory. However, in the special election held on Tuesday, November 28th 1995, Jesse Jackson, Jr. defeated both Palmer and State Senator Emil Jones in the Democratic primary.

While she ran for Congress, Palmer had encouraged and endorsed Obama to run for her state senate seat. When she lost the Congressional race, Palmer wanted to reclaim her seat, but Obama, who had invested much time and money in the campaign, refused to step aside. Palmer had assumed that she would be the next member of Congress from the 2nd Congressional District of Illinois. She had underestimated the impact of Jesse Jackson Jr. Palmer went as far as gathering signatures on petitions trying to get on the ballot for Illinois State Senator, but Obama's campaign team decided to challenge her petitions. When it became obvious that the challenge would succeed, Palmer dropped out of the race, leaving the seat to Obama.

In the Illinois State Senate, Obama was involved in a number of bipartisan proposals, introducing, for example, the so-called Bernardin Amendment.[24] He got involved with Republican State Senate leader Pate Philip in supporting campaign finance reform with a bipartisan group that included Reps. Gary Hannig (D-Litchfield), Jack Kubik (R-La Grange Park), Kirk Dillard (R-Hinsdale), and Edgar's deputy chief of staff, Andy Foster.[25] He supported bipartisan campaign finance reform that cracked down on diverting campaign funds for personal use.[26] He supported legislation that

---

23 Complied by Amanda Vogt from news reports.. "TUMBLING DOWN CONGRESSMAN MEL REYNOLDS TAKES A HUGE FALL :[NORTH SPORTS FINAL Edition]. " *Chicago Tribune* (pre-1997 Fulltext) [Chicago, IL] 29 Aug. 1995, 3.
24 UNIVERSAL HEALTH CARE PROPOSED; [NORTH SPORTS FINAL Edition] Melita Marie Garza, Tribune Staff Writer. *Chicago Tribune*. Chicago, Ill.: Nov 17, 1997. Pg. 5
25 PHILIP HOPING TO GIVE CAMPAIGN REFORM A SHOT SENATE LEADER LOOKING AT BI-PARTISAN PROPOSAL; [NORTH SPORTS FINAL Edition] Ray Long, Tribune Staff Writer. *Chicago Tribune*. Chicago, Ill.: Apr 30, 1998. Pg. 8
26 WHY POLS, PORSCHES AND LUCRATIVE CAMPAIGN CHESTS ARE A BAD MIX; [NORTH SPORTS FINAL Edition] Bruce Dold, *Chicago Tribune*. Chicago, Ill.: May 22, 1998. pg. 27

increased the pay of election judges. He cosponsored many senate bills with Republican State Senator Steve Rauschenberger (R-Elgin). He and Rauschenberger were friends, as were many Republican lawmakers dating back to their card playing days in Springfield. These lawmakers would often play poker in the evening when the sessions extended.

Although I had not directly crossed paths with Barack Obama until 1999, we would later discover some common projects we were involved with, all through my activities with the Beverly Area Planning Association (BAPA). And, we had common acquaintances, such as Larry Stanton, BAPA Executive Director, and Greg Richmond, Chicago Public School System's Director of Charter Schools, who had served with me on the BAPA Board of Directors.

Larry Stanton was a neighbor of Obama's and knew him well. Larry had a personal relationship with Obama, and they would run into each other at bookstores such as 57th Street Books in Hyde Park and other parts of that community. Obama's law firm worked with BAPA on the 19th Ward re-districting boundary fight. The firm won the case, but ultimately a compromise was struck that allowed the 19th Ward, my ward, to maintain its original boundaries.[27]

---

27 Larry Stanton, Executive Director of BAPA, called an emergency meeting of the Board of Directors of the Beverly Area Planning Association. At the time, I was a member of BAPA's Executive Committee. The Ward remapping case was now coming to a head. During my time as a member of BAPA's Executive Committee, we were faced with a crisis that a federal court declared the 1990 census illegal, and the ruling was upheld.

By 1998, we were in Federal District Court. The Chicago ward maps drawn in 1992 were drawn in favor of the so-called all-white wards, according to the lawsuit. To simplify, the courts ruled consistently that an all-black majority ward be established. A federal judge was considering a proposal to remove the eastern portion of Beverly, the so-called East Beverly area of the 19th Ward, from its historic home within the boundaries of the 19th Ward. That is where I lived. We were an organized group of residents and were digging in for a fight. BAPA called for a meeting to discuss the legal strategy.

On July 8, 1998, Andrew Martin & Gary Washburn of the *Chicago Tribune* wrote, "The neighborhood's diversity is particularly evident in a section of the neighborhood known as East Beverly, where whites routinely buy homes back from black families—and vice versa—and where the ratio of blacks to whites has remained fairly stable for nearly two decades."

U.S. District Judge Elaine Bucklo has said she may remove East Beverly from the 19th Ward and make it part of the 21st Ward as part of a complicated plan to increase the number of wards where blacks represent the majority of voters.

Such a move, they say, could create a perception problem for East Beverly that may make whites wary of living there. Instead of being associated with the 19th Ward, which is majority white and served by a white alderman, East Beverly would instead be part of an overwhelmingly black ward with a black alderman, they say.

The fight was led by BAPA Executive Director Larry Stanton and 19th Ward Alderman Virginia "Ginger" Rugai. The leadership that these two individuals displayed was simply incredible. There were twelve people who testified at trial, including myself.

In addition to Obama's indirect involvement with the 19th Ward re-districting case, we had another indirect contact with Obama. While I was on the BAPA Board of Directors, BAPA received a multi-million dollar grant from the Annenberg Challenge, a Board on which Obama served.[28] Even at that time, Obama was often mentioned as an up and coming rising star. Dempsey Travis, real estate tycoon and best-selling author, cited Obama as a bright star and razor sharp.[29]

The *Chicago Tribune* reported in early August 1999 that Obama was seriously considering running for Congress.[30] On Sunday, September 26, 1999, Obama announced his candidacy for the Democratic nomination in the 1st Congressional District, although prior to that time, he had already been campaigning, especially in the 19th Ward, by holding coffees and meeting with diverse groups from the community. One group he met with was called "Unity in Diversity." The group held dinners around the Beverly community, and the idea was to invite an equal number of African-Americans and whites who would not have otherwise socialized. Obama and Shomon were invited to one of these dinners that was attended by Linda Cooper, owner of Café Luna. Cooper recalls the evening fondly. She thought, "Why can't we have more leaders like this in Washington?"

As a member of the Beverly Area Planning Association Board, I would vote on funding these dinners to promote racial unity and harmony.

Obama challenged Rush to a series of five debates, which Rush's aides passed off as an Obama publicity stunt. Obama contended that Rush should welcome the debates since Rush criticized Daley for refusing to debate him in the spring mayoral campaign. Obama aides said the debates should be open to all Democratic primary candidates.[31]

Obama could not motivate Rush to accept his debate challenge, but it was not for a lack of trying on Obama's part. He was relentless in pursuing this debate and trying to exert public pressure on Rush. There just was

28 Yes, this was the same board, Chicago Annenberg Challenge, that Bill Ayers served on with Obama.

29 CHICAGO'S BLACK POLITICAL MOVEMENT WHAT HAPPENED?; [CHICAGOLAND FINAL Edition] Flynn McRoberts Flynn McRoberts is a Tribune staff writer. *Chicago Tribune*. Chicago, Ill.: Jul 4, 1999. pg. 11.

30 2 MAY CHALLENGE RUSH FOR CONGRESSIONAL SEAT; [CHICAGOLAND FINAL Edition] Rick Pearson, Tribune Political Writer. *Chicago Tribune*. Chicago, Ill.: Aug 1, 1999. pg. 3

31 STATE SENATOR CHALLENGES RUSH TO DEBATE HIM; [CHICAGO SPORTS FINAL Edition] *Chicago Tribune*. Chicago, Ill.: Oct 5, 1999. pg. 5

not an interest by the media to report on the non-debate issue. Incumbents typically avoid forums, debates or joint appearances with their opponents because they do not want to give their opponent a platform.

Rush officially announced his candidacy on November 1, 1999. He held a 10:00 am news conference at Pearls Place in The Amber Inn. The Amber Inn is located at the corner of 39th & Michigan Avenue in Chicago's Bronzeville community. Accompanying Rush was then Cook County Board President John Stroger and State Representative Lovana Jones, among other supporters.[32]

In mid-December, Obama again repeated his call for a forum, debate or joint appearance and criticized Rush for ducking a debate. It's hypocritical, said Obama, pointing out how Rush slammed Daley for refusing to debate him.[33]

Between 1992 and 1999, Michelle and I did not have any contact with Congressman Bobby Rush and had never met him. We invited Rush once to a rally at Graver Park in the summer of 1994, but Rush did not respond to our invitation. Many elected officials did attend including then-State Rep. Tom Dart, State Rep. Monique Davis, and Alderman Virginia "Ginger" Rugai.

Cops 'n' Neighbors:
Community Policing in Beverly-Morgan Park

The event received television coverage and resulted in a feature article about Michelle and me and our bookstore in the October 14, 1994 issue of the Chicago Reader titled " Cops 'n' neighbors: community policing in Beverly-Morgan Park." [34]

Grant Pick, the writer of the article, attended that rally at the invitation of Illinois State Representative Monique Davis. Pick had intended to write a feature story about Representative Davis, but after observing Michelle and me that day, he decided to change the focus of his feature. The rally that day in the summer of 1994 was a gathering

---

32 RUSH PLANNING TO ANNOUNCE 5TH BID FOR 1ST DISTRICT SEAT; [CHICAGO SPORTS FINAL Edition] *Chicago Tribune*. Chicago, IL: Nov 1, 1999. pg. 3.

33 EARLY-BIRD CHALLENGER GETS JUMP ON CAMPAIGN FILING; [CHICAGO SPORTS FINAL Edition] Douglas Holt, Tribune Staff Writer. Tribune staff writer Robert Becker contributed to this report. *Chicago Tribune*. Chicago, Ill.: Dec 14, 1999. pg. 3.

34 Cops 'n' neighbors: community policing in Beverly-Morgan Park by Grant Pick. The *Chicago Reader*. October 13, 1994.

that Michelle, Dorothy Riley, a long-time community activist, and I had organized for peace and against gangs and drugs. We had invited a number of local elected officials to gather on a stage to speak to the crowd gathered at Graver Park about how "we can and must" take back our community. "Together We Can" was the mantra. The lineup of speeches was followed by a candlelight vigil march through the heart of the community. Along the route, hundreds came out of their homes to join in this march. We would chant, "Come out of your houses, and join us on the street." The roots of "Yes We Can" and "Come Join Us" were germinating in events like this.

Pick said to us, "You guys are a much more interesting story than State Rep. Monique Davis". Pick had roots in the community when he served several years earlier as the editor of the local newspaper, *The Beverly Review*. The theme of his story was that we were involved in our community, outside of the bookselling world. We were a catalyst, a driving force behind an involved community. The Beverly Hills/Morgan Park community in Chicago has a rich history of community involvement. We were not the first to inject ourselves in the community, and we would not be the last.

This particular march forever identified Michelle and me as community activists and community leaders, even to this day. Commander Dennis Lesniak said in that article, "The Prestas are catalysts, and we use them as an example for other people in the district to follow. Without their kind of commitment, CAPS is going to founder."

We were indeed catalysts.

This rally was the one chance we had to meet Bobby Rush prior to 1999 and, for whatever reason, he did not attend. This reinforced the label that Bobby Rush did not care about nor respect this section of the community.

During the late summer of 1999, one of our friends from the community, Rosa Hudson, a long-time community organizer and activist, made us aware of an event in which Rush would be in attendance. Rosa had a close relationship with Rush and pushed him to come to the community. The meeting, which was to be held at the Beverly branch library concerned HUD housing in the community.

BAPA coordinated the meeting, and in attendance were Willie Winters, Executive Director of BAPA, and Rosa Hudson, President of the Vanderpoel Improvement Association, which was an umbrella group under BAPA.

I attended the meeting with Congressman Rush, but I was unaware at the time of a serious primary challenge, nor had I given it any thought. I found it curious that Rush was in our community, but only as a passing thought. I was coming to hear our sitting Congressman discuss a community issue. The Congressman said he would address the concerns of that evening. Rush made reference to discussing the situation with "Andy," meaning the then-HUD Secretary, Andrew Cuomo. Rush then thanked Willie Winters and Rosa Hudson for bringing this meeting and the community together.

One of Rush's offices was across the street in Evergreen Park on Western Avenue (9730 S. Western Avenue). Obama's campaign office was down the street at 9525 S. Western Avenue, in the heart of the 19th Ward, where he was focusing his campaign and where he would make many personal appearances.

Obama and his group of paid staff and volunteers were working the Metra stations. The Metra stations located in Beverly Hills/Morgan Park are the 91st station, 95th station, 99th station, 103rd station, 107th station, 111th station, 115th station and the 119th station. It was an opportunity to meet hundreds of people in a short period.

Obama's campaign manager for the 2000 Congressional race was Dan Shomon, who was in his mid-30's at the time of the 2000 Congressional race. Shomon developed the political strategy and was Obama's political director. Shomon was a former reporter in the United Press International bureau at the Statehouse and a former spokesman for the state Environmental Protection Agency. Shomon was also involved with then-state Treasurer Pat Quinn and Illinois Senate President Emil Jones Jr. Shomon also worked on some political campaigns, including that of Dawn DeFraties for alderman and Tom Londrigan for state Senate. In 1996, Shomon managed the upset State Senate campaign of Debbie Halvorson over then Assistant Majority Leader and Senator Aldo DeAngelis in Chicago's South Suburbs. Halvorson beat the 18-year incumbent DeAngelis 56-44 percent (an almost 10,000-vote victory margin).

The group of people helping Obama was known as the Obama-ites. The group later became known as the Shomon-ites, named after

Shomon, because he recruited the group over a period of years starting when Obama first ran for Illinois State Senate.

Greg Richmond led Dan Shomon to our door late in fall 1999. They knew each other from having worked on the Illinois Democratic Senate staff, under Senate President Emil Jones. Later, it was Greg who helped establish the Chicago Public Schools (CPS) Charter Schools Office in 1996 and served as its Director until 2003. From 2003 to 2005, Greg served as CPS Chief Officer for New Schools Development, leading Chicago's Renaissance 2010 initiative to close chronically low-performing schools and establish 100 new charter or charter-like schools over five years.

Greg and I served on the Beverly Area Planning Board of Directors together for a year. During that time, Greg and I had worked the "19th Ward Re-map" case where both of us testified in federal court on behalf of trying to preserve our 19th ward boundaries.

Armed with information about us from Greg, Dan stopped by the bookstore to seek our support for Obama.

The very first time Michelle and I talked to Dan Shomon, we gave him a cool reception. We were always skeptical of salesmen, and that is how we viewed Shomon. "What is he selling?" we would ask each other. He made repeated visits to our bookstore in late fall 1999. We rebuffed those efforts by Shomon to lobby on behalf of Obama, but Michelle and I eventually grew fond of Shomon's professional manner and his passion for this man Barack Obama.

But we just were not buying what Dan was selling. He pleaded his case that Obama was a State Senator from Hyde Park and a graduate of Harvard Law School. While at Harvard, Barack was elected the first African-American President of the Harvard Law Review. A community activist and community organizer, just like you guys, he would plead. Obama had a keen intellect with a personality to match, Shomon would argue. Shomon promised to bring him in the store to personally introduce us.

Among his qualities, Shomon would argue, were that he was progressive, responsive, tough, highly organized, and cared deeply about the community. Nevertheless, we were not enthusiastic. From September through Christmas of 1999, Shomon was relentless in pursuit of our support. We took a liking to Dan, and he started to become a fixture at our store, but we still would not endorse Obama. To Shomon's credit, however, he never gave up. The fact was, we did not have an issue with Congressman Rush. We did not have a beef with him. He was the incumbent.

Rush's voting record in Congress very closely reflected our views. Bobby Rush and Barack Obama were ideological equals, and we were not responsive to Shomon's pleas for his candidate. There was no reason to be for Obama. We knew what we had with Rush as our Congressman.

Change comes slowly, gradually, incrementally, and suddenly.

CHAPTER 3

"Barack Obama's An Author, You Know"

~

Then Dan Shomon finally hit on something for us that captured our attention and our imagination. At least it was a beginning of our considering our support of Obama.

"Well he's an author, you know," Dan Shomon said to us one day.

He mentioned that Barack Obama was an author. He wrote a book. A memoir. We were not familiar with the book, *Dreams from My Father*, but we did find some copies were still available from our book distributors.

We then recalled that we had indeed ordered one copy of the book in 1996 when it first came out in paperback, and we bought it from our one of our sales reps, Sean Sullivan, who at the time represented Kodansha Globe. The paperback rights were purchased by Kodansha in 1996. Sullivan represented Abraham and Associates at the time as a commissioned sales rep and Kodansha was one of Abraham's clients. Michelle vividly recalled her conversation with Sullivan about *Dreams from My Father*.

"I don't know if you want to try this book, but it's by a local guy from Hyde Park. It's a memoir," Sullivan explained. "Harvard guy. Community organizer."

Michelle said, "I'll take one. If nobody buys it, I'll read it. I like books by local authors."

Obama was a first-time author and a rookie politician embarking upon his first run for public office when the book was released. Janny Scott did a thorough piece in 2008 in the New York Times concerning the history of the book.[36]

There would not have been any involvement with Barack Obama or his campaign were it not for this book. This book was the glue that bound us to Obama. Without the book, the interest on our part would not have happened.

The book was not a commercial success.

Hardly.

Michelle and I were motivated to read the book and found it to be a good read and very interesting. At the time, we were offered a chance to have Obama come for a book signing, but it never materialized, as often these things do not. Publisher's representatives would routinely encourage book signings of local authors. After we ordered a copy, Sullivan said, "You should call this guy for a signing. I am quite sure he'd come."

But it never happened. Fate was not ready to bring Michelle, me, Obama, and our community together.

Not yet.

After reading the book the first time, I thought that it certainly should have sold better. The writing made for a compelling and engaging story. At that time, the memoir genre sold well, and it was becoming the rage in publishing. It was certainly as good as Angela's Ashes[37] by Frank McCourt. The genre took a step backward many years later with author Jim Frey's book controversy, where he falsified some material aspects of his story.

I recall when I read the book the first time, I felt a great deal of empathy for Barack Obama because he grew up without the benefit of a father. I knew from my own experience what a rich relationship a father and son can have. And my father often talked about the rich relationship he had with his father. My relationship with my own father grew after my tumultuous teenage years. I began to see him in a different

---

36 Janny Scott. "The Story of Obama, Written by Obama: [Series]." New York Times [New York, N.Y.] 18 May 2008, Late Edition (East Coast): A.1. New York Times.

37 McCourt, Frank. Angela's Ashes: A Memoir. New York: Scribner, 1996.

light, and he was always there with his free advice on how to live life. He loved to tell stories that would have life lessons built into them.

Wherever I lived, I always made it a point to call my father, and if he was not available, my mother. I knew all my conversations with my mother were repeated to my father and visa-versa.

My papa was a great storyteller and every story had a valuable lesson. I recall once when I was particularly agitated with a boss, and I told my dad I was going to do this or that to embarrass this boss. He grew quiet and then he said, "Did I ever tell you the story of the Italian farmer and his jackass?" Even if he had, I could not stop him, but it seemed I had not heard this one.

He said that on this particular day in the Italian mountains, in the region near his hometown of Calabria, the farmer was having a particularly difficult time motivating his jackass. Finally, the jackass completely stopped and would not budge. The farmer got behind the jackass and tried to push him and no movement. He tried from the side and from the front. This stubborn jackass just would not move. He had been abused all day by the farmer and yelled at and corrected and apparently, the jackass had enough. Finally, the farmer got behind the jackass, and the jackass kicked the farmer. With one fell swoop the jackass finally moved, but the move was a kick to the farmer's body that knocked him back.

The farmer was angered by the jackass' kick and went to get a saw. In his rage, he sawed the jackass' legs and then taunted him, "See what you get when you kick me, you jackass."

But the farmer, my dad said, was the jackass because he could not plow the fields any longer, couldn't afford to purchase another jackass, nor would any of the other farmers sell him a jackass after what he had done.

And then my dad said, "The moral of the story is don't cut off the jackass' legs, because you are going to need the jackass."

I got it. All of our lives we will deal with jackasses, and they will occasionally kick you, but sometimes you just have to turn the other cheek to the jackass and move on with our work.

The Book *Dreams from My Father* Doesn't Hit
The Tipping Point . . . Yet

Obama's book did not hit the *The Tipping Point: How Little Things Can Make a Big Difference*,[38] as Malcolm Gladwell would say. At least, not yet. It would indeed one day hit a "Tipping Point," but the timing was premature. We later found out from Shomon that Obama had always expected the book to sell well but, to this point, it had not.

Dreams from My Father did not cause a stir or a buzz in book publishing between 1996 and 2004. Transformation and discovery are two predominant themes in the book, and it is well written. After reading the book, it is apparent that Barack Obama is an excellent writer and a student of the English language, but it took many years for his book to discover its audience. It did not travel the typical path of a book, but many successful books don't either.

One example is *The Road Less Traveled: A New Psychology of Love, Traditional Values, and Spiritual Growth*.[39] It took several years for the book to catch fire, but once it did, it sold millions of copies in hardcover. Random House, where the little-known psychiatrist first tried to publish his original manuscript, turned him down, saying the final section was "too Christ-y." Simon & Schuster published the work for $7,500 and printed a modest hardback run of 5,000 copies. The book took off only after Mr. Peck hit the lecture circuit and personally sought reviews in key publications. Reprinted in paperback in 1980, *The Road* first made best-seller lists in 1984 — six years after its initial publication.[40]

Shomon had a sense that Obama's book had great promotional value. It just needed to create the right kind of buzz. It was a great introduction to the candidate. The campaign was giving the book away. Hundreds of them.

Shomon wanted to know if we could order some copies for the Obama Congressional campaign. He said that Obama liked to give them away as introductory pieces.

Sure, we said. How many.

---

38   Gladwell, Malcolm. *The Tipping Point: How Little Things Can Make a Big Difference*. Boston: Little, Brown, 2000.

39   Peck, M. Scott. *The Road Less Traveled: A New Psychology of Love*, Traditional Values, and Spiritual Growth. New York: Simon and Schuster, 1978.

40   http://en.wikipedia.org/wiki/M._Scott_Peck.

Twenty copies, he said.

A number of times Dan came back to purchase more copies, and he was keyed in on gaining our endorsement. We just would not commit to supporting or endorsing Obama at that point. It made no difference in our support whether he bought one copy or a hundred. We would support Obama based on the merits.

Meanwhile, Dan Shomon, Mike Jordan, Doug Price, Barack Obama and some of the other Shomon-ites were working the Metra train stations in the community. They would arrive at the stations at 5:30 am, pass out campaign literature, and solicit votes for Obama. Many of the Shomon-ites were law students of Obama's at the University of Chicago and had been working with him since his first campaign for Illinois State Senate.

This campaign had little money, a sparse organization and little name recognition. There was no buzz. Obama had less than a dozen regular volunteers for the campaign.

One such volunteer was a Shomon-ite, Mike Jordan, and "The Super Volunteer." A true superstar. Oh, not the Bulls guy, Number 23. Back in the 2000 election there was Mike Jordan, Dan Shomon, Doug Price, and a handful of others. Less than a dozen. Mike Jordan would be embarrassed to have his name publicized because he would say the focus should be Obama. Mike is one of the most hardworking, talented, generous and unselfish people on the planet. That is what really makes him a superstar. Mike does not golf very well, does not have a summer home, does not have a boat, and does not fish. His passions are politics and Obama.

Mike Jordan believes in the great movement for real change and for a "chance to believe again."

Mike never stopped believing. He never stopped working. He was tireless and relentless in his efforts for Obama. Obama loved to introduce Mike Jordan to small gatherings of volunteers.

Obama would display that wonderful sense of humor of his, by starting out saying, "And of course, Mike Jordan is here today." The crowd would scan the room to look for Number 23, only to find this fine, humble man, the other Mike Jordan. I call him the "real" Mike Jordan. To Barack Obama, Mike Jordan was as valuable to his team as

Number 23 was to the Chicago Bulls, and it would be impossible to exaggerate this fact.

I called Mike Jordan "the Secret." He is the secret weapon of the Obama campaign. I knew Shomon had a group of high-energy volunteers that cared deeply about Obama.

Doug Price was another veteran "Shomon-ite." Doug, like Mike Jordan, is an insurance agent by trade and a passionate "politico." Doug is one of the most articulate spokesmen for the "Shomon-ites."

Shomon was an excellent recruiter of volunteers and was a true believer in the "The Pied Piper of Hamelin" theory of politics. Dan referred to us as the "Pied Pipers." If you can gather enough "Pied Pipers," you can win an election. In the advertising trade, they are called "influencers." You find a handful of "Pied Pipers" in the community and they will take you a long way and spread your message, although the product must be of high quality. Barack Obama was quality at its "best." The "Pied Pipers" can get a group to pull in the same direction.

Below is the oldest picture of Pied Piper (watercolour) copied from the glass window of Marktkirche in Hamelin by Freiherr Augustin von Moersperg.

~

Pied Piper plot

 In 1284, while the town of Hamelin was suffering from a rat infestation, a man dressed in colourful garments appeared, claiming to be a rat-catcher. He promised the townsmen a solution for their problem with the rats. The townsmen in turn promised to pay him for the removal of the rats. The man accepted, and thus played a musical pipe to lure the rats with a song into the Weser River, where all of them drowned. Despite his success, the people reneged on their promise and refused to pay the rat-catcher. The man left the town angrily, but returned some time later, on June 26, seeking revenge.

While the inhabitants were in church, he played his pipe again, this time attracting the children of Hamelin. One hundred and thirty boys and girls followed him out of the town, where they were lured into a cave and never seen again. Depending on the version, at most two children remained behind (one of whom was lame and could not follow quickly enough, the other one was deaf and followed the other children out of curiosity) who informed the villagers of what had happened when they came out of the church.

Other versions (but not the traditional ones) claim that the Piper lured the children into the river and let them drown like the rats or that he returned the children after the villagers paid several times the original amount of gold.[41]

~

Shomon was looking for influencers for Obama. Nevertheless, he was not looking for just one "Pied Piper," but a whole series of them. "Pied Pipers" sometimes begat other "Pied Pipers." If you gather enough "Pied Pipers of Hamelin," elections can be won and that is the backdrop that eventually led Dan Shomon to our bookstore door.

After some discussions with the Board of Directors of the East Beverly Association, we decided to use our community organizing skills and organize a candidates' forum in the 1st Congressional District. This was a direct result of the intense lobbying Dan Shomon had done with us. Shomon had made us aware of Barack Obama through his store visits. Many in our organization thought we should be sponsoring candidates' forums, and we thought this election lent itself to that.

There is no question now were it not for our initiative to have a candidates' forum, Barack Obama, Bobby Rush, Donne Trotter and George Roby would not have had a joint appearance in our community. Obama had been pleading publicly since September of 1999 with Bobby Rush about a debate, a forum or a joint appearance.

It did not occur in this community until two bookstore owners and some community members organized, that it happened. This would be the first of many grassroots efforts we would entertain on Obama's behalf. We told Shomon about the proposed candidates' forum, and he promised full cooperation on behalf of Obama. We were not going to

---

41   http://en.wikipedia.org/wiki/The_Pied_Piper_of_Hamelin.

deal with it until after the Christmas holidays. Shomon came into the store on Christmas Eve of 1999, bought some book gifts for his nieces and nephews, and was going to the East Coast for Christmas.

After the Christmas and New Year holidays, it was full-speed ahead toward the candidates' forum. We had already made an appointment with Tracy Smith, Executive Director of the Chicago Chapter of the League of Women Voters. Susan Burnet and I went to League headquarters and met with Tracy. We settled on the date and the details. We decided on Tuesday, March 7th at 7:00 pm. We had several sites in mind. It was the League that brought "legitimacy" and "know how" to the candidates' forum. The League of Women Voters also recommended that we work with a group of people called the Citizens Information Service and its Executive Director, Alfred Sousedo. It would take a tremendous effort to force Congressman Bobby Rush's appearance. We put the word out that we would hold the event with or without Rush.

We had several locations in mind, but our first choice was Bethany Union Church located at 103rd & Wood Street in the heart of East Beverly. We called the Reverend Bill O'Donnell, who was the head of Bethany Union Church and asked him if the evening of March 7, 2000 was available. Reverend Bill said yes, and suggested we hold the forum in the smaller auditorium to make it look fuller, instead of the much larger chapel. If the larger chapel was not filled, it would look empty. Reverend Bill taught me a valuable lesson.

We told Reverend Bill we had a limited budget, but he said whatever we could contribute to the church would be appreciated. We would set up a collection plate at the door. The East Beverly Association did donate to the church, as did one of the co-sponsors, the Beverly Improvement Association.

Shomon was pleased that we would be organizing a debate, although we made it clear that we would not endorse or work for any candidate until after the forum. Shomon was convinced that Rush would not attend the candidates' forum.

We would invite any and all the Democratic candidates on the ballot. This included the following:
- Congressman Bobby Rush, former 2nd Ward alderman, 2nd Ward Democratic Committeeman, and

- State Senator Barack Obama, a second-term State Senator and civil rights attorney; author, Harvard Law graduate, and
- State Senator Donne E. Trotter of the South Chicago neighborhood, intergovernmental liaison for the Cook County Department of Public Health and a third-term state senator; and
- George C. Roby[42] who was a retired Chicago police officer from the Calumet Heights neighborhood.

I did not know Mr. Roby, but I insisted we invite him and the others agreed. Anyone that went to the effort of gathering petitions for placement on the ballot and raised money for the campaign, deserved to take part in the event. I had a great deal of respect for Roby who accumulated more than the necessary number of required signatures for the ballot.

On January 22, 2000, we sent the four candidates invitations to the Candidates' Forum. The first response was from Dan Shomon on behalf of Barack Obama. He accepted in person at the store. "Yes, we'll be there."

Shortly thereafter, Donne Trotter and George Roby also accepted.

Congressman Rush Will Be Unable to Attend

Congressman Bobby Rush was a different story. I received a letter from Bobby Rush's campaign manager, Louanner Peters, that Rush would not be attending.

~

Dear Mr. Presta:

We are in receipt of your Jan. 22 letter seeking the Congressman's participation in a Candidates' Forum sponsored in conjunction with the League of Women Voters and the Citizens Information Service.

We thank the East Beverly Association for the invitation. We regret we are unable to participate. As you can imagine, we have and are still receiving a large volume of requests for Candidates' Forums from churches, community groups, media, and civic organizations, and it is impossible to facilitate all. As an example, we received three different requests for forums co-sponsored

---

42 Dan Shomon told me that George C. Roby's petitions passed the scrutiny by the Obama campaign. All the signatures were valid. Roby was a retired police officer that had become a perennial candidate for political office.

by the League of Women Voters, one of them in conjunction with your affil-
iate, the Beverly Area Planning Association. I understand from your discussions today with our Press Secretary, Maudlyne Ihejirika, that confusion
among your representatives led to the duplicate requests.

While we are unable to participate in this particular Candidates' Forum,
we remain very interested in facilitating a meeting with your organization,
allowing the Congressman to share his accomplishments and record of the
past four terms, and his vision for the future. As you know, the Congressman
has worked very closely with Beverly community organizations through the
Beverly Area Planning Association, particularly on the issue of dilapidated
HUD properties threatening property values. He looks forward to meeting
with your organization.

Again, thank you for the invitation.

Sincerely,
Louanner Peters
Campaign Manager

~

Through the entire process, the campaign refused to commit to
coming to our candidates' forum. Whether it was by phone or letter,
the answer was always the same: the congressman will be unable to
attend a candidates' forum, but we will come and speak to your group.
Without the other candidates, of course. We were undeterred. We
would use the empty chair if necessary. The empty chair would create
media interest. It is likely had Bobby Rush agreed to attend right from
the get go, our candidates' forum would have attracted little or no
interest. Nor would attendance have been as great as the 600. The buzz
we created was, "We were sponsoring this candidates' forum, and Bobby
Rush is refusing, once again, to show respect to our community." This
aspect was misplayed by the Rush campaign.

Obama was endorsed by the IVI-IPO in the 2000 Congressional
race.[43] Obama was vigorously trying to drum up media coverage of the
campaign, but still the race failed to excite the media.

Trotter and Obama charged that Rush failed to define himself during
his seven years in office. Evan Osnos of the *Chicago Tribune* wrote the
longest piece on February 20, 2000, citing charges Trotter and Obama
were making against Rush, but clearly showing there were no deep-

---

43   IVI-IPO BACKS MOORE, OBAMA IN CONTESTS; [CHICAGO SPORTS FINAL Edition]
     Chicago Tribune. Chicago, Ill.: Feb 15, 2000. pg. 3.

seeded disagreements between the three men.[44] This lack of disagreements and a lack of corruption or scandal with Rush, made it increasingly difficult for Obama or the other candidates to gain a foothold with the media. All the candidates were progressives.

After Rush became aware of our forum, he agreed to debate on February 20th, 2000 at Trinity United Church on 95th Street, Obama's church. Rush had to cancel at the last minute to fly to Georgia to be with his sick father who passed away that same day, Sunday, February 20th. Jimmy Rush, Bobby's father, died in Albany, Georgia at Phoebe Putney Hospital.

Earlier in the campaign, in October of 1999, Bobby's son, Huey Rich, was shot and killed. It was an unspeakable personal tragedy for Rush. The campaign was difficult for Rush because of these personal tragedies. It is unfathomable to imagine first losing a son in such a tragic way and then losing a father. And the threat of losing the job you loved, Congressman from Illinois' 1st District.

All of his campaign appearances were canceled.[45] In the February 21st article by Evan Osnos, Obama declared about Rush, "Seniority without vision doesn't get you much." That was the best Obama could do against Rush.

On March 6, 2000, the *Chicago Tribune* endorsed Obama for Congress. Our candidates' forum would be the next day. The coveted endorsement would be the *Chicago Sun Times* because of its African-American readership.

Up until March 7, 2000, there was precious little publicity or attention given to this 1st District Congressional race. Certainly there was no television coverage. This candidates' forum was the beginning of the media coverage for Obama in this campaign. The reason was simple because of the question: Would Rush show up?

Rush had inadvertently brought attention to this race and to Obama because of this simple misstep of saying he was too busy to attend because of his Congressional responsibilities. The media would be in attendance

---

44   Evan Osnos, Tribune Staff Writer. "RUSH COULD FACE HIS TOUGHEST TEST 2 KEY STATE SENATORS AMONG PRIMARY FOES :[CHICAGOLAND FINAL Edition]." *Chicago Tribune* [Chicago, Ill.] 20 Feb. 2000, 4C1.
45   RUSH'S FATHER DIES AFTER FALLING ILL; [CHICAGO SPORTS FINAL Edition] *Chicago Tribune*. Chicago, Ill.: Feb 22, 2000. pg. 3

in full force because we had put the word out that Bobby would not be there. Rush's office was flooded with media requests for an interview as to why wasn't he going to attend this candidates' forum, and he had no answers. Newspaper reporters and television producers were calling me at the store and wanted to know what I knew about Rush: Was he coming or not coming?

We had great difficulty dealing with the Rush group. Up until the day of the forum, it was understood that Rush would not be attending. "Absolutely not," Maudlyne Ihejirika, his Press Secretary would tell us. "The Congressman will be in session in Washington doing the people's business."

Shomon repeated, "I told you so."

The Rush group failed to return telephone calls. We encountered the same problem in the summer 1994. They didn't say no. They said nothing.

"He was in Washington tending to Congressional business," said members of his staff to the League of Women. We put the word out to the media, through the League of Women Voters and the Citizens Information Service, that Rush would not be attending the forum. It was our intention to pressure the Congressman to attend in any way we could or bring enough attention to the forum.

We leaned on him. And it worked. On forum night, over 600 residents attended. The crowd was not committed before the debate for either candidate. This is the strength of this event. Many did have a bias against Rush because of the prevalent feeling that "Bobby never came around." Requests for funding of local projects, known as earmarks, went unanswered according to local elected officials. The earmarks for the District went everywhere but our section of the community, argued these officials.[46]

Most of the major local television outlets were there and the print media were there including the *Daily Southtown* and the *Chicago Sun Times*. The hook for the media was "Where's Bobby?" Rush made a miscalculation. Rush underestimated Obama and most of all ignoring our community, again. This would come back to haunt him. Rush

---

46   The elected officials talked to me off the record and wished to remain anonymous.

would win the Election, but he would be wounded by the accomplishments of Obama here in the 19th Ward.

On forum night, we didn't just get a huge crowd. We had pressured Bobby Rush into attending in spite of the fact I received a letter saying he would not be there. Our strategy to get Rush there worked. Louanner Peters, his campaign manager, approached me right before seven o'clock and said the Congressman would not be there on time, so could we delay the start of the forum until the Congressman arrived. I respectfully declined. This was the same person that had written me a couple months earlier saying that Rush would not be able to attend. I had just met Obama minutes earlier. Why could Obama make it on time, and so could Trotter and Roby, but Rush couldn't?

Other Rush aides had tried to stall me because he was on his way. I told them, the forum starts at 7:00 pm, with or without Rush. One Rush ally after another approached me to lobby me to delay the proceedings, but I steadfastly refused. I was in charge of this event and would have none of this. The crowd was ready for the event. I was very involved in the event and did not want to lose my focus on making this the best event it could be. There was no legitimate reason to delay the start for Rush since all the candidates knew the rules in advance. They even asked if I would like to talk to the Congressman on the cell phone. Now he returns phone calls. I would have been glad to under normal circumstances, but I was working the event. I declined the request to talk to him, citing my attention to the candidates and the crowd. We were getting overwhelmed by the crowd, which far exceeded our expectations that evening. We had spread the word through the community about Rush and the possibility he would not attend. Much of the curiosity was, "Why won't our Congressman come to our community?" This was politically damaging to Rush and set the stage for election day.

Obama Takes the Stage and His Star is Shining Brightly: A Rising Star is Born

The forum started promptly at 7:00 pm. There was standing room only. The church did not have enough chairs to accommodate the crowd. They told me they had 500 chairs total, so we got a good idea of the size of the crowd. Many were standing in an attempt to get a glimpse at the proceedings. The session was called to order by Carol Maier, President of the League of Women Voters of Chicago, and there was complete silence. Sandra Robinson, a Board member for the East Beverly Association, was the timekeeper. Tracy Smith of the League of Women Voters would hold up the 'Stop' sign. The moderator was also from the League of Women Voters.

The television cameras for the event were everywhere in the hall. Newspaper reporters and photographers were also wandering around, but once the event started, we asked everyone to please be seated. Every word the candidates were saying was heard throughout the hall. Obama had answered a number of questions much to the delight of the crowd.

Barack Obama discussed the need to end "scorch-earth politics." He also introduced themes that would become his trademark: bring voice to the voiceless and power to the powerless. He also brought up the idea that we are all connected regardless of where we live.

Our friend, neighbor, and customer, Lyn Wozniak, who is married to Larry Wozniak, is a mother of two and a retired surgical nurse, attended the candidates' forum and had a typical response to the forum.

For Real!!

It all started in 2000. A bunch of guys had decided they wanted Congressman Bobby Rush's job. So, accompanied by a rather large number of my neighbors I went to see the forum these guys had challenged him to. #1 got up to speak. I thought to myself, he looks like my chum Jim. He started to talk and that's when it happened! In the 1st episode of "The West Wing" Josh is enlightened by the candidate and goes and drags his friend out of a board meeting, and they go to work for him. This was it! This guy's for real! Wow!! I thought.

My friend John was involved in his campaign, I saw him the next day and said, "I'm in!" Bobby Rush won anyway.

John told me the day after the primary that #1 (Obama) was going to run for something else. So, in March of 2000 I said, "Count me in!"

Our friend Lyn Wozniak continues:

He begins with an explanation of his name Barack Obama. I actually hadn't wondered about it but the name rang a bell. Anyway, he begins telling us why he should be our congressman. That's when it happened. "Holy Moley," I think. "He makes a lot of sense!!"

Remember I left off with the tall skinny guy saying that he was Barack Obama and that he wanted Bobby's job.

I caught my friend John's eye and pointed to the guy speaking. John nodded in the affirmative. This was the guy John had said earlier was, "Someone to keep our eye on, hope for the future, etc."

Our friend Lyn Wozniak continues:

Well!, all of a sudden there's a commotion in the lobby. We are all distracted and turn to see… Bobby! Complete with an adoring entourage following behind him applauding vigorously. The video cameras rolling. The works. I've seen that before, in the days of the 'machine', it was for Hanrahan that time.

The woman from the League of Women Voters took the podium and pointedly told Bobby that he was rude, late, and since he wasn't there to take a number, he would be last, and to sit down and shut up (she put it more politely). We applauded. Obama didn't even twitch. He smiled, thanked Bobby for coming, and continued to convince me of the reason to vote for him. As it turned out, I wasn't the only one convinced that night. That's where it all started.

What nailed it down was Bobby's next move to dazzle us. When it was his turn, he said he was late because the police stopped him. I couldn't believe it, he was going to play the race card. He hadn't done his homework. This is an area where integration works about as well as it can. Further, some of the biggest supporters of the police are my African-American neighbors. I looked at one of them. She had on her 'How dare you/Who do you think you are!' looks. She and I had mentioned to one of Bobby's aides once about his absence at an Anti-Drug rally in the neighborhood.

Three precincts vote in this room. Obama carried them all by a big margin in the primary.

— Lyn Wozniak,
Super Obama volunteer 2000, 2004, 2008

∼

I often speculate that if Bobby had been there on time and not insisted that he would not attend and graciously accepted our invitation, how would that have changed things? What if Rush accepted our August 1994 invitation? Would Rush have established a relationship in the community? Would that have driven Obama down a different road?

Likely, it would have diminished Barack Obama's star that evening and he might have been just another one of the candidates running for

Congress. Obama would have blended. Now he stood out.

Several questions had already been asked and answered when Rush finally showed up. Had Bobby attended on time, he may have been the star of the evening. Politicians often received poor advice and such was the case with Bobby Rush when it came to this forum. He failed to take full advantage of the power of incumbency.

The *Chicago Sun Times* Lorraine Forte wrote in the March 8th, 2000 edition about the March 7th event and reported that Rush arrived thirty minutes late. The answers, she wrote, "revealed few political differences."[47]

This was Barack Obama's night. It was his "coming out" party. This was his celebration. Of the 600 people in attendance, a great majority of them would become "Pied Pipers of Hamelin for Obama." This obscure State Senator from Hyde Park with the funny name had clearly made a huge impact on this crowd. He was the star of the evening and for a half hour, he was it. For Obama, a half hour is enough time to win you over.

He dazzled the crowd and, frankly, dazzled Michelle and me.

Here is what Kathy Konopasek who is our friend, neighbor, customer and Obama volunteer had to say about that evening and about Obama.

Obama on the House

Beverly community members and business owners, John and Michelle Presta were extremely enthusiastic about this guy from Hyde Park. The saying "All politics is local," may be true, since I was immersed for two years in Hyde Park for employment, and had two wonderful summers as a University of Chicago scholar, but as long time Beverly resident and well informed citizen. The Hyde Park community and their elected Illinois State Senator Obama, seemed to be completely in left field.

However, I had complete trust and belief in the opinion of our local Reading on Walden Bookstore owners. They had been active in the community for years, spearheading the community policing strategy and taking a risk by opening a small business. They turned me on to Barack and I found myself volunteering with them and attending their grassroots meetings.

There was a turning point for me, when at a meeting put together by the

---

47   Better late than never: Rush, rivals debate; [5XS Edition] LORRAINE FORTE. *Chicago Sun-Times*. Chicago, Ill.: Mar 8, 2000. pg. 24.

Prestas on March 7, 2000 at a local church Obama was debating our representative, Bobby Rush. I was surprised at how acidic Rush's people were toward Obama. One Rush member implied that it would be a detriment to our community to have someone like Obama be our representative because of his Hyde Park connection. Obama lost that race.

But when Obama decided to run for the Senate, John and Michelle's enthusiasm, work and support continued. It was truly grassroots, authentic and catching. So much so, that on my tiny home in Beverly, I took the measurements for my five front porch windows and purchased self-adhesive letters O-B-A-M-A and posted and illuminated the sign. What made my support statement special is that the house is parallel to the popular Metra Rock Island commuter railway. Passengers could not help but see the future Senator's name in lights going to and from downtown Chicago each day.

Indeed, all politics are local. I thank John and Michelle for their insight and citizenship in our community.

— Katherine Konopasek

Kathy was one such convert that evening, some in response to the negativity of Bobby Rush, but mostly to the positive aspects of Obama.

Obama continued to score points with Michelle and me. He was able to use our bookstore as an example in answering a question about the Internet sales tax issue. We were being schmoozed, and it worked. More impressive is that he was the only one of the four candidates that understood the question. The question was about the Internet sales tax and not about a tax on the Internet. Obama understood the distinction. The other three candidates didn't get.

Internet taxation was a raging issue for us back in 2000 because we had just started our online bookstore web site and this small company called Amazon.com had a clear competitive advantage over us. I had written that question because I wanted to know where my future Congressman stood on the issue.

Barack Obama got it.

We spent three months organizing and promoting this event, and it showed. We had no idea prior to that evening what an impact this evening would have on Obama's future and our own our future. The reactions continued to pour in. Robert Davis, a friend, neighbor, customer, community activist and labor union activist, is a long-time Obama supporter.

John:

I think Reading on Walden Bookstore was my daughter Hollie's first bookstore. I remember bringing her to the store when she was a toddler and she wanted every book that she could reach. It appeared to me that she was picking books by the book covers because I knew she couldn't read. That experience has lasted her entire life. She still reads excessively. I will always remember the demonstrations we had on our block against drug selling. You and Michelle were at our house. I was at that debate in 1999 (I think) where Barack was running for congressman against Bobby Rush where he lost every district except ours. I also remember how you guys convinced us to work on his behalf. Barack will always be connected to you and Michelle for forcing me to stand out in the cold campaigning for him on Election Day and waiting at Sutherland School for a printout of the result. I also remember some of his opponents trying to get me to leave the polling place I was working saying, "You can leave. He is going to win." I knew they just wanted me to leave so they wouldn't have to compete.

—Robert Davis,
Super Obama volunteer 2004, 2008

As our relationship developed with Obama, we were told by a lobbyist from Springfield what an enormous grasp Obama had on the workings of state government. "He's a student of state government," he told us. "And I imagine he is a student of anything he tackles. Quite an impressive man."

Obama made it his business to find out how Springfield and the State of Illinois worked. He knew all the right buttons to push in state government in order to achieve constituent services. He received high marks from his constituents. And he demanded the same high standards from his staff.

He is also a policy wonk, much like former President Bill Clinton. He can explain an issue from both sides and from many angles that perhaps were not considered. Most of all, he kept those he dealt with at ease. He looked people straight in the eye. He is a WYSIWYG politician.

We also could not help but notice that Obama would never leave a room until he was sure to have shaken hands with everyone or hugged and/or kissed them hello or goodbye depending on the situation. He made sure he acknowledged everyone who took the time to come to an event. This evening at Bethany Union was no exception. He shook every hand that evening. Many people in attendance wanted to say hello. We were still putting chairs away and cleaning up the facility and noticed Obama was still talking with and greeting people.

At one point as I putting away chairs, Obama came over and said, "Thanks again for doing this." No sooner had he said that, another person from the audience was tugging at him. He had made an impression.

After the forum in which Obama received a great deal of publicity, his campaign seemed to pick up some momentum. We were collecting names of people that wanted to get involved with Obama. Lyn Wozniak was one of them.

Count Me In!!
By Lyn Wozniak

The primary was over. I was talking to John and his wife Michelle. When Michelle told me about the vote, I remarked that it wasn't our fault that we still had Bobby.

By the way, we were redistricted again and now have Lipinski. My neighbors have all said that we're cool with that.

John then remarked that Obama was planning to run for something else. Count me in, said I. Put my name on the list.

$\sim$

Well, we didn't have an Obama list of volunteers. At least not yet, nor was that how we defined it. But thanks to Lyn, it got us thinking. That would come later, although we saved all the names we collected that night.

One of the reasons incumbents do not like to hold debates, forums and joint appearances with their opposition is exactly what occurred that evening. Congressman Rush had little choice but to attend the forum, in response to the media pressure that we helped to exert with the aid of the League of Women Voters and the Citizens Information Service. Our strategy in including the League of Women Voters legitimized the event in the eyes of the media.

Without this candidates' forum, the campaign would have come to a complete dead end. The campaign, up until March 7th, was on a near political media blackout. Moreover, it was not until this forum that there was considerable attention to Barack Obama. In the coming days, he would have some other joint events, including radio interviews and a television appearance on the Chicago Tonight show broadcast from Chicago's PBS station, Channel 11. The media's love affair with Obama was blossoming in its early stages. After the March 7th forum, the congressional race received non-stop media attention on television, radio, magazines and newspapers. The man with the funny name was getting attention. The attention can be directly traced to this evening of March 7th, 2000, in the Beverly Hills community, at this non-denominational church at an event organized by two small bookstore owners. While the attention was not enough to save this campaign, it would be invaluable in future campaigns.

The candidates' forum was a no win situation for Rush. If he attended, the media would start paying attention to this bright young star in the Democratic Party. Had Rush not attended, the media would have paid exclusive attention to this bright young star.

The day after the candidates' forum, Phil Kadner of the *Daily Southtown* wrote a column about the event that I found inexplicable. It was as if we attended different events.

There's no 'Bulworth' in Congressional Debate

Warren Beatty may be a handsome guy, but he could never win a congressional election, especially if he ran as the outspoken "Bulworth."

I thought about Beatty's movie character as I watched a debate the other night between four Democratic candidates running in the First Congressional District primary.

The candidates all seemed to be intelligent guys with interesting backgrounds.

Bobby Rush (D-Chicago) is the incumbent. He was a Chicago alderman before running for Congress in 1992, but is probably best known as a former Black Panther.

Rush never mentioned his Black Panther background. It could be that he assumes everyone knows about his radical roots. Or it could be that he doesn't think it would help him win re-election.

Rush also failed to mention that he holds two masters degrees.

The congressman, who showed up for the debate about 30 minutes late, didn't say anything radical. He talked about the money he had brought back to his district from Washington, D.C. and his support for the Brady Bill, which requires a waiting period to purchase a handgun.

A lot of the time, he seemed to have difficulty collecting his thoughts or recalling details, which could be a tactic designed to draw support from other middle-aged men who have the same problem.

Did Rush say anything memorable? Not that I can recollect, although it's possible that he did and I forgot.

Barack Obama, a state senator, has Sidney Poitier good looks and is one of the most articulate candidates you are ever likely to hear on the campaign stump.

But in his summation at the end of the night, he accurately noted that his views on political issues are not much different than those of the other three candidates.

He supports more laws controlling the availability of guns, backs some ill-defined notion of national health care and thinks it's time to lift the economic embargo against Cuba (as did the other candidates).

Obama mentioned that he teaches a law class at the University of Chicago, but neglected to mention that he was the first black editor of the Harvard Law Review.

Obama explained that his unusual last name was inherited from his father, who is from Kenya. His mother, he added, is from Kansas.

If Obama said anything memorable, or newsworthy, it slipped my mind.

Donne Trotter, another state senator, wore a Paul Simon-type bow tie and was almost as eloquent as Obama.

He came close to criticizing Rush, claiming that it's not enough to sponsor legislation if you are a congressman, you have to actually pass legislation.

Trotter claims to have been a key proponent of Kid Care legislation in the General Assembly, which guarantees that no child in Illinois will be denied medical care due to a lack of money.

George Roby, the fourth candidate, was in many ways the most interesting member of the group.

A retired police officer, he is running on the ordinary guy platform. He probably had the weakest position on gun control.

While the other fellows in the race plan to spend more than $100,000 on their campaigns, Roby said he plans to spend about $10,000 of his own money.

One of the first things he did after filing his nominating petitions for office was buy a used copying machine to print his own literature, he told the crowd.

Roby is the longest shot in the race, yet he still didn't say anything that made him stand out from the rest of the pack.

The debate, sponsored by the League of Women Voters and the East Beverly Association, was not a debate in the traditional sense.

Candidates were not allowed to ask each other questions.

Instead, they were each given a list of 15 questions in advance and given one minute to answer each question.

On the positive side, there was no negative campaigning. No one made outrageous claims about an opponent. No one tried to use scare tactics, "Vote for me or Social Security will come to an end."

Talking to a handful of residents after the meeting, I would say Obama was the most effective in pleading his case.

"I think Obama would be the more likely to sway opinions in Congress because he's more eloquent," said one woman, pretty much summarizing Obama's own closing remarks.

Rush's late entrance (he claimed his car was stopped by police for speeding) probably hurt him with fence sitters. It looked staged, even if it wasn't.

Debates like this one are better than nothing.

But smart candidates realize that you shouldn't say anything that's likely to anger a lot of potential voters.

The four Democrats running in the First District were all smart enough to avoid that trap.[48]

~

When I questioned Kadner about this years later, it was clear Kadner recalled the column. Kadner reiterated what he wrote and defended the column. It was obvious that Kadner was not in Obama's corner. "You know, my column still irritates Obama," Kadner told me. "He called me complaining about the column."

Tracy and Much of the Crowd Are Mesmerized by Obama

Add me to the list. I was irritated with Kadner's column too. Kadner's view of the candidates' forum was the front row, but it was obvious he didn't see the excitement going on behind him. The crowd was mesmerized with Obama. For example, Tracy Smith of the League of Women Voters was in the front row and saw it much different.

Wow, that seems like a lifetime ago! I remember that evening well. It was the first time I worked with him and the night I realized he was something special. I was timekeeping and kept losing track of the time when he spoke because he was so engaging. We did a forum at the Chicago Urban

---

48   Phil Kadner. "Phil Kadner : There's no 'Bulworth' in congressional debate." *Daily Southtown* (Chicago, IL) March 8, 2000.

League as well. Bobby Rush was calling him "Professor" like it was a
shameful thing to be.

— Tracy Smith,
Chicago League of Women Voters,
Executive Director, 2000

One method in defeating an "entrenched incumbent" is the sneak attack. In Chicago, it sometimes happens in local aldermanic campaigns when a sitting alderman does not tend to his constituents, fails to meet the opposition every step of the way, doesn't return telephone calls or ignores the "Pied Pipers" of the community. Amazingly, even those races are typically close. After this reception for Obama, it should have been obvious to Congressman Rush that this Obama opponent was no slouch. With Obama, we called it the "**to know him is to love him**" theory. This bore out in much of the polling later on, and it went something like this: when the voters got to know Obama whether through the media, through his book, from speeches, or meeting people personally, he resonated with the voters. Rush had to be careful he did not let this Obama person become a runaway train. His attendance at this forum saved the campaign for Rush, but he made a tactical error initially in ignoring Obama. Rush quickly responded. He could not and would not let Barack Obama steal this race from him.

Immediately after the candidates' forum, I approached Shomon and told him the words he wanted to hear.

"Michelle and I endorse Obama."

"You have my endorsement. And Michelle's too. And whoever else we can recruit." He was excited. We had agreed that evening that we would pass out yard signs to neighbors and friends and call people we knew on his behalf. Time was working against us with less than two weeks in the campaign. We had never worked a campaign before. We did not know what the campaign already knew: the odds of winning were long. It was likely too late, but we would not give up so easily. While Obama had definite strengths in his home turf of Hyde Park and Thomas Dart and his crew had flooded the Mount Greenwood community with Obama yard signs, the campaign was weak elsewhere.

It was symbolic that the campaign was located in this community. In retrospect, a second and third office in another part of the Congressional district would have been a big help.

And money.

Lots more money certainly was needed. Money to purchase signs, hire staff, and advertise on television and the radio. The fundraising part of the campaign was mediocre at best and was a glaring weakness of the campaign. More effort should have been made in that area. Fundraising is not the most pleasant task in a campaign, but it is necessary for success. Shomon often mentioned the shortage of funds. In any future campaigns, fundraising would receive a higher priority.

There was something different about Obama, and we could feel it instinctively. There was no question that he would have a bright future in politics. We were on the same pages with the issues, and it was obvious he was an outstanding speaker. He had great empathy, and it was something that he conveyed to people whether one-on-one or to a large group. He resonated. What Obama would say to Michelle and me in private would be the same if a microphone were in front of us. He has one personality. And he possessed great discipline.

Shomon often said, "I didn't know how many copies I would have to buy before I got your endorsement." That issue just would not have made any difference to us. We didn't judge people by the number of books they bought or didn't buy. We did know that we liked the book and that it was well written and literate. The genre of the memoir was gaining steam in the book business, and we had a growing feeling that this book was "quality."

Several other joint appearances were being held in areas where Rush was much stronger. The Congressman did not have an organization of his own. Many Ward organizations came to the Congressman's rescue. He was at the mercy of various ward organizations. One elected official who was in his corner was Cook County Board President John Stroger, who overwhelmingly delivered his ward for Rush.

Change comes slowly, gradually, incrementally, and suddenly.

CHAPTER 4

Barack Obama's "Coming Out Party:" The Candidates' Forum

~

After the candidates' forum, Michelle and I decided that we would support State Senator Barack Obama This also meant we would volunteer our time to the campaign, although there were less than two weeks to go in the race. We understood that winning for Obama was a long shot. Nevertheless, I did not like Bobby Rush's behavior through this whole forum process, and as I look back to this type of behavior, I realized that this is typical incumbent behavior. I didn't buy into the "Bobby doesn't deliver" arguments. The *Chicago Reader* published an article on March 16, 2000 titled "Is Bobby Rush in Trouble? Two formidable opponents in the race for his congressional seat are banking on it."[49] Rush disputed accusations that he doesn't "bring home the bacon," citing federal money to resurface 95th Street, helping Evergreen Park get a new zip code, and work on building a new post office in Alsip. He also secured funding to rebuild the extensive number of Metra stations in the Beverly community.

Phil Kadner fueled the "Black Panther" thing in his column, but I didn't buy into that either. I just saw this 'rising star,' Barack Obama. It was much less anti-Bobby Rush sentiment on my part and overwhelmingly pro-Barack Obama.

---

49 *Chicago Reader.* Mach 16, 2000. Is Bobby Rush in Trouble? Two formidable opponents in the race for his congressional seat are banking on it.

Judge Sheila Murphy Was the First Candidate Reading on Walden Supported

Our decision to support a political candidate for any office was not arrived at lightly. Up until this election, our store windows were clear of anything political, except for one brief time in 1996 when we agreed to display a sign for our friend, Circuit Court Judge Sheila Murphy. Sheila was the presiding judge at the Cook County Courthouse in Markham, Illinois. We admired Sheila's stance on the death penalty. Sheila did not just talk the talk. She walked the walk as evidenced by her courageous act on June 24, 1996, when she released Verneal Jimerson[50] and called it "an egregious denial of due process," and dismissed the charges."[51] This led to the release of three others in the case, Dennis Williams, William Rainge and Kenneth Adams, who were also exonerated by DNA evidence. This act directly led to the death penalty moratorium in Illinois that is in effect to this day and hopefully will lead to the abolishment of the death penalty Illinois.

Sheila was running for Judge of the Appellate Court in 1996 and finished third in a close race. Sheila is also featured in a book by noted author and scholar Thomas Cahill, *A Saint on Death Row: The Story of Dominique Green.*[52] Sheila represented Dominique and worked tirelessly to commute his sentence. Dominique was executed on October 26, 2004 by the State of Texas, despite thousands of hours of work on his behalf. Texas Governor Rick Perry refused a last-minute appeals in spite of pleas by many prominent people, such as Bishop Desmond Tutu of South Africa.

We were selective about our political choices. After the candidates' forum, we began our relationship and our undying support for this obscure State Senator with the funny name.

Michelle and I never viewed the name Barack Obama as a liability. We frankly thought it was a cool name and did not understand all the fuss. We saw it clearly as being an asset. Once you repeated the name Barack

---

50 Jimerson was on death row for 18 years.
51 Andrew Fegelman, Tribune Staff Writer. "DEATH ROW INMATE EXONERATED CHARGES DISMISSED AGAINST MAN IN '78 RAPE, KILLINGS: [SOUTHWEST SPORTS FINAL, SW Edition]."
52 Cahill, Thomas. *A Saint on Death Row: The Story of Dominique Green.* New York: Nan A. Talese/Doubleday, 2009.

Obama a couple of times, it sang like a song, and it stuck with you. The name is poetic. The name is lyrical. It could not be confused with any other name. He stood out. And after all, standing out above the crowd is a treasured political asset. It made for a great icebreaker in his famous stump speeches. "My name is Obama. Some call me Yo Mamma. Some call me Alabama." It usually got laughs before he went onto the serious issues of the campaign. Some campaign aides felt the name was a liability, we strongly disagreed. It is an asset. It is a treasure.

The day after the forum, we received dozens of telephone calls. People were stopping by the store to say that they were there. What was that nice man's name again? Barack Obama. Oh yes, Barack Obama, they would repeat. We would repeat the Obama mantra that "A Star is Born." This went on through Election Day. He had created this tremendous buzz. I had no doubt that he would do very well here. We passed out yard signs, buttons, window signs and literature. And we talked about him everywhere we went. Every minute of those thirteen days leading to Election Day, we promoted the candidacy of Obama every step of the way.

19th Ward Committeeman Thomas Hynes, according to inside sources, convened a special meeting with the 19th Ward precinct captains in an attempt to rally the precinct captains behind Bobby Rush. Thomas Hynes and the official 19th Ward organization was supporting Bobby Rush, but Hynes was unable to control the events in the ward. It would have been an embarrassment for Hynes politically to have Obama win the ward. It was as much a power struggle for Hynes as an entrée for Obama in this part of the city. There was already a large faction in the western part of the 19th Ward that was supporting Obama. With this latest development and our group starting to form and working with Obama, he could win the entire ward, and win every single precinct. The meeting was in direct response to this dramatic development in the community with Obama — the overwhelming support he was receiving on the west end of the ward with Tom Dart's crew and on the east end of the ward with our crew, and the tremendous impact the candidates' forum had. As one Hynes ally told me at the time, "We are quietly supporting Obama."

'A Star is Born' mantra was being whispered.

"Did you hear that guy?"

"You've got to see this guy."

"Class act."

"A Rising Star."

Thomas Dart, then a State Representative in the Illinois House, was the chief organizer on the west end of the 19th ward with Dan Shomon, in the area known as Mount Greenwood. This caused a split in the 19th Ward organization. The support for Obama was as much for Obama as it was against Bobby Rush.

This was the Illinois game of political musical chairs. There was so much young talent in the state of Illinois and precious few slots. There was Dan Hynes, with a slight edge as State Comptroller. He had won a statewide office, which would take him a long way to higher office. There was then State Senator Lisa Madigan, the daughter of Illinois House Speaker Michael Madigan. Thomas Dart was an up and coming Illinois State Representative, and he was a strong advocate for women's rights, children's rights and many other progressive social issues.

Obama had to be included in the hunt, too. Obama would make his mark and move up a notch in Illinois politics if he won this important Congressional seat. Tom Hynes had to cut people like Obama off at the pass. He could not allow Obama a chair in the "political game of musical chairs," because it was obvious that Barack Obama had much going for him: looks, intelligence, charm, background. Now this young man Barack Obama was coming into Tom Hynes' back yard and making a strong showing.

Tom Hynes did not have any special affection for Bobby Rush, in spite of his public show of support for Rush. My observation was that Tom Hynes was advancing his son's career at the expense of much more talented candidates, including some in his own ward.

The precinct captains complained to Tom Hynes that Bobby wasn't there for them, so why should they support such a man? Tom Hynes assured them that Rush would be there for them going forward. Tom Hynes had many motivations in attempting to keep his captains at bay, but the overriding reason was the advancement of his son, Dan Hynes, who had recently been elected State Comptroller in 1998. He did not want to offend the regular Democrats. Tom Hynes wanted and needed their support if he expected his son's career to advance if he ran for Governor or United States Senate.

After Rush's performance at the candidates' forum at Bethany Union Church, Rush started to find his campaign legs. He received a boost that was to change the campaign dramatically, in his favor. It was this evening that he realized Obama was a formidable opponent. Rush observed all the people glad-handing Obama after the event and had to notice how he resonated with the crowd. The crowd was not necessarily pro-Obama. Before the evening, they had never heard of him. It was not an anti-Rush crowd either.

We deliberately advertised the event as a non-partisan presentation, and that is what it was. The organizers, including the League of Women Voters, as is their practice, did not take a position on the candidates and that included me. The crowd came as interested community members wanting to make a choice on Election Day. None of the promotional pieces for the event advocated one candidate over another. To my knowledge, no stories appeared in the local newspapers about any of the candidates.

What happened next sealed the deal for Congressman Rush. President Bill Clinton went on a radio ad blitz on African-American radio for his friend Rush. This was not something that President Clinton did very often, but Rush had personally appealed to Clinton for his help, and Clinton consented.

Rush's call for help was a direct result of the overwhelming show of support that Obama received at our candidates' forum. The effect of this cannot be underestimated. Clinton was wildly popular in the African-American community. He had a personal relationship in the Chicago African-American community, having spoken at many of the churches there. He knew many of the African-American ministers by first name. So for President Bill Clinton to endorse Bobby Rush, this was bad news. Clinton was affectionately called "the first black president," an honorary title and a tremendous show of respect that was given to him by Toni Morrison. She was the winner of the Nobel Prize for Literature in 1993. The award is given for the lifetime achievement of an author. In 1988, Morrison won the Pulitzer Prize for Fiction for her work on *Beloved: A Novel.*[53]

Clinton's standing in the African-American community was without question in 2000 or today. This was huge.

Shomon was clearly upset at President Clinton's intervention in this campaign. I never got the sense that anyone blamed Clinton because they understood that this was how politics worked. The difficulty of defeating an incumbent is that they become entrenched. They develop political friendships and network with each other.

"This is clearly a boost for my efforts to be reelected here," Rush said.[54] President Clinton's endorsement and radio commercial blitz was a blow to the Obama campaign. I believed at that point that the Obama campaign staff was beginning to feel defeat was close at hand for Obama's hopes for a seat in Congress. The radio commercials began on the Monday the week before Election Day and played nonstop. It was a payoff for the loyalty that Congressman Rush had shown the President before and after the Bill Clinton impeachment trial in the Congress. Bobby stood by the President's side in a strong show of support after the United States House of Representatives voted to impeach President Clinton in 1998.

We saw Shomon the day the Clinton commercials aired, and he was down in the dumps. "This is terrible," he said. "The most popular Democrat in the state of Illinois is endorsing Bobby Rush. This is not good."

Shomon had asked me to bring him whatever copies of the *Chicago Sun Times* I could spare on the morning of March 16th, 2000. I was able to get 75 copies of the *Chicago Sun Times*. He was hopeful that the *Chicago Sun Times* endorsement would go the Obama campaign's way. It could reverse some of the impact of the Clinton endorsement. An endorsement of Rush probably would be the death knell to the campaign.

I opened the paper that morning at 2:30 am to the editorial page and was one of the first to find out.

The *Chicago Sun Times* was endorsing Congressman Bobby Rush for

---

53   Morrison, Toni. *Beloved: A Novel.* New York: Knopf, 1987.

54   CHALLENGERS DEBATE RUSH ON HIS VOTING; [CHICAGOLAND FINAL Edition] Evan Osnos, Tribune Staff Writer. *Chicago Tribune.* Chicago, Ill.: Mar 12, 2000. pg. 4.

reelection and it was a disappointment and the fatal body blow to the Obama Congressional campaign that never found its campaign legs.

> In 1992, Bobby Rush challenged then-Rep. Charles Hayes in the 1st Congressional District by saying the incumbent 'doesn't have the fire in the belly we need.' In 2000, Rush finds himself on the receiving end of the same claim. His opponents for the Democratic nomination, State Senator Donne Trotter and State Senator Barack Obama, have both failed to make their case. Rush merits reelection.
> Trotter and Obama, both state senators and both impressive but...[55]

But . . .

I had read enough. I was disappointed, too.

I dropped the papers off at the Obama headquarters at 9525 S. Western Avenue that morning as Dan had asked. It was very early morning and Dan was not there, but I am guessing Dan had already heard.

The *Chicago Sun Times* was an endorsement Obama coveted. He clearly would have traded the *Chicago Tribune* endorsement for the *Chicago Sun Times* endorsement. The *Chicago Sun Times* was very important and influential in the African-American community at that time. *The Chicago Sun Times* endorsement had a great deal to do with the influences of Conrad Black and David Radler, who were clearly conservative and Republican leaning. Black and Radler were the publishers of the newspaper and dominated the editorial pages. Endorsing Obama, a future rising star in the Democratic Party, which is not what Black and Radler would have wanted, would have strengthened the Democrats. Whether Black and Radler were that astute politically is not known, but it is definitely a possibility. Their actions later in 2000, endorsing President Bush over Vice President Al Gore, brought out the true colors of Black and Radler.[56]

In spite of the *Chicago Sun Times* endorsement, we did our best to boost Shomon's morale. Shomon is a very astute political guy, and he

---

55 Editorials. "Another term for Rush." *Chicago Sun-Times* March 16, 2000, LATE SPORTS FINAL, EDITORIAL: 35.

56 Conrad Black was a major stockholder in the *Chicago Sun Times* and David Radler was his CEO. Both are convicted of felons, related to the operation of the company. Radler turned states evidence against Black.

can read the writing on the wall. He already knew they had little or no ground troops in a great majority of the 1st Congressional District. Hyde Park had its share of foot soldiers. Tom Dart was doing a great job getting out the yard signs, literature and Election Day help, and more importantly, the votes in the Mount Greenwood area. Along with some Evergreen Park and Oak Lawn politicians, it was clear that these areas would deliver for Barack Obama. We really had no idea how big.

And although we had only signed on after March 7th, we would quickly put together a grassroots effort that would deliver the eastern part of the 19th Ward in an overwhelming manner for Barack Obama.

Much of it was the positive response from the Bethany Union Church forum that we held. Because we had started so late in the process, our impact was limited, although we got the word out rather quickly in the two weeks before the election through word of mouth. A buzz was running through the community, created in large part to Obama's performance at the March 7th forum.

We attended a small fundraiser on the evening of March 13th at Cafe Luna, then located at 1808 W. 103rd Street. Shomon had asked us to attend so we can spend time with Obama. It was at this event we met Mike Jordan, a friend and a super-Obama worker.

Some of the elected officials that were supporting Obama also attended, including State Rep. James D. Brosnahan (D) 36th District; Oak Lawn City Clerk, Jayne Powers; and State Rep. Tom Dart. Jeff Dixon, son of former United States Senator Alan Dixon, also attended. We also invited some of our friends. Less than 20 people were there, but from Barack Obama's demeanor, you would think we had a full house.

We greeted Obama that evening, and he asked us questions about our bookstore. We discussed politics: local and national issues. He was pleased with the reception at Bethany Union Church on the 7th, and we told him we decided to get on board with the campaign. Michelle and I were impressed with this fine young man. Again, I was left with the impression that Barack Obama is a "What You See is What You Get" politician, or in the current vernacular, WYSIWYG.

Some of those attending this mini-fundraiser were the Mooney family: Caroline, Tim, and daughter Rebecca. Here is Caroline's take on that evening and her impressions of Barack Obama and other matters.

Caroline and Tim are white, and they adopted an African-American child, Rebecca. Caroline describes how Barack Obama passed the "Rebecca Mooney" test that evening.

The New Millennium and the Rebecca Mooney Test

Let me preface this by saying, at the time, we had known the Prestas only a couple years.

At any rate, John and Michelle invited us to a meet and greet for a guy running for Bobby Rush's seat. They were very enthusiastic about the candidate. I, on the other hand, am a "glass half-empty" kind of girl. John and Michelle told me about how smart Barack Obama was; I think John gave me his whole CV in like 10 minutes (you know how those Democratic true believers are).

Therefore, we decided to go, but not before I told John and Michelle that their candidate has to pass The Rebecca Mooney Test, which is where the rubber meets the road for us.

Let me explain. We have a unique family configuration. My husband Tim and I are Caucasian. Our daughter Rebecca is African American. We adopted her the day after she was born. For us, she was and is a miracle. My beautiful, talented child is now nearly 11 and over these past years, we have witnessed racism on every imaginable level. I have been in department stores, home improvement stores, grocery stores and convenience stores waiting to check out while my child was looking at the displays near the cash register and had clerks confront her asking, "Where is your mother?" or "What are you looking for?" like she shouldn't be there. When I say I am her mother and she is not doing anything, suddenly they become very sheepish and walk away. In predominantly white neighborhoods, people gawk at us in slack-jawed amazement, and think we are either nuts or should be somehow nominated for sainthood. IN THE NEW MILLENNIUM!

As obnoxious as all this is, in the African American community things are much more complicated. My day-care provider is African American. When her other clients saw that Rebecca was going home with Those White People every day, there was quite a hue and cry until she asked them directly, "Where were you when that child needed a home?" Which, of course, she can do because she is African American. We go to many black cultural events each year, but are starting to cut back, because we get a LOT of hostility when we go. We get the sideways looks, and again, the gawking, not with slack-jawed amazement, but with anger. Strangers grilling us on how Rebecca came to be part of our family, what we are teaching her about African American culture, what church do we go to, on and on and on. Therefore, our radar is always up.

We moved to Beverly to be in a diverse, stable community where there were more mixed race families and families with trans-racial adoptions, but still, you get the picture. People are what they are, and on certain issues, you cannot hide your true self.

Therefore, we go to meet Barack Obama. He is a smart person and talks to us about all kinds of things, but none of them is about stuff that falls into the category of "nunya." He met my beautiful child and did not bat an eyelash. We talked politics for a while, and I got to be a "glass half full" kind of girl for a change. Barack Obama is an interesting guy. He has a vision and the ability to convey that vision in a way that you believe he has the means to deliver. He is good at finding common ground and coalition building. I think his appeal is that he makes us feel that we CAN be our better selves, as individuals and as a nation.

— Caroline Mooney
Obama Super Volunteer

⌒

"I have a little girl at home about your age," he told Rebecca. Obama has passed the "Rebecca Mooney" test with Rebecca's parents. The Mooneys' never forgot that night and were great promoters of Barack Obama after that date. And for me, Obama passed the Rebecca Mooney test with flying colors (no pun). He didn't blink. Not one eyelash. He didn't comment that the parents were white and the child was African-American. He embraced little Rebecca Mooney and saw her as a child, period. Not African-American, not white. Just a beautiful child.

Another person in attendance was our friend and neighbor Bob Bruno. He had spent some time that evening talking with Obama and Shomon and from that point forward Bruno was in Obama's corner. I had taken a photo of Bruno, Shomon and Obama. He had treasured that photo. He was interested in meeting Obama because he attended the candidates' forum on March 7th and was impressed with Obama's performance. He picked up a yard sign that night and was an Obama supporter after that evening.

Bruno was a retired salesman with American Greeting Cards. Bruno held court every night at 11:00 p.m. at the local Dunkin Donuts and typically stayed there from 11:00 p.m. to 1:00 a.m. If you walked into Dunkin Donuts during those hours, he knew you and greeted you. And he knew your name. I always knew that he was a successful salesman, and to spend five minutes with him you knew why. He was now selling Obama to anyone who would listen.

Bruno knew about the candidates' forum from me because most

nights I was in Dunkin Donuts on my way to my newspaper distribution job for the *Chicago Sun Times*, one of my other jobs. It was a chance to get a great cup of coffee and great conversation. He wanted to know what was going on in the community. He was a long-time member of the East Beverly Association. Bob's late wife, June Bruno, was also an active part of the Beverly community. Bob and June Bruno were active members of the community for many years. June greeted and welcomed me to the community within days of my moving into my house and said please call her if I needed anything or had any questions about the community. The community was filled with people like Bob and June Bruno.

When Bruno heard about the candidates' forum, he wanted to attend. He had a degree of dissatisfaction with Bobby Rush. He asked if he could be accommodated there because at this point in Bruno's life, he had a difficult time with his physical health. I did accommodate him, as I did for many events and helped him to the front row. I escorted him to the front row for his ringside seat to American History.

Bob Bruno typified the Obama supporters. Because of health issues, he would not be able to canvass door-to-door for the campaign, but he was valuable to the Obama campaign by talking about Obama to everyone and anyone who would listen. Bob Bruno's platform was Dunkin Donuts.

"You got to meet this guy," he would tell people. "This guy can be President of the United States one day."

He Connects With People

As Michelle and I left the mini-fundraiser at Café Luna that evening, it was our consensus that we were talking to a future President of the United States. From that evening on, his being President of the United States one day was the elephant in the room. Michelle and I had discussed it that evening for the first time at great length. We were both thinking it and now we were discussing it. And we would discuss it with others, too. Michelle and I were excited by Obama. I already knew of his background from the book and knew that he had a keen intellect. And his grasp on the burning issues of the day was astounding. He had it.

And he connected with everyone he met.

I could not help but notice that this man looked you right in the eye when he spoke. Obama had a trait that is a gift: he makes the person he is speaking with feel that they are the only person in the world. He is totally focused on the person in front of him. I had told Obama that we were getting an overwhelming reaction from the candidates' forum and that people wanted to know where to sign up for the campaign. I really did not understand any of it at the time, but it is clear now: the Barack Obama bug bit me.

We kept hoping for a miracle. What we didn't know at the time, but what Obama and Shomon knew, was that outside of the 19th Ward and Hyde Park, the campaign was weak, lacking money, and lacking resources to cover the entire 1st Congressional District. They had both concluded that they could not win. Obama and Shomon had forgotten to tell us, but we would not have believed them anyway. Such was our passion for Obama. And it all happened in such a short time. But time was running short for Obama. Election Day, March 21st was right around the corner.

John Stroger, Ward Committeeman of the 8th Ward, had effectively pulled all his troops out for Bobby Rush in the 8th Ward, another role reversal that four years later would turn dramatically in Barack Obama's favor. But in 2000, Stroger delivered for Congressman Rush. Overwhelmingly.

The Southside Irish Parade

On Sunday, March 12, 2000, Obama marched in the 22nd Annual South Side Irish Parade. Obama attended mass and had breakfast at the home of BAPA Executive Director Willie Winters. Tom Dart escorted Obama to the home of Jack and Maureen Kelly for Irish Soda Bread and breakfast casserole before marching in the parade. He later marched in the parade with a group of Democrats, mostly allies of Tom Dart who had organized the western part of the 19th Ward on Obama's behalf and delivered for Obama in a very big way.

As Barack Obama was marching in the parade, he spotted Michelle and me in the crowd at the corner of 107th and Western. Obama enthusiastically pointed at us and waved. He shouted out our names and quickly came over to us and gave us a hug. He then continued south down on Western Avenue. We were able to photograph that event as it happened.

Beverly was one giant block party Sunday, as about 300,000 people descended on the neighborhood for the 22nd annual South Side Irish Parade. Neighbors hosted open house parties before and after the parade, which moved south on Western Avenue from 103rd to 115th streets. Bagpipers in kilts drank beer on front lawns and praised the weather. Teens wearing Mardi Gras beads with hair dyed bright green for the occasion stopped to talk on streets closed to traffic.

On Tuesday night, March 14, 2000, the candidates in the 1st District congressional race hit the television airwaves. Once again they showed little disagreement on the issues. "I don't think there are a lot of ideological differences," said Obama, who appeared on WTTW-Channel 11's "Chicago Tonight" with Rush and Trotter.

This lack of ideological differences is what made the campaign so difficult for Obama. There was no question in our minds that in spite of the outcome of this race, Barack Obama still had a very bright future in Democratic politics. He was a "Rising Star" of the Democratic Party.

Shomon had invited Michelle and me to the victory celebration in Hyde Park, but Dan Shomon and Barack Obama were aware that it would not be a victory celebration. Shomon and Obama hadn't let Michelle and me in on the secret: Obama would not defeat Rush, and they both knew it.

Michelle and I found out the hard way: on Election night.

Words Seldom Heard: Obama Loses an Election

Barack Obama lost to Bobby Rush by a wide margin. He did well in a few pockets, like the 19th Ward, Evergreen Park, Oak Lawn and Hyde Park. Obama failed to carry the rest of the District. After the defeat, Dan Shomon told Michelle and me, "Remember, you will always have a friend in Springfield. Feel free to call him anytime."

Steve Neal of the *Chicago Sun Times* wrote that Obama would be heard from again. Obama hinted on election night that he might make another run in the 1st Congressional District. That would have been a mistake, as evidenced by Rush's overwhelming win in the March 21 primary. It is most difficult to oust a sitting congressman. Rush would probably be stronger in 2002.

Obama's defeat was a crushing blow to us, nevertheless. For the previous two weeks, we had worked the campaign hard on behalf of Obama. We had put in a full three months working on this campaign if you include the time spent organizing the candidates' forum. We liked it. It was our first real full-fledged campaign. We were infected by the political bug. We wanted to do this again. It was like handselling a good book: an easy sell. A hidden gem. The selling of Barack Obama. It was like selling Harry Potter to teens and pre-teens. It just had to be displayed properly.

We were assuming that Obama would defeat Rush, but we later found out that it would have taken a miracle. Miracles do not just happen in politics. Miracles happen from great campaigning and a message that resonates with the voters that the voters actually hear. Miracles happen slowly, gradually, incrementally and suddenly. It just wasn't the time for Obama to win, and we didn't "get it."

Miracles in campaigns don't just happen. It is a process.

Change comes slowly, gradually, incrementally, and suddenly.

~

We did not get on board with the campaign until very late in the process, but for the short period we were involved, we made a huge impact. After his defeat, we wondered aloud how much we could accomplish in a campaign given much more time. What if we had fourteen months to prepare and spread the word about our new friend, Barack Obama. What if we had signed on in September when Obama first announced his candidacy and what if we had more time to organize volunteers. Spread ourselves to the rest of the 1st Congressional District. Pass out more yard signs. Pass out more literature. Make phone calls. Knock on doors. Spread the word. Raise more money for the candidate. It was a daunting task for us. It was strange because we had spent such a relatively short period working for him.

We could feel that it was our destiny to promote the candidacy of Barack Obama. Something was happening. We must have been smitten.

"We were bitten by the political bug."

"We were bitten by the Obama bug."

Regardless of any discouraging words people would have for me or for Michelle about Barack Obama, it went in one ear and out the other. I was wearing blinders when it came to this man. I had friends who explained to me why Obama didn't win and why he would not amount to anything.

One friend would berate me over and over, "Johnny, you just have to give up on this Obama guy. He's going nowhere." I just could not, would not accept this explanation.

We truly believed that we could help Obama win a future campaign. Before the candidates' forum on March 7, 2000, Barack Obama was a virtual unknown and, had it not been for that forum, he would have remained an unknown in our community. It gave Obama some hope for the future. We were the catalyst for Obama in this community. We were a shining example of what could be accomplished. Michelle and I were both community organizers, and we did "get it."

That forum upped his profile, not just in our community but around the city too, because of the television coverage given the race after March 7th. Rarely does an incumbent get much coverage because the media considers the race not to be close. After the candidates' forum, television stations covered the race as a direct result of the profile that was raised in the forum. "Would Bobby Rush show up?" was the question. The same man that accused Mayor Daley of "dodging" debates and joint events was now attempting to dodge debates and joint events. The candidates' forum was having the "domino effect" on the campaign and putting Barack Obama on the map. Especially outside of the 1st Congressional District. He was slowly, surely starting to be known throughout the community.

A candidate like Obama needs to merely get his foot in the door. And we took pride in the fact that we helped Obama do just that. Obama had the rare ability to energize and inspire a crowd. It was a natural-born gift. He also had the ability to make a person feel special, like that person is the only person in the world.

We had lost, and we were disappointed. I still believed that one day we would be there to share a great victory with Barack Obama. We could just feel that Obama would someday be a winner in this Illinois game of political musical chairs, and possibly beyond Illinois. It was clear to us that once Obama vaulted onto the national stage, he would be a player.

The fact was, by the time we signed onto the campaign, Obama had no chance of victory. Victories do not occur overnight. They build. They gain momentum.

Change comes slowly, gradually, incrementally, and suddenly.

We Just Couldn't Wait for the Next Campaign

It would be less than three years before we would work another campaign for Barack Obama. We just could not wait for another opportunity to work with this outstanding young man.

And we kept his book on our shelves. In spite of the fact that the book was out-of-print. In spite of the fact that it was not our "modus operandi." Books stay for so long and then move on. Sometime sixty, ninety days, at the most, unless they show salability. It is that simple. We could not and would not give up on this book for emotional reasons. No one ever advised us not to get emotionally involved with our books. We would not and could not give up on the book or on Barack Obama.

The excitement was contagious. If we could accomplish so much for him in less than two weeks, what could we accomplish working an entire campaign from start to finish? The campaign did not reach beyond the 19th Ward. Tom Dart and his crew did a great job in a door-to-door effort on the western end of the district, and we were able to get the word out quickly first with the candidates' forum and then by spreading the word out to the eastern part of the district and through our vast network of friends. The campaign was stretched thin.

What was encouraging was that after the March 7, 2000 forum, dozens of people came into or called us at the store to ask about this bright young State Senator Barack Obama. We were preaching the gospel of Barack Obama. We knew something special was happening.

Barack Obama lost on March 21. He was knocked to the canvass by a more experienced opponent. But, on March 22, Obama pulled himself off the canvass and would never be defeated again: reminiscent of his idol, the boxer, Muhammad Ali.[57] Obama would do the knocking out

---

57   One of Obama's favorite photos that hangs in his office is of Ali standing over an opponent he
     had just knocked out.

in the future.

The defeat was crushing for Obama, but Al Kindle, a campaign aide for the Congressional race, told Obama shortly after his defeat to Bobby Rush, "You lost the skirmish, but you won the war." It seemed to cheer up Obama, according to Kindle. He had appeal with white people and people of all races. With the encouragement of friends like Al Kindle, Obama pulled himself together.

Obama was born anew on March 22, 2000. On that day, he went around the community in search of people who had displayed Obama for Congress signs and knocked on dozens of doors. Moreover, he thanked them for their support. Linda Kozloski recalls a knock on the door one day and it was Barack Obama thanking her for displaying an "Obama" sign in her window. Linda and her husband, Tom Bohn, invited Obama in the house, and they chatted for about fifteen minutes. It was an unforgettable moment for Tom and Linda etched in their memories forever. It inspired Linda to tirelessly promote Barack Obama.

Obama started his next campaign, going door-to-door, thanking voters, running for an unknown office. He went on an unknown journey. Obama started on a journey knocking on doors and slowly, surely building a grassroots organization.

Change comes slowly, gradually, incrementally, and suddenly.

David Mendell reported in his book[58] that Barack Obama had always aspired to be the mayor of Chicago. He wanted to be like Mayor Harold Washington, who pulled together a coalition of African-Americans, whites, progressives. But for many reasons, Obama had abandoned that dream and had much loftier ambitions. He was zeroing in on statewide office.

There were rumors, though, that Obama would run for Illinois Attorney General, and the rumor was fueled by an article that *Chicago Sun Times* columnist Steve Neal wrote on April 19, 2000. Steve Neal's theme was that Obama would be heard from again.[59]

We also started our own campaign for Obama that day. We bonded with Obama through his losing campaign. We were committed to

---

58 Mendell, David. *Obama: From Promise to Power.* New York: Amistad, 2007, page 128-129.
59 Attorney general may be Obama's calling. *Chicago Sun-Times* - April 19, 2000 Author: Steve Neal, page 8.

Obama, and we were committed to this book he wrote. We were convinced that both the man and the book would one day resonate with the public. We also hung "Obama for Congress" buttons in the store as a reminder to the public and ourselves.

After Barack Obama's defeat, we decided to purchase a dozen copies of his book, gave them to Dan Shomon for Barack's signature and put them on the shelf. For nearly three and half years those signed copies stayed on our shelf.

Unsold. And yet, we could not bring ourselves to return them. And the "Obama for Congress" buttons were kept in place indefinitely.

And the books stayed on our shelves.

Michelle would dust them on a regular basis. With each dusting, we kept the book and the hope of Barack Obama alive. We would not give up. We kept hope alive.

The books stayed there for a very long time. We refused to give up just because of a defeat because we did not feel defeated.

Change comes slowly, gradually, incrementally, and suddenly.

CHAPTER 5

Barack Obama and the Iraq War — "War is not the Answer"

~

September 2002. It was obvious that the Bush Administration was beating the war drums. President George W. Bush had developed political muscles by taking advantage of the political environment surrounding the tragic 9/11 attacks. Michelle and I would tell whoever would listen that this war proposal being bandied about in Washington, DC was a "dumb idea."

And we had an unexpected partner in our opposition to the Iraq War.

Barack Obama, of course. He was going to speak out in October of 2002 and deliver a major speech in downtown Chicago, a speech that far into the future would help him secure the Democratic nomination for President. And help to separate him in the Presidential General Election some six years later.

It was just one more thing that Barack Obama did that endeared us to him. The opposition to the Iraq War.

War is never a smart idea and should only be used as a final resort when all else has failed. The alternatives had not begun to be exhausted. President George W. Bush, I am ashamed to say, was taking us to war without justification, and citing his doctrine of preemption. Hit before you get hit.

This proposed war made no sense. It bothered Michelle and me deeply. How could such smart people in the Congress vote for this "dumb war." The United Nations inspectors were there, and they had made great progress over the years, it seemed to us. Now President George W. Bush was demanding that Sadaam Hussein disarm his weapons. What was he going to disarm? Were not the weapons inspectors doing their job? I had not heard that they were complaining at the time that the Weapons of Mass Destruction (WMD) were still in Iraq. If Sadaam was that strong with these weapons, why didn't he use them in 1991 after the ill-fated invasion of Kuwait? He didn't have them then, and he doesn't have them now, we reasoned.

We had watched images claiming to have destroyed much of Sadaam Hussein's arsenal. What was this really all about? Is this President George W. Bush a madman? He would have to be if the noises he was making were of war. Pre-emptive strikes was the buzzword. The new "Bush Doctrine." Hit before being hit. Especially if you think, your opponent is strong. Is this what we are teaching our children? Hit before being hit?

Our hope was that Bush was kidding and simply acting like a big shot just showing off America's muscles. We were hoping that he was making idle threats. He had already declared war on al-Qaeda and had a military presence in Afghanistan. Why was Bush now neglecting our real enemy — the man and the organization that attacked us: Osama Bin Laden. Weren't we taking our eye off the ball?

Stop it Bush, we would say. Just stop it Bush.

And our new friend, Barack Obama, was going to make a major speech in October about this Iraq War. It showed the good judgment he had.

Michelle and I were not supporters of President George W. Bush. The Florida recount and the ensuing decision of the United States Supreme Court was devastating for us and many of our friends. Bush had plenty of help becoming the 43rd President of the United States from his five friends on the United States Supreme Court. It was a coup d'état by a slim majority of the United States Supreme Court. They took our government from us for political purposes.

President George W. Bush was war mongering. Bush was influenced by Dick Cheney, and moreover, he had assistance from Donald Rumsfeld and Paul Wolfowitz.

Fight.

Attack.

Invade.

Overthrow Sadaam.

Disarm now. Sadaam was vehement that he didn't have anything to disarm.

How could America, with such a rich history, even propose an unprovoked attack? President Bush was threatening a pre-emptive strike against Iraq. It was an act of barbarism. It seemed to us this was not a shining moment in history.

The House of Representatives vote was not so surprising since it was a rubber stamp for Bush, but the vote in the United States Senate was a huge disappointment. The United States Senate is the deliberative body, and the Senate should know better.

The Senate didn't know better, and they rubber-stamped the war. A disappointment for us was that New York Senators Hillary Clinton and Charles Schumer could vote to go to war.

Dick Cheney, who in my view had undue influence over President Bush, took advantage of the nation's ugly mood. There were few voices out there opposing the war. Even the first Iraq War, the so-called Desert Storm, was approved by a close vote. It would be difficult to argue against Desert Storm. We had the support of an international coalition that was extraordinary indeed. Desert Storm was a shining moment for the 41st President, President George H. W. Bush.

President George W. Bush announced that our new policy, the Bush Doctrine, is that preemptive strikes will protect us on our homeland. He called it the "Bush Doctrine." I was asking the hard questions of why. It was not a happy time for us. We felt robbed of the election of Bush over Gore, and now this nonsense. We kept asking ourselves, each other, some of our closer friends in the store, what could we do to stop this? What can we do to stop this insanity?

Many of us asked, "What about anti-war marches?" Others would say, "Don't call it anti-war marches, call it peace marches." The mood of the nation just was not right. There was not much of an interest in opposing this insanity. Not in the year 2002. Few politicians were speaking out against the war. There was the rare "voice in the wilderness," speaking out against this "dumb war."

We attended a rally in October of 2002, sponsored by the Illinois Council Against Handgun Violence in downtown Chicago. Many politicians were there. We met then-candidate for Congress, Rahm Emanuel, who was running for the seat vacated by Governor Rod Blagojevich. We approached Emanuel and introduced ourselves. We expressed to him our dissatisfaction with the upcoming war resolution and like sheep, Congress was ready to approve this attack.

We asked Emanuel how we could stop this senseless act from occurring. Can we as citizens take action to send a message to Congress that this war stuff is intolerable? Emanuel listened and then he said, "You can't. It's going to happen."

We were stunned by Emanuel's response. We knew that he was in tune with the Washington establishment, having served as an aide to Bill Clinton in the White House. He would be someone I would consider the consummate insider. We did not know him and had never met him before, but we knew of him. The character on West Wing, Josh, was loosely based on Rahm Emanuel, he told us. This man was plugged in.

And when I asked him if we can do anything about it, he said, "You can't. It's going to happen."

"You can't. It's going to happen."

We could not believe he said that, "You can't. It's going to happen."

It's going to happen. The public sentiment was clearly in favor of letting Bush do whatever it took to protect the homeland. George W. Bush could do no wrong. Bush could now say anything or do anything, and the American people would buy it. We noticed some of our customers were showing indifference. This attitude, indifference, is far worse than these pro-war attitudes. It is much more difficult to fight indifference.

We saw Obama at this very same rally two years earlier, in the fall of 2000.

We had gotten to the Dirksen Plaza early. We were cosponsors of the event and giving away a $100.00 gift certificate to our store to a student who wrote an anti-gun essay.

We noticed hundreds of cordoned off chairs in the VIP section. We saw one lone figure sitting there reading, and as we got closer, it was Barack Obama. He was sitting in the third row.

Alone and reading.

Years later, when I think back to that moment, I think of how few moments he would enjoy like that again. That image of Obama sitting there alone with the empty seats would have made a striking photograph. We still have that image etched in our minds. No one was with him, and no one but us noticed him.

We approached Senator Obama, and he said, "Hello. It's the Prestas, of course. How's the bookstore?"

He would always ask about the bookstore.

We told him again that whatever office he would run for, please let us know, and we would be there for him. We gave him our business card, and then he thanked us. We did not see him in person again until July 2003.

Our "friend in Springfield," gave a speech on October 2, 2002 in Federal Plaza,[60] organized by the Chicagoans against the War in Iraq that unequivocally opposed the Iraq war and opposed Congressional action authorizing military action. Congress was in the process of handing President Bush a blank check. Was Rahm Emanuel listening?

We had promised "our friend in Springfield" that no matter what he ran for we would be there for him. With this single act of courage on Barack Obama's part, he showed that he was there for us. Combined with this brave stance on the War and this personal integrity that we found, we would be on board for his next political move.

We also loved Obama for his integrity. Once during the 2000 Congressional campaign, Dan Shomon told us that some dirt was uncovered about Obama's main opponent, Bobby Rush. Shomon was excited about the prospect of bringing it to light. When he brought it to Obama's attention, Obama rejected it immediately and ordered Shomon not to publicize it. I don't know to this day what this dark secret was, but to Shomon's credit, he did not repeat it to us either as Obama had ordered. That would be the same as leaking it.

---

60   Known as the Federal Plaza in front of the Kluczynski Federal Building, which is a skyscraper in downtown Chicago located at 230 South Dearborn Street.

Obama reeked from integrity. I never once heard him discuss acquiring money for himself. He never discussed empowering himself, but often discussed how people need to empower themselves.

Prior to the announcement for the 2004 United States Senate race, Shomon related to us a story about a local candidate who wanted to cut a deal for himself with Obama. It was framed as follows: if I support you, then you must support me. Obama told Shomon to tell this candidate, "I would love your support, but it must be unconditional. Thanks, but no thanks."

Obama had little patience for these type of deal-making stunts and typically rejected them. It was what we loved about him. And now he was opposing this "dumb war."

I have viewed portions of the Iraq War speech on television and on the internet. I was pleased that Obama was getting some television coverage. He created a "buzz" on the internet. He had not received coverage like this since the forum at Bethany Union Church on March 7, 2000.

Obama gave the best speech of his life. The speech created quite a buzz in the community especially among those who opposed the war. One such organized group was the **South Siders for Peace**.[61]

He declared the Iraq War a "dumb war." Yet he said in the first sentence of his speech that he "is not opposed to war in all circumstances." And four paragraphs down, Obama repeated it again. "I don't oppose all wars." And again for emphasis in the beginning of the sixth paragraph, "I don't oppose all wars." I knew this was a sign that he had larger political ambitions. Obama wrote this speech himself.

Barack Obama's speech on October 2, 2002 opposing the war in Iraq

Good afternoon. Let me begin by saying that although this has been billed as an anti-war rally, I stand before you as someone who is not opposed to war in all circumstances.

The Civil War was one of the bloodiest in history, and yet it was only

---

61   MISSION STATEMENT: Based on the southwest side of Chicago, South Siders For Peace is a community group of activists united in our opposition to the invasion and occupation of Iraq, and to war in principle as a means of resolving international conflict.
     Together we seek ways to build a more just, honorable, and peaceful society, and to promote our views through the undaunted exercise of our First Amendment rights.

through the crucible of the sword, the sacrifice of multitudes, that we could begin to perfect this union, and drive the scourge of slavery from our soil. I don't oppose all wars.

My grandfather signed up for a war the day after Pearl Harbor was bombed, fought in Patton's army. He saw the dead and dying across the fields of Europe; he heard the stories of fellow troops who first entered Auschwitz and Treblinka. He fought in the name of a larger freedom, part of that arsenal of democracy that triumphed over evil, and he did not fight in vain.

I don't oppose all wars.

After September 11th, after witnessing the carnage and destruction, the dust and the tears, I supported this Administration's pledge to hunt down and root out those who would slaughter innocents in the name of intolerance, and I would willingly take up arms myself to prevent such a tragedy from happening again.

I don't oppose all wars. And I know that in this crowd today, there is no shortage of patriots, or of patriotism. What I am opposed to is a dumb war. What I am opposed to is a rash war. What I am opposed to is the cynical attempt by Richard Perle and Paul Wolfowitz and other arm-chair, weekend warriors in this Administration to shove their own ideological agendas down our throats, irrespective of the costs in lives lost and in hardships borne.

What I am opposed to is the attempt by political hacks like Karl Rove to distract us from a rise in the uninsured, a rise in the poverty rate, a drop in the median income – to distract us from corporate scandals and a stock market that has just gone through the worst month since the Great Depression.

That's what I'm opposed to. A dumb war. A rash war. A war based not on reason but on passion, not on principle but on politics.

Now let me be clear – I suffer no illusions about Saddam Hussein. He is a brutal man. A ruthless man. A man who butchers his own people to secure his own power. He has repeatedly defied UN resolutions, thwarted UN inspection teams, developed chemical and biological weapons, and coveted nuclear capacity.

He's a bad guy. The world, and the Iraqi people, would be better off without him.

But I also know that Saddam poses no imminent and direct threat to the United States, or to his neighbors, that the Iraqi economy is in shambles, that the Iraqi military a fraction of its former strength, and that in concert with the international community he can be contained until, in the way of all petty dictators, he falls away into the dustbin of history.

I know that even a successful war against Iraq will require a US occupation of undetermined length, at undetermined cost, with undetermined consequences. I know that an invasion of Iraq without a clear rationale and without strong international support will only fan the flames of the Middle

East, and encourage the worst, rather than best, impulses of the Arab world, and strengthen the recruitment arm of al-Qaeda.

I am not opposed to all wars. I'm opposed to dumb wars.

So, for those of us who seek a more just and secure world for our children, let us send a clear message to the president today. You want a fight, President Bush? Let's finish the fight with Bin Laden and al-Qaeda, through effective, coordinated intelligence, and a shutting down of the financial networks that support terrorism, and a homeland security program that involves more than color-coded warnings.

You want a fight, President Bush? Let's fight to make sure that the UN inspectors can do their work, and that we vigorously enforce a non-proliferation treaty, and that former enemies and current allies like Russia safeguard and ultimately eliminate their stores of nuclear material, and that nations like Pakistan and India never use the terrible weapons already in their possession, and that the arms merchants in our own country stop feeding the countless wars that rage across the globe.

You want a fight, President Bush? Let's fight to make sure our so-called allies in the Middle East, the Saudis and the Egyptians, stop oppressing their own people, and suppressing dissent, and tolerating corruption and inequality, and mismanaging their economies so that their youth grow up without education, without prospects, without hope, the ready recruits of terrorist cells.

You want a fight, President Bush? Let's fight to wean ourselves off Middle East oil, through an energy policy that doesn't simply serve the interests of Exxon and Mobil.

Those are the battles that we need to fight. Those are the battles that we willingly join. The battles against ignorance and intolerance. Corruption and greed. Poverty and despair.

The consequences of war are dire, the sacrifices immeasurable. We may have occasion in our lifetime to once again rise up in defense of our freedom, and pay the wages of war. But we ought not – we will not – travel down that hellish path blindly. Nor should we allow those who would march off and pay the ultimate sacrifice, which would prove the full measure of devotion with their blood, to make such an awful sacrifice in vain.

~

One bright spot for us was the vote of one of our United States Senators, Dick Durbin, against the war. I will not forget this important vote by Durbin. It was an unpopular vote politically. But it was the right vote. The speech Durbin gave opposing this action was exceptional.

Other votes in favor of the resolution were disappointing. John Kerry and John Edwards, among others. The redeeming value of those votes is that they both regretted their vote and disavowed their support for the war.

The following are heroes who voted down this resolution to strike before being struck. The 23 United States Senators that opposed the war. They are

- Daniel Akaka (D-Hawaii)
- Jeff Bingaman (D-New Mexico)
- Barbara Boxer (D-California)
- Robert Byrd (D-West Virginia)
- Lincoln Chaffee (R-Rhode Island)
- Kent Conrad (D-North Dakota)
- Jon Corzine (D-New Jersey)
- Mark Dayton (D-Minnesota)
- Dick Durbin (D-Illinois)
- Russ Feingold (D-Wisconsin)
- Bob Graham (D-Florida)
- Daniel Inouye (D-Hawaii)
- Jim Jeffords (I-Vermont)
- Ted Kennedy (D-Massachusetts)
- Patrick Leahy (D-Vermont)
- Carl Levin (D-Michigan)
- Barbara Mikulski (D-Maryland)
- Patty Murray (D-Washington)
- Jack Reed (D-Rhode Island)
- Paul Sarbanes (D-Maryland)
- Debbie Stabenow (D-Michigan)
- The late Paul Wellstone (D-Minnesota)
- Ron Wyden (D-Oregon)

In the House of Representatives, 133 members also opposed the war. Not all were Democrats. Another hero of ours, Congressman Dennis Kucinich (D-OH), organized the Democrats in the House that opposed the resolution.

We needed people like Obama representing us in Congress after this war fiasco. We needed people in Washington, DC who showed good judgment. We need someone thoughtful and not given to rash behavior. If I could see the errors of this "dumb war," why couldn't the majority of Congress see it? How could they give this President a "blank check" and an "open-ended" commitment? To advocate pre-emptive striking as part of our foreign policy is un-American with no historical precedent. If we are at a high moral standard, pre-emptive striking puts us at the opposite end of that sphere.

I never stopped believing in Obama. The books were still on our shelves when Obama gave the speech at the Federal Plaza on October 2, 2002. We were holding on. We also had the books when Congress authorized military action one week later. We made one addition.

We added the "War is not the Answer" sign in our store window, placed one in our yard at home, and promised not to remove them until all our troops are safely home. That is the only way to support our troops.

One of the books that influenced my strong anti-war feelings is *Slaughterhouse-Five: Or the Children's Crusade, a Duty Dance with Death.*[62] The book was about Vonnegut's experiences as a World War II Prisoner of War and is filled with anti-war sentiment through the uses of literary imagery. This book was the first to get me thinking about war and its destruction. This book brought the Vietnam War into perspective for me, many years later. I think of this book as a good reason to not go to war. World War II was not a "dumb war", but many "dumb things" happened during the war, such as the fire bombing at Dresden, which Vonnegut discusses in the book and that he personally witnessed.

Some other good books on "dumb wars" and "just wars" in our history were bestsellers in our store.

Two of those books were by the late Stephen Ambrose. Ambrose was a prolific historian with tons of transformational books.

D-Day: June 6, 1944: The Climactic Battle of World War II[63] is a skillful account of a key battle in a "just war," World War II. This monumental narrative provides a compelling portrait of the strategic dimensions of the invasion that changed the course of World War II, skillfully melding eyewitness accounts of American, British, Canadian, French, and German veterans, materials from government and private archives, and

---

62   Vonnegut, Kurt. *Slaughterhouse-Five; Or, The Children's Crusade, a Duty-Dance with Death.* [New York]: Delacorte Press, 1969.

63   Ambrose, Stephen E. *D-Day, June 6, 1944: The Climactic Battle of World War II.* New York: Simon & Schuster, 1994.

never-before-utilized sources from the home front. This book was followed up by its sequel, *Citizens Soldiers*.[64] These two books chronicled the most critical eleven months of World War II. This war had the strong support of the American people and was certainly considered to be a "just war."

The Iraq war, we strongly believed, would prove to be a "dumb act." It would take time.

Change comes slowly, gradually, incrementally, and suddenly.

Obama Loves Books and Bookstores, Too

Books and bookstores were always a large part of Barack Obama's life. As a subtext, bookstores were important in the life of Obama in the Chicago area. Bookstores and Obama are the perfect fit. Obama was involved with bookstores such as 57th Street Co-Op Books in Hyde Park, where Obama frequently browsed through the "new arrival" table at the front of the store. Obama's friend, Brad Jonas, owner of the used bookstore, Powell's Bookstore of Chicago, also carried the paperback version of *Dreams from My Father: A Story of Race and Inheritance*.[65] Once during that period, we had no sooner walked in to Powells, we nearly tripped over the stacks and stacks of the book, *Dreams from My Father: A Story of Race and Inheritance,* that were spread all over the floor. They were priced to sell at $5.00. Jonas had bought nearly 4000 copies of the paperback version of the book in the late 1990's, through the book remainder sales channel. And it seemed all 4000 copies were on the floor.

"Obama was a frequent buyer of the book that he gave away to voters during his run for State Senate, Congress, and the run for the United States Senate. I offered to give the books to Obama, but he insisted on paying for them," said Brad Jonas.

"I really wanted to just give him the books, because I found that special quality in him that I saw in few politicians: he listened. The first time I met him, he had met my daughter, and when I saw him again about a year later, he remembered her and asked about her. This man

---

64 Ambrose, Stephen E. *Citizen Soldiers: The U.S. Army from the Normandy Beaches to the Bulge to the Surrender of Germany, June 7, 1944-May 7, 1945*. New York, NY: Simon & Schuster, 1997.
65 Obama, *Dreams from My Father*.

was impressive."

Obama paid a $1.00 for each book, but Jonas added, "I must tell you I paid far less for them."

After his defeat at the hands of Bobby Rush, Michelle and I would say, it'll just take a little longer for Obama to get to the White House. We consistently told Obama personally or through personal messages that we would send through friends that we would be there for him, so please let us know of your plans. He would always ask how the bookstore was doing and he always said thank you. We often thought of his book, the book that sat on our bookshelf: untouched by the hands of customers and unsold.

During the three years we were waiting for Obama to make his move, we would speculate about for which office he would declare his candidacy.

We would ask people who would see Obama to find out what his plans were. One such person was our friend, Ronald Carter. I would have contact with Ron in the neighborhood. Ron was the publisher of the *South Street Journal*, a small African-American-oriented newspaper in the Bronzeville community. He started with the paper in 1994 and has struggled financially nearly every year since its founding. But Ron's passion for journalism, and his passion for social justice has kept the paper afloat all these years.

Ron would repeatedly ask Obama about his future plans. And Ron always mentioned our name to Obama. On one such occasion Ron cornered Obama and asked if he were running for mayor. The Prestas want to know.

Obama told him, "Well Ron, that isn't in my plans. I have something else in mind." Ron dreamed of seeing the Harold Washington coalition rebuilt one day and was hoping that Obama would do it. In our conversations, I told Ron that Obama was the only one around who could rebuild the coalition and defeat Daley.

One rumor for 2002 was that he would run for Illinois Attorney General. Statewide office was the next obvious step for Obama. I had discounted his running for Illinois Attorney General in 2002 because he could lose his state senate seat. That meant Obama would have to choose between running for office and possibly losing it all, and keeping his "safe" state senate seat. I felt from what I knew about him and given his youth, that he would not give up that seat. When he ran for Congress in 2000, there really was no risk of losing his state senate seat. So, it was obvious to me that whatever move he would make would not be in the 2002 races: governor, state treasurer, comptroller, attorney general were all out of the question as we saw it.

As far as Illinois Attorney General, Illinois House Speaker Michael Madigan had different plans for that seat. He would aggressively promote his daughter Lisa Madigan, an Illinois State Senator. Speaker Madigan was relentless in lobbying for support for his daughter and convincing people to stay out of the race. He could not convince John Schmidt against running, so his daughter Lisa would have some competition. Schmidt was not as formidable as say Barack Obama or State Rep. Thomas Dart. Speaker Madigan was known to have made hundreds of telephone calls, calling in every favor that was ever owed him. It is not known if Obama was promised or offered anything to stay out of the Illinois Attorney General's race, but it would have made little difference since this would have been a high-risk race for Obama. But Obama could read the tea leaves. In actuality, it was all or nothing. Obama is not a gambler but is in fact conservative in his political choices. Obama's choice to run for Congress was a low-risk decision.

State Representative Tom Dart was also interested in Illinois Attorney General but was convinced by Speaker Madigan to drop the idea in favor of running for Illinois State Treasurer. However, Dart would be taking on an "entrenched incumbent," Judy Baar Topinka, a Republican, but very popular. She was going to be difficult for most Democrats to defeat. For Thomas Dart, this was an all or nothing maneuver.

Bobby Rush had not forgotten that Tom Dart had worked against him. First, Dart was Mayor Daley's campaign manager in 1999 when Daley soundly defeated Rush for Mayor of Chicago. In the year 2000, Dart helped Obama organize the western part of the 19th Ward and delivered a huge majority in the area he worked. These two events did not go unnoticed. Bobby Rush got his revenge against Dart in the race for Illinois State Treasurer. Steve Neal reported on September 27, 2002 that Bobby Rush would support Judy Baar Topinka against his nemesis, Tom Dart.[66]

The 2002 election for Illinois State Treasurer was going to be challenging for Dart, regardless of Rush's support or non-support. While Rush liked to think that being involved with then-Illinois State Treasurer Judy Baar Topinka meant a lot, Rush's involvement had a minimal effect on the election. Topinka was the incumbent and a popular political figure in the State of Illinois. She could be the Illinois State Treasurer for as long as she wished. She was a well-liked, popular, moderate Republican in an increasingly blue state.

Michelle and I were sure that Obama would not challenge Rush again in 2002 or 2004 for Congress. There was no upside and all downside in challenging Rush again. Obama assessed correctly that he could not defeat Rush for Congress in the 1st Congressional District.

Obama had set up a strong base in the 19th Ward and the surrounding suburbs because of the work done by Dart and by Michelle and me. Obama was becoming stronger in his home district of Hyde Park. This would allow Obama to then campaign in the parts of the District where he was weak. Groups like Tom Dart and ours would carry the day out here, while Obama could organize the rest of the district. This was a start of Obama's building of networks around the city. Rush was starting to feel a strong sense that Obama was building momentum, in spite of the 2000 defeat.

There was a victory for us in this devastating defeat. We could not defeat Rush at the polls and as of 2002, he was no longer our Congressman. That was a result of the work that we accomplished in the 19th Ward.

In the 2002 redistricting of the Illinois Congressional Districts, Rush had strongly lobbied to eliminate the 19th Ward from his District, thus diminishing the chances that Obama would take him on again. But what Rush could not know was that Obama was no longer interested in being a member of the House of Representatives. Likewise, the Hyde Park home of Illinois State Senator Barack Obama, who ran against U.S. Representative Bobby Rush for Congress last year, is now two blocks

---

66   Steve Neal. "Rush bolts party to help pal Topinka - Dem congressman says her programs help his community." *Chicago Sun-Times.* September 27, 2002, EDITORIAL: 45.

outside Rush's recrafted district in Chicago.[67]

This was also more of a symbolic move because Obama could always run for Congress and challenge Rush and then move into the District after he won. Rush's message was clear: stay away from me.

> Rep. Bobby L. Rush (D-Chicago), whose 1st Congressional District has been represented by an African American for 72 years, is picking up the black-majority 18th Ward from Lipinski in the new map. Rush, who won a lopsided primary last year over state Sen. Barack Obama, is giving up the 19th Ward on the far Southwest Side, where Obama trounced him.[68]

So for Obama, the United States House of Representative seat was politically restrictive. Still, the speculation was running rampant. Illinois Attorney General was a strong possibility, as Steve Neal reported previously in 2000.[69] Illinois State Treasurer was another possibility. Michelle and I did not believe either was well advised. We also did not believe he would run for anything in 2002 for the simple reason that he would risk losing his state senate seat.

Obama learned a valuable lesson from Alice Palmer. You just do not give up what you have. Palmer had an ambition to be a Congresswoman, but Jesse Jackson Jr. and Emil Jones stood in her way. Alice Palmer had underestimated Jesse Jackson Jr. and never dreamed she would be defeated in her race for Congress. Underestimating your opponent and overestimating yourself are not good things.

But Obama, as he stated many times, was more interested in pursuing a career in public service and not in pursuing wealth. It was clear that Obama wanted to be in public service and would not be happy in private practice, lucrative or not. Money, I always had the impression, was not a motivating factor for him. He was destined for greater things in public service. We were hoping for that, too.

---

67 Dan Mihalopoulos, Tribune staff reporter. "Political opponents cast out by remap :[North Sports Final Edition]. " *Chicago Tribune* [Chicago, Ill.] 27 Jun 2001,1.1. *Chicago Tribune.*

68 Steve Neal. "Map allows Dems to retain 6 seats - Lost seat means Johnson, Phelps go head-to-head." *Chicago Sun-Times.* May 23, 2001, LATE SPORTS FINAL, NEWS: 21.

69 Attorney general may be Obama's calling. *Chicago Sun-Times* - April 19, 2000 Author: Steve Neal, page 8.

In Obama's October 2nd speech against the war in Iraq, in an interview with cable television talk show host and internet blogger Jeff Berkowitz, Obama only laid out a prophetic scenario about this "dumb war" that he opposed. He also gave strong hints of what he was going to do.

He would often say that he did not oppose all wars. He saw some wars as being legitimate, sighting the Civil War and World War II specifically. He could not agree with those that would say "War is not an Option."

In late 2002, there was some speculation that Obama was eyeing the Mayor's race in February 2003. It would mean that he could keep his state senate seat. Of course, running and losing would cause him great political harm. Congressman Rush, although he defeated Obama, was weakened by his defeat to Daley in 1999. Since Obama had already witnessed what happens to a candidate when they lose against Daley, I do not believe that he gave serious consideration to this race. The Mayoral race had a very short time span, and it might not be enough time to develop the type of support he needed. If he announced too early, his opponents could line up against him.

Most importantly in the mayoral race, he would again be taking on a powerful political force, Mayor Daley. I also strongly felt that the mayoral race would not benefit Obama on the national stage, and we thought that Obama belonged on the national stage. Although, if Obama ran for Mayor, we would have supported him, and Obama was the only person we would have supported over Daley at that time. And we believed that Obama could have defeated Daley.

The question was, if after Obama had worked so hard to be Mayor of Chicago, could he then run for United States Senate. The implications of that would have been devastating to Obama's future and any national ambitions. He would have looked overly ambitious.

The timelines between the mayoral race and the senate race were too close. The mayoral race could zap all of his resources that he would need to defeat Daley, and he would have nothing left for the United States Senate race. Obama would also be returning to the same donor base within a short period, and that would be difficult.

We are grateful that we did not have to make that choice because we still saw him as a force on the national scene. And, we were convinced that once he got his foot in the door, he would be there to stay.

So in our analysis, that only left the United States Senate. Obama was likely to seek the soon to be vacant seat of Republican Illinois Senator Peter Fitzgerald. We observed that Republicans were looking to unseat the very unpopular Senator. That would set the stage for Obama. In our second meeting with him back in March 2000, we saw that special something. Now it was time to bring out those qualities to the people of Illinois. We were certain his indomitable spirit would show.

Meanwhile, in 2002, Obama did not discourage talk about his running for any office, including mayor, because it kept his name alive. In retrospect, it was obvious to Michelle and me that Barack would make his move in 2004.

Michelle was convinced that running for the United States Senate would be Obama's best bet. She told people around Obama that he should run for Senate to which they would say, "He's already in the Senate."

"No, No. Not the Illinois Senate," Michelle would say, "The United States Senate. He can run without losing his seat. Besides, Fitzgerald is vulnerable."

The Path to the United States Senate is The Road Less Traveled

We were hopeful Obama would make the right choice in 2004. When Obama lost his Congressional election to Bobby Rush on March 21, 2000, it was a crushing defeat for this bright young star. And like many bright stars, he picked himself up, dusted himself off, and began a great journey down *The Road Less Traveled*.[70]

One of Obama's idols is the famous boxer Muhammad Ali. Ali never thought he would or could lose but, when he did, he picked himself up, dusted himself off, and began his journey back to the world's heavyweight championship. Defeat was not an end for Ali, it was a beginning. Muhammad Ali was in fact defeated a number of times during his boxing career. Ali saw those defeats as part of the journey.

---

70   Peck, *The Road Less Traveled.*

Although Ali did not like losing, he also did not fear losing. A defeat was a chance for renewal, and it was a new beginning. Obama had many of the same traits as Ali.

On March 21st, Barack Obama was knocked out decisively by Bobby Rush. He was stunned, disappointed, frustrated but never defeated. Obama was strengthened by those around him who encouraged him. Al Kindle was a constant source of encouragement for Obama.

Kindle, who has known Obama for 20 years, saw many positives in the 2000 Congressional defeat. A positive aspect of the defeat was Obama's glimmering performance in Chicago's 19th Ward. It was not just Obama's performance in the 90% white section of Mount Greenwood, but it was also coupled with a strong showing in the area east of Western Avenue known as Beverly Hills/Morgan Park. The demographics were 70% white and 30% African-American there. He also performed strongly in the area called East Beverly, where Michelle and I reside. It was an even stronger hold for Obama. This area was nearly 50% white and 50% African-American, a community with a near-perfect synergy of whites and African-Americans.

Kindle told Boston.com that, "Barack didn't come out of this with a whole rosy picture. He was [angry] at himself, I believe, for committing to a race he didn't go ahead and deliver, and go ahead and win. It wasn't like Obama was sitting at the dinner table saying, 'OK, what next?' "[71]

Obama had no idea on March 21st who his next opponent would be or when he would have another opportunity. All he knew is that it would happen. And we knew, too.

Michelle and I were as crushed by Obama's decisive knockout by Rush as if we were in the ring with him and we were knocked out ourselves.

We knew that there was something special about Obama. He represented a new brand of politics. He represented a new brand of hope. He connected. We had delivered East Beverly by a resounding margin for him and Tom Dart had delivered Mount Greenwood by even more impressive margins. Dart was helped in

---

71   http://www.boston.com/news/nation/articles/2007/10/12/early_defeat_launched_a_rapid_politi-
      cal_climb/.

the 19th Ward by Cook County State's Attorney and Beverly resident, John Sommerville.[72] Obama had done well in his home area of Hyde Park. He was knocked out in the rest of the Congressional District.

That night he dusted himself off, shook off the cobwebs and pondered his future. It was time to move on to the next fight, his next challenge.

I clearly recall our own feelings about losing to Rush. We had actively worked the campaign for two weeks, but it was a very intensive two weeks where we ate, slept and drank Obama. We poured all of our time and energy into the Obama Congressional campaign during that period. We gave Obama the best two weeks of our lives. We talked to people non-stop about this guy Obama, and we won over many converts. We were spreading the gospel according to Obama. We had, of course been involved with organizing the candidates' forum for a much longer period of time, but since we insisted on being non-partisan before the forum, we did not take part in the campaign prior to March 7th. But as stated earlier, Michelle and I had never worked a political campaign prior to 2000 and that one meant a lot to us.

We knew that with the right kind of marketing and the type of grassroots effort that we put forth in the 2000 campaign, Barack Obama could be elected to a higher political office or any political office he sought. We discovered something that we would keep repeating: "**to know him is to love him**." He would draw many volunteers like us to help him. Everyone wants to help Barack Obama. If we could accomplish what we did in two short weeks, what would happen if we had a month to prepare. We needed time: two months, six months, a year, or longer. Then imagine if there were dozens of people and groups that join. The multiplying of volunteers increasing exponentially. Selling Obama was like hand selling a "hot book." The content of the book is awesome. You just have to get the customer to at least peruse the book,

---

72 John Sommerville would later challenge Alderman Ginger Ruagi in the 2003 and 2007 aldermanic elections, but would fall short of defeating Alderman Rugai. I had supported Rugai in both races and had actively campaigned on Alderman Rugai's behalf. In the 2007 election, Barack Obama, had officially endorsed Alderman Ginger Rugai for 19th Ward Alderman. Both candidates reportedly had sought the coveted Barack Obama endorsement. A representative from the Obama camp had asked for my input prior to the endorsement announcement.

then hopefully buy it, and then buy multiple copies to give as gifts.

There are rare moments in life when something just feels right. It cannot be explained. Being on board with Barack Obama was the right thing to do. We got on board for the ride of our lives. We would have good seats for this ride.

March 21, 2000 was a disappointing day for Obama and for us. It was a low point of a great life. This is a day of mourning. Tomorrow would be a new day.

March 22, 2000 was a new day. It was a re-birth. It was the start of something big.

March 22, 2000 started Obama on the road toward his next political venture. He knocked on doors after the election. He never once looked back and dwelled on his defeat, although he learned from his mistakes. He grew not only as a person but also as a political candidate. Whether Obama knew at the time that he would be running for the United States Senate is unknown. The occupant of the Senate seat, Peter Fitzgerald had not yet started stumbling politically. It is just that he was a Republican, and that alone in Illinois makes an incumbent vulnerable. Fitzgerald had not learned the art of political schmoozing. I sensed that he would have been very good at it. But he didn't seem interested in it. He gave the impression that, "If I do a good job, why wouldn't I get reelected?"

Because that isn't how it works. He would need to build networks and alliances. Accept every invitation possible. Shake lots of hands. Have an aggressive staff. Didn't seem that this was Fitzgerald's style. Incumbents lose for more complicated reasons than they are in the wrong party. It is a whole slew of issues, mostly non-political.

Barack Obama quickly learned that "entrenched incumbents" were difficult to defeat. Illinois rarely elected a Republican to the United States Senate, but when they did, there was a tendency to stick with the incumbent, even a Republican.

Jospeh Meegan, who with Saul Alinsky organized the Back of the Yards, were famous community organizers. Both Meegan and Alinsky brought community organizing to a new level. I had spent hours talking and listening to Joe Meegan.

He taught me the riches that could be made in community organizing and being a committed member of the community. The riches were not money, but a deep feeling inside that gave a person a "rich" satisfaction in achieving great things for a community. He made a strong case for "community organizing" for me. Meegan credits his friend, Senator Everett Dirksen of Illinois, with being instrumental in helping to pass the school hot lunch program, a pet program of Meegan's. It was Dirksen who was instrumental in the passage of the Civil Rights Act of 1964. Dirksen had been lobbied heavily by President Lyndon Baines Johnson.

Senator Fitzgerald was no Everett Dirksen. Fitzgerald had not learned his lessons. Dirksen would have been a shining example for Fitzgerald.

But it was obvious that Obama is a great "student" and will learn these valuable lessons. Obama would learn a great deal from a stunning defeat.

The candidates' forum at Bethany Union was obviously a great marketing tool for Obama, went a long way toward getting himself known in our community, and gave him confidence that he could woo a crowd outside his home district.

Change comes slowly, gradually, incrementally, and suddenly.

CHAPTER 6

Barack Obama Announces for United States Senate

~

The official announcement for Barack Obama to run for the United States Senate was January 21, 2003. Obama was joined by such political heavyweights as Illinois Senate President Emil Jones, Illinois Senator Denny Jacobs (D-East Moline), Illinois Senator Terry Link (D-Lake County), U.S. Rep. Jesse L. Jackson Jr. (D-2nd), Senator James Meeks (D-15th), Rep. Danny K. Davis (D-7th), Aldermen Arenda Troutman (20th), and Toni Preckwinkle (4th), Cook County Commissioner Jerry Butler and many others, black and white, from around the state, as reported by the *Chicago Daily Defender* newspaper reporter Chinta Strausberg. Strausberg reported that, in the spirit of Dr. Martin Luther King Jr., Illinois State Senator Barack Obama (D-13th) Tuesday announced he's running for U.S. Senate and accused the Republican incumbent of "buying" his seat four years ago and vowed to "take it back."[73] The group standing with Obama was a coalition of African-American and white elected officials from throughout the state of Illinois.

And the *Chicago Tribune* reported on January 22, 2003 that "Democratic State Sen. Barack Obama of Chicago formally announced his candidacy for the U.S. Senate on Tuesday and contended Republican

---

73 Chinta Strausberg. "Obama to challenge Sen. Fitzgerald. " *Chicago Defender* [Chicago, Ill.] 22 Jan. 2003, 5.

incumbent Peter Fitzgerald had "betrayed" voters on bread-and-butter issues. [74]

The announcement caught us by surprise and after some research, we discovered that Shomon was the campaign manager: again. We had no contact with Shomon from the last time we saw him when he stopped by our house to deliver the signed copies of *Dreams from My Father: A Story of Race and Inheritance,* which was several days after the 2000 Primary Election Day. He had told us that Barack wanted to thank us for all that we did and greatly appreciated our efforts, and we received a personal note also thanking us for our efforts.

The Daily Herald reported who some of the potential opponents for Obama would be. It reported that if Obama is to face Fitzgerald, he must first win a crowded Democratic primary that's likely to include state Comptroller Dan Hynes, wealthy investment banker Blair Hull and former Chicago school board President Gery Chico. Cook County Treasurer Maria Pappas also may run. [75]

The potential field that Obama would be challenging was problematic. First, there was Blair Hull, who was a multi-millionaire who had befriended Governor Blagojevich and Chicago Mayor Richard M. Daley. He had donated hundreds of thousands of dollars to the Blagojevich campaign and allowed Blagojevich to use his private jet to fly around the state and campaign during his 2002 bid for governor. He also was a friend of Mayor Daley and donated to the Daley campaign. It was said that Daley had encouraged Hull to run for United States Senator. There was an expectation on Hull's part that he would be endorsed by both Blagojevich and Daley as payback for his support of them. This was the first of many incidents that showed the political naiveté of Blair Hull.

It was widely assumed that Mayor Richard Daley would endorse a candidate in the race for United States Senate. He had a personal friendship with Blair Hull. An argument could also be made that Daley would support Dan Hynes. In fact, Janny Scott of the *New York Times,*

---

74 Legislator in race to unseat Fitzgerald ; Democrat seeks 2004 nomination for U.S. Senate; [North Sports Final Edition] Rick Pearson and John Chase, Tribune staff reporters. *Chicago Tribune.* Chicago, Ill.: Jan 22, 2003. pg. 4.

75 Democratic candidate says Fitzgerald 'betrayed' state; [All Edition] Eric Krol *Daily Herald* Political Writer. *Daily Herald.* Arlington Heights, Ill.: Jan 22, 2003. pg. 11.

who in 2007 and 2008 had written a number of articles about Obama's early years, mistakenly reported this.

> Mr. Obama has also cultivated a working relationship with Mayor Richard M. Daley. Mr. Daley, who backed an opponent of Mr. Obama in the 2004 Senate primary, this year endorsed Mr. Obama for president — around the time that Mr. Obama endorsed Mr. Daley for re-election, annoying some supporters and passing over two black candidates considered unlikely to win.[76]

In fact, Daley remained neutral in the race. When I wrote to Janny Scott pointing this out, here is what she had to say about the assumption that Daley supported Hynes.

> "I was led to believe by a number of people that the Mayor was allied with Hynes, though I understand that he does not generally endorse people in primaries. Anyway, thank you for clarifying that," wrote *New York Times* reporter Janny Scott.

~

It was an understandable mistake based on an assumption that Daley would support the party organization.

Another candidate was Gery Chico, who with Paul Vallas, had turned the Chicago Public School system around and who was very popular among teachers and would presumably have teacher's union support. Chico's stance on the issues were closely aligned with ours. In addition, there was Maria Pappas, the Cook County treasurer, who was a popular woman who could capture the female vote in Cook County.

But the most challenging competitor of all for Obama, and a problem of sorts for us, was Dan Hynes, Illinois State Comptroller. Hynes was born and raised in our community and was very popular here. He was considered the front-runner by many and considered by "experts" to be the prohibitive favorite. Hynes would be an obstacle for Obama that needed to be overcome. It was presumed that Hynes would easily capture the area, but we clearly had other ideas and were conceding nothing. The argument that the Hynes people consistently made was

---

76   Janny Scott. "A Biracial Candidate Walks His Own Fine Line: [Series]." *New York Times.* 29 Dec. 2007, Late Edition (East Coast).

that Hynes was the only candidate in the race that won statewide office. Twice. Once in 1998 and again in 2002, both times by overwhelming margins. Hynes would be a favorite too because he could tap into the labor union leadership's access to campaign money. And it would surely go to Hynes because of the relationships his father, Tom Hynes, had built over the years.

Obama had not run statewide up until this race. We had early on adopted the motto that "Dan Hynes is not only the candidate in the race to have won statewide office, but we are sure he will be the first to have won and lost statewide office." This was the attitude we adopted.

Shortly after the announcement, I saw Bob Bruno, Obama's friend from 2000, at his Dunkin Donuts. "Hey, why didn't tell me Obama was running for United States Senate?" Before I could tell Bob I didn't have advance notice, he said, "And don't forget to get me a sign for the yard."

"That Obama guy is going a long way, you know," Bob told us. "He's a good guy."

Yard signs would not be available for months, but when they did come out, Bob was the second to get one (we were the first). I would see Bob often at his Dunkin Donuts, nearly every conversation turned to Obama, and he was hungry for campaign updates.

I called our friend Harvey Mader in Evanston, and I knew that Harvey had a close, personal relationship with Congresswoman Jan Schakowsky. I asked Harvey if he could ask Schakowsky to endorse Barack Obama for the United States Senate race. It just made total political sense to me. At this point, I really had no idea if they knew each other, but I assumed they did. Obama and Schakowsky's terms overlapped in the State Legislatures between 1996 and 1998, although they served in different chambers, Obama in the State Senate and Schakowksy in the State House.

Mader would try an emotional pitch with her since he remembered that Senator Paul Wellstone, another close friend of Mader's, deeply regretted not endorsing Schakowsky sooner and endorsing her when it would have mattered most.

We would call Mader often after January 2003 and each time we would bring up Schakowsky's possible endorsement of Obama. We knew how tenacious Harvey could be, especially if he believed in the cause.

By the time Obama made his announcement that he was running for United States Senate, the dozen or so signed copies of *Dreams from My Father: A Story of Race and Inheritance* were still on our shelf. And still collecting dust. And Michelle was still dusting them. From the end of March 2000 through the announcement in January 2003, those books had a lonely life on our shelves. Many customers would certainly recognize the book and comment on it. "Isn't that the guy from the church in 2000?" But the books were just not selling. The hardcover version had been out-of-print for quite some time. Oh, customers would look at it and say, "Is this what's his name, Obama, I think, who was at the church with Bobby Rush in 2000?" But dust would continue to accumulate on these books until Michelle wiped it off. Finally, the trade paperback went out of print, too. The book would not get back in print until several years later.

During this 2004 United States Senate campaign, Kelly Clute would bring his then three year-old daughter, Sofia, to our bookstore. Every time she would come near the bookstore, she would tell daddy, "I want to go to Obama's Bookstore." Sofia gave our bookstore the nickname. Sofia's dad was a loyal customer and an enthusiastic early Obama supporter and volunteer. Obama resonated with small children, there must have been something special about him. Adults sometimes had a difficult time remembering his name, but we noticed his name flew right off the tongues of children.

We had become known in the community as "Barack Obama's Bookstore," and this we owe to Sofia Clute. To this day, we are known in the community as the people who brought Obama to the community.

Senator Peter Fitzgerald Offended Foes and Friends

Obama would have had to know that Peter Fitzgerald would become unpopular. Fitzgerald not only offended Democrats, which is actually what he is supposed to do, but he also offended members of his own Republican Party, which is not what you are supposed to do. He had filibustered a massive spending bill because it included funds for the Abraham Lincoln Presidential Library. That offended Senate Republicans and really offended House Speaker Dennis Hastert. He did it to bring to light the Republican-controlled Illinois state government's failure to promise competitive bidding for the project.

Fitzgerald also voted against a massive bailout measure for most of the major airlines, following the September 11th terrorist attack. Standing alone out of all members of the U.S. Senate, Fitzgerald delivered a speech entitled "Who will bail out the American taxpayer," arguing that the airlines would simply go through the money and remain financially unstable. The bill passed 99 to 1.[77]

A good rule in Illinois politics and in national politics is: do not oppose Abraham Lincoln for any reason, even if you believe it is fiscally irresponsible. Abraham Lincoln does not have a price tag. When it comes to Lincoln, money is no object. Senator Fitzgerald was politically tone deaf. If we had to title a book about the Fitzgerald years, it would be entitled, *All the Wrong Moves*. It is not impossible for a Republican to hold onto a seat in the United States Senate in Illinois. Illinois has a recent history of such Republican Senators as Everett Dirksen, Charles Percy and Peter Fitzgerald.

Fitzgerald defeated Senator Carol Mosley Braun, who was also an aloof politician who failed to build a political base during her term in office. Senator Braun had voted the right way on the issues that were important to us, but she did not distinguish herself as a legislator, and she rarely made appearances in Illinois. She was invisible until election time in 1998. It is a good idea for United States Senators to make appearances in their home state. Braun had become the caricature of a politician. Constituent services are a key ingredient to any legislator's long tenure in any legislative body. Legislators that do not have any type of political organization shouldn't act that way. It seems, interestingly enough, that Fitzgerald was following Braun's example. Braun was a Democrat and Fitzgerald a Republican. From 1992 through 2004, our United States Senator from Illinois was virtually invisible. Constituent services were poor from both Senators, and they seemed to take the folks back home for granted.

Braun and Fitzgerald were both unpopular within their own party, which is a prescription for defeat. The similarities between the two United States Senators, Braun and Fitzgerald, were striking. One was

---

77   http://en.wikipedia.org/wiki/Peter_Fitzgerald#cite_note-1.

left wing and voted consistently that way, and the other was right wing and voted consistently that way. But it takes more than doing the right political stuff, and it proves voters do not judge politicians solely based on political viewpoints.

Michelle and I recalled sitting at a local coffee shop before the 1998 general election and listened as a number of 19th Ward precinct captains were discussing the race. The derogatory remarks that were being made about Braun made it obvious the local Democrats would not lift a finger for her reelection. At the time, Michelle and I were quite perturbed by this response.

Braun had isolated herself in Washington, D.C. and had virtually ignored her constituents until it came to Election Day. A great politician knows how to make Election Day anticlimactic. If Election Day becomes the big climax, there is definitely a problem with the candidate. Fitzgerald, in 1998, was able to defeat a vulnerable Braun by pointing out all these foibles and not having to necessarily focus on the issues. But Fitzgerald also isolated himself in Washington.

Both Braun and Fitzgerald, it seems, landed in Washington, D.C. and never looked back toward the people back home. Fitzgerald learned very little from the mistakes of his predecessor. Fitzgerald didn't seem to care.

Incumbents who provide constituent contact and services and know how to get involved in the community win reelection year after year. And that is how they become "entrenched incumbents." Even Republicans in blue states. A great example in Illinois was Senator Everett Dirksen who was an institution in Illinois and was loved by Republicans and respected by Democrats. The Great Society of Lyndon Baines Johnson in the 1960's would not have happened without the support of a Republican like Everett Dirksen. The Civil Rights Bill of 1964 also had Dirksen's support. When Dirksen passed away, Adlai Stevenson ran for his vacated seat, and Stevenson won.

Fitzgerald could have been the United States Senator from Illinois for a longtime. One of several fatal blunders Fitzgerald committed was moving to the Washington, D.C. area. Fitzgerald was ignoring his constituency back home. This, coupled with his ignoring his own party leadership, made for a politically deadly formula for failure.

And this set the stage for Obama's candidacy for United States Senate.

There were rumors running rampant in the media that Fitzgerald would not run for reelection because of very low approval ratings, in the 20% range. Party leaders were strongly encouraging Fitzgerald to step aside. Finally, on April 15, 2003, Fitzgerald officially announced that he would not run to reclaim his United States Senate seat. It was now officially an open seat, although one could argue it didn't matter either way because Fitzgerald couldn't win.

The Birth of the Netroots

An inauspicious event occurred that at the time went unnoticed but would eventually affect the Obama campaign in 2004.[78] A veteran campaign manager, Joe Trippi, had started something on behalf of Howard Dean. It was called a blog. It was a relatively simple thing to set up. The date was March 15, 2003.

> Welcome to the Dean call for action blog! This is the official place where we at the campaign can let people know when, where, and how you can help. We are going to need as much support from the netroots and grassroots as we can possibly get. Please check back here regularly.
>
> Saturday's call to action:
>
> 1. Thank you California!!!! If you haven't heard, Howard blew the roof off the California convention today. The next few days should have some great stories, and we'll be posting the speech on the website soon. When it's up, read it, and pass it around.
>
> 2. The most important thing you can do right now is let everyone know about this blog. Email your friends, other Dean supporters, and anyone else you think might be interested, and let them know to check this site. Please post a link on any blogs or websites that are appropriate, and make the link prominent on anything you maintain yourself. Get the word out!
>
> 3. Between now and March 31, we need to raise as much money as possible before the FEC filing deadline. A member of the New York Dean 2004 meetup issued a challenge to raise a million dollars over the internet as fast as possible. The challenge is for everyone on the net who supports Howard Dean to contribute whatever they can (and add one penny to their contribution so the campaign knows this is money coming from the internet). The biggest thing the netroots can do for Howard is contribute and raise as much money by the March 31 deadline. Spread the word, get the contributions in, help Howard

---

78   Which would have implications in the 2006 and 2008 national campaigns.

any way you can. A sample letter to cut and paste and send out is below.

4. Howard was blown away by the New York City meetup. He turned to us and said, "look at the power of the net!" Now we've got to show how the power of the net translates into winning. Our campaign is going to need organizations in every state and every city and town. At this stage, we may not have as much money as other candidates, but we have more netroots support and grassroots support than all of them combined. Meetup is a critical part of our organizational ability. In some areas it may be simply a good place to recruit, in other places it will turn out to be our organization. Join meetup today and make sure you go to the April 2 meetup in your city! Please go through your address books, your listservs, and spread the word to join the dean2004 meetup in every town. We will be posting an action plan for the April 2 meetup on this blog.

We'll post again soon—keep coming back!

— Joe Trippi, Campaign Director[79]

~

Joe had said a mouthful. He was using terms like "grassroots" and "netroots" and "blogging" and "email communication" and "contribute" and "join the dean2000 meetup." They made use of linking to other sites. Howard Dean would have his own website. And it would knock the political world on its ass.

This would be a more efficient way for campaigns to raise funds and recruit volunteers. Meetup.com was one of the first social networking websites.

The Howard Dean campaign for President would attract lots of attention because of all of these factors. They would influence other campaigns, and the Obama campaign was no exception. Those campaigns that ignored the Howard Dean phenomenon did so at their own peril.

The web site tools now available to those that dared took the "Pied Piper" theory of Dan Shomon to a new level. It was now "Pied Pipers on steroids."

By April 5th, 2003, Howard Dean had an impressive amount of people signed up for "Meetup.com." 13,000 people signed up for Howard Dean by April 5th compared to less than 800 for Senator John F. Kerry.[80] Howard Dean's campaign was receiving national attention at

---

79 http://deancalltoaction.blogspot.com/2003_03_09_deancalltoaction_archive.html.
80 Id.

this point.[81]

Working the Open Seat

Meanwhile, the Obama campaign was plugging along the old-fashioned way. Raising money with phone calls. Recruiting volunteers one at a time. Hiring new staff. And for our part, we planned a fundraiser at World Folk Music Company. We had briefly considered having a candidates' forum again, but we thought it was too early in the campaign process. What would benefit Obama would be slowly, surely recruiting volunteers for the long campaign. At this point in the campaign, there would likely be little interest in a candidates' forum, so we opted for the fundraiser and the recruiting of volunteers and friends for Obama.

It was April 2003, and one of the bestsellers in our store was *Armageddon: The Cosmic Battle of the Ages*[82] by Tim LaHaye and Jerry B. Jenkins. This was the 11th volume in the "Left Behind" series. Also appearing on the bestseller list was Dan Brown's *The Da Vinci Code: A Novel*.[83] The murder of a curator at the Louvre leads to a trail of clues found in the work of Leonardo Da Vinci and to the discovery of a centuries-old secret society.

Even as we were sure that Obama had an unlimited future in politics, although there were many doubters. And in the back of our minds we still thought about that "Presidential thing." Obama was very young and had nothing but road in front of him.

But we would hear the mumbling, "He's a nice guy **but** . . . " and "We are certainly impressed with his credentials and qualifications **but** . . . " comments from people.

But. And then the "buts" stopped with the questions.

"How could he win?"

"How could he raise the money?"

"How can he defeat Hynes?"

"How can he defeat Hull?"

81 Lesser-known candidates getting word out on the Net Former Vermont governor mobilizing support through Web site, Carla Marinucci, Chronicle, Political Writer, *San Francisco Chronicle*, page A-3, Saturday, April 5, 2003.
http://sfgate.com/cgibin/article.cgi?f=/c/a/2003/04/05/MN295458.DTL.

82 LaHaye, Tim F., and Jerry B. Jenkins. *Armageddon: The Cosmic Battle of the Ages*. Wheaton, Ill: Tyndale House Publishers, 2003.

83 Brown, Dan. *The Da Vinci Code: A Novel*. New York: Doubleday, 2003.

And the comments.

"He doesn't have an organization."

"He's got a funny name."

"He hasn't paid his dues."

"He should wait his turn."

When it came to Obama, Michelle and I had blinders. We only saw the road ahead, and it appeared to us that the road was clear. The road he was taking was *The Road Less Traveled*.[84] He had started early enough to raise the money needed, spending the winter months of 2003 personally making the phone calls to donors, according to Dan Shomon. Obama was not going to let money stand in the way of victory.

It was obvious that the Hynes people would run the campaign as if he was the heir to the throne. He even ran as if he were the incumbent. While Obama was spending his time talking about the issues all over the state of Illinois and throughout the African-American community, Hynes was eerily silent on all the issues. It would turn out to be a tactical error. The charge could easily be lodged that you didn't know where he stood.

Bill Clinton is Still a Force in Illinois Politics

And after all, Bill Clinton was on Dan Hynes side. "How could he lose?" seemed to be the attitude of the Hynes camp. And with the growing presence in the United States Senate of Hillary Clinton, it was becoming apparent that the Clintons were unbeatable. Look at what happened in 2000 when Bill Clinton endorsed Bobby Rush. Michelle and I feared this more than any other opposition in the race.

In addition to the stiff challenge that Hynes would give through his money and organization, Obama would be challenged for African-American support from another candidate in the race, Joyce Washington, a health care advocate and former candidate for Lieutenant Governor. Washington had made an impressive showing in that race for Lieutenant Governor, garnering over 350,000 votes in losing to Patrick Quinn in 2002.

First, it was the African-American ministers who urged Washington to withdraw in the name of unity. One such request came from Bishop

---

84 Peck, *The Road Less Traveled*.

Trotter, a cousin of one of Obama's former opponents, State Senator Donne Trotter, in the 2000 Democratic primary. He said Joyce Washington should get out of the race. He's the most qualified, said Trotter, and his record in our community speaks for itself.[85]

And others chimed in. Activists and ministers urged Washington not to run for U.S. Senate because they had already given their support to Senator Obama. In January 2003, speaking on behalf of a number of African-American ministers, Sean Howard, a Democratic political consultant who managed Washington's campaign, urged her to stay out of the race. "Everyone pledged their support for Obama in 2002," said Howard. He said only a unified front could defeat U.S. Senator Fitzgerald (R-Ill.) who in January 2003, was still in the race. [86]

Many other party leaders and activists were not happy about Washington's candidacy, which many saw as someone trying to draw votes away from Obama. They continued to urge her to withdraw in the name of party unity. Rev. Jesse L. Jackson Sr. urged Washington to step aside and back Obama—an act Washington vowed never to do.[87]

And then there was the concern of Rush's endorsement of multi-millionaire Blair Hull. The fear was that Rush could galvanize African-American support against Obama. With Washington in the race and now Hull getting an endorsement from a prominent African-American politician, Obama's base was in jeopardy should the plans succeed. Rush had originally endorsed Washington in the race and then switched to Hull. Allies of Rush warned Rush that he was eroding his own base by going against an African-American candidate who had the backing of many African-American officials. Rush had previously turned against those who aided Obama in the 2000 campaign as payback for their support. When former State Representative Thomas Dart ran against sitting State Treasurer Judy Baar Topinka, Rush supported Topinka.

I felt that all these factors were merely obstacles that could be

---

85 Trotter, Washington butt heads over Obama Chinta Strausberg. *Chicago Defender*. Chicago, Ill.: Jul 22, 2003. pg. 3.
86 Activists say no to Joyce Washington Strausberg, Chinta. *Chicago Defender*. Chicago, Ill.: Jan 29, 2003. Vol. XCVII, Iss. 187; pg. 3.
87 Rush backing of Blair 'divides Rep's base'; Congressman's allies critical of his Senate choice Strausberg, Chinta. *Chicago Defender*. Chicago, Ill.: Jul 24, 2003. Vol. XCVIII, Iss. 57; pg. 2

overcome with an effective grassroots effort, which was something we were adept at performing. We would start in our community, spread the word, and recruit not just volunteers but also activists.

"Pied Pipers." Lots of them. Everywhere.

Blogging, Meetups, Emails, Internet Fundraising

But how could we spread the word quickly about Obama from our little bookstore perch. The internet was slowly becoming a force in political campaigns, and I had taken notice of the Howard Dean campaign that had started something new called "blogging."

Change comes slowly, gradually, incrementally, and suddenly.

Not only "blogging," but also this guy Dean was even raising money. Small amounts. He was raising small amounts from hundreds and thousands of people. This could revolutionize political campaigns, I would tell Nate Tamarin, deputy campaign manager of the Obama campaign. In addition, Howard Dean was making great use of something called "Meetup.com." Meetup.com is a website that "helps people find others who share their interest or cause, and form lasting, influential, local community groups that meet regularly face-to-face" according to the Meetup.com website, www.meetup.com.

"Meetup.com" was not originally set up for political campaigns, but for Howard Dean it sure turned out that way. Campaigns needed to not rely on these devices exclusively, but use them as just another campaign tool. They underestimated the value of a grassroots effort. The internet could go a long way in aiding a grassroots effort by recruiting volunteers and "Pied Pipers."

And because this time Obama had announced fourteen months in advance of the primary, he had a fighting chance.

Shomon Explains the Obama Campaign Strategy

Talking to Obama campaign manager Dan Shomon helped to boost our confidence. After the Obama campaign announcement, we contacted Shomon and asked what role we could play in the campaign. Dan came to our house shortly after the contact and brought materials and window signs to us and openly discussed Obama's candidacy.

He showed us a brochure developed by "political consultants" that said "A Chance to Believe Again." He said Obama was not satisfied with this slogan, but for now it would have to do. Dan explained the planning of the campaign and what would be needed to win the Senate race.

First, the fundraising was a higher priority than in the Congressional race, Shomon explained. He said Obama blocked out several hours a day for making fundraising phone calls to his lists. He would spend a considerable amount of time with the personal phone calls. It was what Barack did best: sell him. This proved to be effective. The process was tedious and time-consuming but was essential at mounting an effective campaign. And the dividends this produced proved to be worthwhile in that Obama raised a substantial amount of money and also recruited many high-powered volunteers.

Dan would also be hiring campaign staff and seeking a more permanent office location. As it turned out, the most important hire Shomon made was a young man named Nate Tamarin. He would be our contact person throughout the campaign. Tamarin would have a great future in the Obama camp.

The Politics of the 19th Ward Organization

Shomon's first question to us was: Are you sure, absolutely sure, you want to get involved with this campaign? After all, you will be opposing not only Dan Hynes but also the powerful 19th Ward organization. Hynes had lined up support for his bid early in the process as Steve Neal of the *Chicago Sun Times* reported on January 20th, 2003. Hynes, who was set to launch his exploratory committee in February 2003, sought to raise $5 million to $8 million for the Obama fundraising formula to victory March primary. David Mendell, in his book, laid it out step-by-step: the Obama fundraising formula to victory with three million, he had a 40% chance of winning with five million, a 50% chance of winning, with seven million an 80% chance of winning, and with ten million said, "I guarantee you I will win."[88]

Of the Democratic contenders, Hynes had lined up the most organizational support, including a majority of the state's county

---

88   Mendell, David. *Obama: From Promise to Power*, p. 154.

Democratic chairmen, party leaders in the suburbs and collar counties, and key ward committeemen including Congressman William O. Lipinski (D-Chicago), the most influential member of the city's congressional delegation. The Hynes family has a record of accomplishment of winning statewide elections. Tom Hynes, Dan's father, managed President Bill Clinton's 1996 re-election in the state.[89]

The Hynes family and the Clinton family had a relationship that dated back to the Saint Patrick's Day parade[90] in 1992. President Clinton's endorsement during the 2000 campaign in favor of Rush was the final nail driven into the Obama campaign. Again in the 2004 election, the name surfaced again with the early presumption that Clinton could be called upon to help Dan Hynes, whether through personal appearances, fundraising events or just simply talking up the Hynes candidacy to others.

Tom Hynes had been grooming his son Dan for bigger things since 1998, when Tom slated his son as Illinois State Comptroller. Tom made sure the field was cleared for Dan. The talk always was that he would become the governor of Illinois or United States Senator from Illinois one day: probably sooner rather than later. Tom had even brought Dan into the bookstore during the 1998 campaign, introduced us to him, and purchased some books. Judy Hynes, Dan's mother, owned and operated an Irish import business, Hynes Irish Cottage, on a business strip near us. Judy was a mainstay in the community, and the Hynes family was highly respected.

The 19th Ward Political Organization is one of the strongest and best funded of the political organizations in the city. So many members of the 19th ward organization not only held countywide and statewide offices, but the influence of the 19th Ward even reached into the White House, with Thomas Hynes being a member of the Democratic National Committee. Hynes received his appointment through President Bill Clinton.

Michael Sheahan at the time was the Cook County Sheriff. Dan Hynes

---

89 It is no accident Hynes won re-election by such an overwhelming vote. *Chicago Sun-Times* - January 20, 2003 Author: Steve Neal, page 31.

90 The Southside Irish parade was one of the biggest Irish parades in the country outside of Dublin or Boston. It started as a small parade with a few wagons and children.

was born and raised in the 19th Ward and was now the State of Illinois
Comptroller. Kathleen Meany is a member of the Cook County Water
Reclamation District. Paul Vallas had run for governor in 2002 and nearly
defeated Rod Blagojevich in the Democratic primary that year. Thomas
Hynes, the 19th Ward Committeeman, was the Cook County Assessor
and is now in private law practice. And Jeremiah Joyce who was a former
19th Ward Alderman and a State Senator, was now a personal confidant
to Mayor Daley. "Jerry" Joyce is a top-notch political strategist. His son,
Kevin, is a state representative from the district and is discussed as a
Congressional candidate. Kevin had worked in the Clinton White House
under Rahm Emanuel.

It was against this backdrop that Dan asked the question: Are you
sure you want to stick your neck out, go against the wishes of the 19th
Ward organization and support an outsider against one of your own?

Yes we did, we told Shomon. We wanted to support Obama. We
would support Barack Obama.

We explained to Shomon that we understand all the politics of the
situation but the fact was we were not against anyone. We were not
against Dan Hynes. Nor Blair Hull. Nor Gery Chico. Nor Maria Pappas.
Nor Nancy Skinner. Even Joyce Washington.

Shomon did not have to elaborate any further. We did indeed
understand what this meant. I had worked the 2003 aldermanic
campaign on behalf of the 19th Ward sponsored candidate and an
incumbent.

Alderman Virginia "Ginger" Rugai faced her most serious challenge
since her first election (after Daley appointed her to succeed Cook
County Sheriff Michael Sheahan). I had volunteered to work her
campaign, and I was essentially working for the 19th Ward Organization.
My interest in helping her reelection was my admiration of her work
ethic on behalf of the 19th Ward. There were no particular favors or
special services she performed on our behalf. It was not because of a
job or position I held or a contract I received. Another plus for Rugai
was that she was a full-time alderman, that she had no other sources of
income.

I was for Rugai, not against anyone.

Shortly after Rugai's election in a closer race than she was used to in 2003, I informed her staff that I would be supporting Obama for the United States Senate. I was on good terms with Rugai and her staff, and I felt I could let them know about this as a courtesy. I was already aware of the fact that favorite ward son, Dan Hynes, would most certainly be supported by the ward organization. Rugai would be supporting Hynes out of her loyalty to the 19th Ward organization, although Rugai supported Obama in 2000 for Congress against Rush.

> In 1999, State Senator Jeremiah Joyce suggested I meet with a young man with an impressive resume who was running for our Congressional District. Barack Obama and I met and discussed the concerns of our district. He struck me as an incredibly bright and charismatic man, someone I could proudly support to represent us in the House, and someone with a great future. Barack won our 19th Ward, but was unsuccessful district-wide. Today, I am one of a very few people who can claim to have backed both Rich Daley in 1983 and Barack Obama in 2000. Like Mayor Daley, Barack learned a great deal from a difficult defeat and both hopefully will continue to greater heights in public service.

Jeremiah "Jerry" Joyce had told Alderman Rugai that this Obama guy could one day become President of the United States. Jerry Joyce is an astute political observer and strategist. He is someone that Mayor Richard M. Daley can confide in and not worry about reading it in the newspaper the next morning.

Dan Hynes Runs for U.S. Senate as the "Incumbent"

There was a feeling on Hynes' part that he was an incumbent and that he was entitled to the job. He campaigned as an incumbent. In order to be an "entrenched incumbent," you must first be the incumbent. Obama certainly noticed that Hynes was running that way. It took the longest time for Hynes to make public statements about the issues. We asked Shomon about that and he said, "Oh you are not going to hear anything from Hynes for quite a while. That is the strategy." A flawed strategy, I thought.

Being mum on the issues is a fine strategy for an incumbent, but Hynes wasn't the incumbent.

To Know Him is To Love Him

What we would slowly discover about Barack Obama then, and it still holds true today, is that "**to know him is to love him.**"

Change comes slowly, gradually, incrementally, and suddenly.

I always thought that would be a great theme song for him, "to know him is to love him."

Obama needed to campaign aggressively throughout the state of Illinois. He had difficulty during the Congressional campaign reaching large numbers of people. Clearly, when he did meet them, such as the highly successful candidates' forum at Bethany Union Church on March 7, 2000, he connected. And he had a great persona on television.

We sensed even then that Obama represented a new kind of politics. He represented a different kind of politics and speaking out against the politics of "slash and burn." Therefore, we were on board for this historic run for the United States Senate.

Shomon believed Obama's chances were very good, and we believed the same. He remembered how late we got on board for the Congressional race and he was excited to have us there from the very beginning. After we were finished with Dan, he turned around again and looked at us again and said, "Are you sure you want to go up against the 19th Ward?" he asked. We did not really blame Shomon for repeatedly asking us the question.

"Yes," we said. "We are supporting Barack Obama for United States Senate." We had reserved our seats for this viewing of American history. And Dan knew at that point that we would never turn back. Nor would he ask us the question again. We were Shomon-ites. And Obama-ites.

In mid-February 2003, Hynes announced the formation of an exploratory committee for United States Senate.[91] Hynes would begin the race with a formidable lead with name recognition, organization and fundraising. Hynes would be the only candidate in the race to have won statewide office, a point he made constantly while trying to convince voters. He also had a relationship with most of the Chairmen of the Democratic Party organizations in the state from Chicago to

---

91   Hynes readies for Senate race; [RedEye Edition] *Chicago Tribune*. Chicago, Ill.: Feb 13, 2003. pg. 38.

Springfield to Cairo. The Democratic Party apparatus would be in full swing in their support of Hynes for the United States Senate.

And even after the announcement, Hynes was eerily silent on the issues.

Of course, we were in. The battle would be uphill all the way. None of the early polling in the campaign was bright for Obama. Steve Neal reported in his column on April 2, 2003 that Obama was polling at 9% of the vote. Hynes is favored by 24 percent, followed by Pappas with 21 percent, former Chicago Board of Education President Gery Chico and health care executive Joyce Washington, each with 5 percent, and commodities millionaire Blair Hull with 1 percent.

The same poll showed that "**to know him is to love him.**" The plan was to get him to as many places as possible, at first face-to-face, but near the end of the campaign, through television by blitzing the airwaves two weeks before Election Day. Obama was still a virtual unknown in most parts of Illinois, and that would be the challenge. According to the poll, the Democratic race could become even more volatile as voters learned more about the other candidates. Obama, who has an impressive legislative record and strong support from the black community, surged when voters were told about his background.[92]

The column also showed a definite bias on Steve Neal's part in favor of Obama, something that Neal would show up until his untimely passing on February 18, 2004 before the Democratic primary.[93]

"Barack Is Excited!"

We reinforced our commitment to Dan Shomon, and he conveyed this to Barack Obama. Shomon left us a message on our home phone shortly thereafter, a message he would leave quite often during the months leading up to the fundraiser we had set for July 20, 2003 at World Folk Music Company. We would get these frequent messages from Dan Shomon saying, "Barack is excited."

"Barack is excited."

We were on board. In early February 2003, we put an Obama sign

---

92 Pappas nears Hynes, but it is still early - This poll indicates that Pappas is a contender rather than a spoiler. *Chicago Sun-Times* - April 2, 2003 Author: Steve Neal, page 53.
93 It made me sad that Steve Neal would not see Obama through to the winning campaign.

in the window of our store, and it stayed there until the day he was elected to the United States Senate in November 2004. We posted it next to the "War is not the Answer" sign, which we had posted since the day America invaded Iraq.

One of the key issues that resonated with us with Obama then was his total opposition to the war in Iraq. He called it "a dumb war" and explained the consequences of going to war with Iraq. His analysis of what would happen if we invaded Iraq was prophetic. Even then, I thought he sounded Presidential. But one office at a time.

Relationships that Obama had made over the years were now coming into fruition. Conrad Black and David Radler, who would both be indicted for depleting the company of its assets and cash without the knowledge and consent of the Board of Directors, previously controlled the *Chicago Sun Times*. They were clearly not fans of Barack Obama. Obama had developed a close relationship with then Editor-in-Chief of the *Chicago Sun Times*, John Cruickshank, who started in early 2003. Cruickshank saved the *Chicago Sun Times* from extinction. He worked under Radler and Black, but he was not tainted by the scandals. In fact, when they were ousted, he took immediate charge of the paper. In 2004, Cruickshank discovered a "massive circulation scandal" and not only uncovered the scandal, but reported the fraud immediately.

This change of Cruickshank at the helm of the *Chicago Sun Times* would prove to be another one of many lucky moves for Obama when he launched his United States Senate campaign. Cruickshank was a man of impeccable integrity and he struck up a personal friendship with Obama. And it would pay dividends for Obama's race for United States Senate.

Everything in the Senate race was slowly, surely starting to go Obama's way.

The Beginnings of the Grassroots Efforts

The difference between the 2000 campaign and the 2004 campaign can be summed up: luck, hard work, Shomon's great planning, fundraising, building an organization, hiring great staff, and an awe-inspiring grassroots effort. It was this grassroots effort that extended far beyond anyone's imagination and planning. Michelle and I would be at the center of this grassroots efforts.

The 2000 Congressional campaign consisted of nothing but luck, unfortunately, **bad luck**.

The 2004 United States Senate consisted of nothing but luck, fortunately this time, **good luck**.

During the 2000 campaign against Rush, it seems Obama had plenty of luck, all bad luck. The 2004 Senate campaign also had plenty of luck: all good luck. Obama had grown during the time after the Rush campaign and the time he announced for the United States Senate. Obama made his own luck. Luck is the residue of hard work. Obama had lots of residue after March 21, 2000. Rush's announcement on July 24, 2003, that he would accept the position of co-chairmanship of millionaire Blair Hull's U.S. Senate campaign drew a violent reaction from Obama's media friend, ally, and columnist Steve Neal. "He is a sellout. Rush has exposed himself as a smalltime hack and petty grudge-holder."[94]

July 3rd 2003 Parade in Evergreen Park

Dan Shomon had called us shortly before July 3rd, 2003 and asked if we would like to march in the Independence Day parade in Evergreen Park, Illinois. And did we know of any Obama supporters who wanted to march with him.

We made dozens of phone calls for volunteers to march with us that day but, because of the short notice and because of the holiday, we did not find any takers. But Michelle and I were excited at the opportunity to march with Barack Obama and company. Obama was marching in other parades that same day. The energy of this man was inspiring.

Before the start of the parade, we had an opportunity to talk with Obama about many things. It would be an hour and a half before we would start marching, so we spent the hour and a half discussing politics, the campaign, the upcoming 2004 Iowa caucus, Howard Dean, the other candidates in the Senate race, and many other issues.

When we arrived and saw Obama, we both received a big hug from

94 Bobby Rush a Sellout, Steve Neal, Columnist, *Chicago Sun-Times*, Chicago, Ill.: July 23, 2003. pg. 25.

him, and he thanked us for coming. We had not seen him since that day in Federal Plaza when we saw him sitting alone and reading. "How's the bookstore?" he asked.

We then had Shomon take some photos for us, and we continued our long discussion while we waited for the parade to begin. In discussing the upcoming campaign, Obama wondered aloud why Blair Hull would spend such large amounts of money in downstate ads in the middle of the summer. Who would remember at election time, he would say. Of course Hull was trying to establish name recognition, and it was accomplishing a little of that. Hull was failing to brand himself, and he was not defining an opponent. The Hull ads made little sense to Obama.

There was little purpose or direction to the ads. They temporarily boosted Hull's numbers, especially downstate, but that would not last. Hull was targeting Dan Hynes' popularity downstate. But more than a year before the 2004 general election, businessman Hull used $6 million of his own money in an attempt to become Illinois' next U.S. senator, according to his latest campaign finance report.[95]

Obama told us that his strategy was to do better incrementally. "If we can perform 10-20% above expectations everywhere, we breeze through this election," he told us.

He would remind us of Lance Armstrong pedaling up a steep incline in the Tour de France. Obama just kept coming and steadily passing up opponents one at a time, receiving donations one at a time, recruiting volunteers, one at a time. Slowly, steadily and with tremendous self-confidence. The man never stopped believing in himself, and we never stopped believing in him.

Change comes slowly, gradually, incrementally, and suddenly.

Winning downstate would be nearly impossible for someone who has zero name recognition. If he could slowly build alliances, grassroots organizations and find a few good "Pied Pipers," he would win.

Change comes slowly, gradually, incrementally, and suddenly.

If Obama was polling at 10% downstate and could improve that to 20-30%, that would be significant. He was confident that he would

---

95 SENATE CONTENDER USES $6 MILLION OF OWN MONEY; [ILLINOIS FIVE STAR LIFT
    Edition] Dennis Conrad, The Associated Press. *St. Louis Post - Dispatch*. St. Louis, Mo.: Jul 16,
    2003. pg. B.3.

come out of Chicago with a large majority of the vote. Obama was expecting a great majority of the African-American vote, in spite of the fact that Joyce Washington was in the race. That was a major component of the plan that Dan Shomon developed. He had been laying the groundwork in the African-American community for months up until this point. He was planting the seeds of the grassroots efforts in the African-American community, and frankly, Joyce Washington was not and could not.

Blair Hull was also in the parade that day. He walked past our group and shook hands with Obama. Hull, it would turn out, would also attempt to make inroads in the African-American community and would make some progress at the outset, but ultimately that plan would fail. We would later find yard signs littered along the highways and the parkways, only to be disposed of by City of Chicago sanitation trucks because political signs in parkways are prohibited.

Al Kindle, a campaign aide to Obama on loan from Toni Preckwinkle's office told us once, "As soon as black people discover that Hull is not black, they will turn to Obama in droves." Whether it was by design or whether Hull was passing himself off in the African American community as an African American candidate, part of the confusion was that Bobby Rush had signed on to the Hull campaign as co-chairman.

We met a couple of African-American women early in the campaign when the discussion turned to the Senate election. We told them we were supporting Obama for Senate. They told us, "well he has never done anything for us in our neighborhood." Turns out he was not even in their state senate district.

So, are you supporting anyone for United States Senate? Michelle would ask have you heard of Barack Obama? Yes we had, but we really like this nice man, Blair Hull. What a nice man! He came to our church to talk to us. And do you believe he gave us money: $1000.00. What a nice man!

This was not an isolated incident. This was Hull's method in an attempt to buy the election with a different style of campaigning.

He would pay storeowners a fee for posting his political signs in their window. By Election Day, however, Obama signs quickly replaced the

Hull signs simply because they wanted Obama and were more in synch politically with Obama. They knew nothing about Hull except that he gave away money.

Obama had been spending most mornings on the phone raising money and weekends speaking at African-American churches in Chicago and the suburbs. He knew most of the ministers and pastors on a first-name basis. He would meet as much of the congregations as possible. Obama, it turned out, was everywhere. Regardless of the event and the size, he would be there. Among the churches and church leaders he would visit were the following.

Apostle John T. Abercrombie, Truth and Deliverance Christian Church in Chicago

Rev. David Bigsby, Calvary Baptist Church of Glenwood

Bishop William Bonner, Greater Mt. Olive COGIC in Aurora

Bishop Arthur M. Brazier, Pastor, Apostolic Church of God in Chicago

Rev. Roy R. Brown, Progressive Church Baptist in Aurora

Rev. Clay Evans, Fellowship Missionary Baptist Church of Chicago

Rev. Charles Ford, St. Paul COGIC in Chicago

Bishop Simon Gordon, Triedstone Full Gospel Baptist Church

Rev. Marshall Hatch, New Mt. Pilgrim Missionary Baptist Church

Rev. Jesse Hawkins, St. John AME Church in Aurora

Apostle R. D. Henton, Monument of Faith Evangelistic Church in Chicago

Rev. Jeffrey Hodges, King of Glory COGIC in Chicago

Rev. Paul Jakes, St. Paul Missionary Baptist Church

Bishop Jerry Jones, Apostolic Assembly of Jesus Christ in Chicago

Rev. Joseph Jones, Pleasant Ridge MB Church in Chicago

Rev. Charles Johnson, Starlight Missionary Baptist Church

Bishop Willie Jordan, St. Marks Baptist Church

Rev. Alvin Love, President, Baptist Convention of Illinois

Rev. George Marshall, Gayles Memorial MB Church in Aurora

Rev. T. Ray McJunkins, Union Baptist Church in Springfield

Rev. O. C. Morgan, Evening Star MB Church in Chicago

Rev. John Norwood, Mt. Zion Missionary Baptist, Evanston

Father Michael Pfleger, St. Sabina Catholic Church in Chicago

Reverend Tony Pierce, Christian Family Center Church, Peoria, Illinois

Rev. John Rouse, Mt. Zion MBC in East St. Louis

Rev. Obie Rush, St. Paul Missionary Baptist Church in East St. Louis

Rev. Don Sanford, Faith United Baptist Church in O'Fallon

Rev. Mark Smith, Family & Faith Christian Church in Aurora

Rev. Stephen J. Thurston, President, National Baptist Convention in America

Bishop Larry Trotter, Sweet Holy Spirit Full Gospel Baptist Church

Rev. Marvin E. Wiley, Rock of Ages Baptist Church in Maywood

Apostle H. Daniel Wilson, Valley Kingdom Ministries International

Rev. Jeremiah Wright, Trinity United Church of Christ in Chicago

Rev. Herman Watson, Mt. Sinai Baptist Church in East St. Louis

"You never know who the one person you would meet who could impact the campaign," Obama told us that day. He treated everyone he met equally: with respect and he made sure he looked everyone in the eye. Every person was important to Obama.

Obama also discussed the 2004 Howard Dean campaign that day. Dean was already in Iowa campaigning. His "grassroots fundraising" on the Internet and his "Meetup.com" was already making an impact, and was being discussed widely on the news. Dean was the front-runner at that moment, and it was obvious that Obama was paying close attention to the race. Obama's observation was that Dean seemed to be overly dependent on technology. The internet is a great tool, he said, but you also needed that personal touch and contact, too. Obama's assessment was that Dean didn't have ground troops.

It was that day that we discussed the issue of "Meetup.com" with Obama and Nate Tamarin. Glenn Brown, an early volunteer and fan, had already raised the issue with Nate Tamarin. He said that Brown was persistent about it and was insisting this was the future and the future was now.

"There is no downside," I opined to Tamarin. "None." I told Nate I would be happy to help with "Meetup.com" in anyway that I could.

And, if the Obama campaign got on board with this early in the process, the other campaigns would have to play catch up with them. The likelihood is the other campaigns would ignore it. The other beauty of the "Meetup.com" portion was that it was a way to recruit volunteers or, as Dan Shomon called them, "Pied Pipers." Many, many "Pied Pipers." The "Pied Pipers" of "Meetup.com."

They were interested in this "Meetup.com" thing. This time period was the very early stages of the Internet boom in social networking, fundraising and advanced technology. The concept of "grassroots fundraising" had not yet been introduced. "Netroots" was in its infancy.

The Obama Campaign Was Technologically Illiterate

Obama then made a comment at the parade that I had never forgotten. In retrospect, it showed how quickly Obama identified weaknesses and turned them into strengths.

"We are technologically illiterate," Obama said. "We need to learn from these things."

My comment was that all the campaigns are "technologically illiterate," so we were all on an even playing field. I recalled back to the 2000 Al Gore for President campaign and signed up for their email newsletters and never received even one. I didn't see the Hynes campaign embracing this because they think all they need is the "organization" to lead them to victory. The "organization" alone will not cut it either, I felt.

"Obama for Illinois Technology Committee" Forms

All the campaigns were learning, some faster than others. Shortly after this event, Obama's campaign posted a notice on their website recruiting volunteers for an "Obama for Illinois Technology Committee." It took a few months, but a meeting was scheduled for October 2, 2003 and posted on the Obama for Illinois website. The response was overwhelming and many called to offer help well before October 2nd.

Upcoming Events . . .
Thursday, October 2 (2003) at 5:30 p.m. – First meeting of the Obama Tech Advisory Committee, 310 S. Michigan, Ste. 1720. We're looking for your ideas on innovative ways to connect with voters over the Internet. If you have experience with building or designing websites, e-mail communications or graphic design we want your input!

The committee's purpose was to improve "technology literacy." It was certainly early enough in the campaign for them to catch up. They were recruiting volunteers who had expertise in computers and were willing to donate their energy and time to take the campaign and technology to the next level.

Glenn Brown had set up the "Meetup.com" account that week, and the ramifications of this was incredible. I am sure he initially started the "Meetup.com" with the intention of meeting in his community, but what ended up happening is that it spread throughout the Chicago land area, to the suburban areas, the collar counties. There were even "Meetup.com" groups outside the state of Illinois including in the nation's capital of Washington. D.C. and New York City. It would be incredible. Much of the "grassroots fundraising" success could be traced to "Meetup.com." Here is how Glenn remembers that time.

I asked Dan Shomon, Obama's campaign manager at a 4th of July event, if I could try and start the Meetup, he gave me permission to do so. After the meetup got created I was surprised to see about 50 people sign up within a month. We had about 15 at our first meeting. A couple months later we had enough people to make the lead paragraph on a description of meetup.com in the *Chicago Tribune*. Within 6 months we had more people than all of the presidential candidates except Howard Dean. Meetups were happening in Chicago, Springfield, Champaign-Urbana and even Washington DC. All of this was BEFORE the primary election, mind you. After the primary, and especially after the Keynote speech things really exploded. In Chicago, we were reserving whole sections of restaurants or using their party rooms. We were getting over 100 people at the Chicago Meetups.

What was truly amazing is that the campaign really had little direct involvement until after the primaries. Nate Tamarin provided us with campaign literature and gave us direction in terms of volunteer activities, but the Meetups largely grew organically and without a whole lot of effort.

In the end I think the idea of meetups were pretty good as far as it went, but they paled in comparison to the organizing ability of the Presidential campaign explosion.

— Glenn Brown

But what Glenn Brown accomplished was the start of something big. And he not only set up the Meetups, but in a short time set up an "Obama for Senate Yahoo Group" that was also instrumental in bringing more "Pied Pipers" into the fold.

Jim Cauley is Hired as The New Campaign Manager

We were also informed that day that Obama would be hiring a new campaign manager whose purpose was to bring in "national experience" to the campaign. That person would be Jim Cauley, who was aggressively pursued by David Axelrod to join the Obama campaign, according to David Mendell.[96] Cauley was a native of Pikeville, Kentucky and a political science graduate of the University of Louisville. Cauley was also campaign manager and the six-month chief of staff for U.S. Rep. C.A. "Dutch" Ruppersberger, D-Md. Earlier he was campaign manager for Mayor Glenn Cunningham of Jersey City, that city's first African-American mayor. Cunningham later was elected to the New Jersey State Senate. Cauley was also general consultant to Baltimore Mayor Martin O'Malley's 1999 campaign and, in 1992, was a field operative for Bill Clinton's presidential campaign in half of Kentucky. Cauley, we would later learn, advocated holding back the money for as long as possible, then unleash. The plan at that point was to do the opposite of Hull. Spend virtually nothing on television commercials, then wait two to three weeks before Election Day and bombard the airwaves with commercials. Hopefully, the campaign would have done all the right things in lining up volunteers and raising money. Unexpected events like "Meetup.com" and the "Yahoo Group" would develop great numbers of volunteers. And that is in large part thanks to Glenn Brown.

---

96 Mendell, pg. 183-185.

Mike Jordan Loves a Parade and Calls On the Crowd to "Meet Senator Obama"

Once the parade started, Obama went to work with the crowds. I was in awe. He would swing from one side of the crowd to the other and with Super Volunteer Mike Jordan leading the way, putting Obama for Illinois stickers on children in the crowd. Obama was shaking as many hands as possible and Mike would point at Obama and say, "Meet Senator Obama" and continue stickering children and sometimes adults.

"Meet Senator Obama", Jordan shouted to the crowd.

Non-stop. All through the parade route from the 9700 block of Harding to 9500 block of Harding and east down 95th Street to Francisco and then north down to 93rd Street.

I caught glimpses of Hull and Hynes marching in the parade. They did not appear to have many volunteers marching with them. And I did not notice them resonating with this crowd as Obama was. They were both rather stoic and just waving to the crowd from the middle of the road. Obama, on the other hand, was like a whirlwind moving from one side of the parade route to the other. Shaking hands. Talking. Laughing. Looking people in the eye. Making a connection.

I could not help but notice that Obama never bypassed anyone in a wheel chair and would spend a couple minutes exchanging pleasantries. The crowd obviously liked this tall, skinny kid with the funny name. We all had our Obama for Illinois blue shirts on, and the crowd was soaking it in. Thousands of people would remember the name. Anyone who was in the crowd that day would remember him and all the energy shown by the Obama contingent. All the blue shirts saying "Obama for Illinois." As we marched, we saw many of our friends in the crowd, and they would yell out to us, "Is that the guy you were talking about?" Indeed Obama was, we would nod. Slowly. Surely.

When the parade was over, Obama shook each one of our hands (and again he hugged Michelle and me) and thanked us all for coming and sharing this day.

He was off to his next parade.

Full of life.

Full of energy.

Full of enthusiasm.

Slowly, surely building the momentum toward primary Election Day. Patient and confident that he was on the right path toward victory.

Change comes slowly, gradually, incrementally, and suddenly.

This was the first time since 2000 that we spent time with Mike Jordan. He is a likeable guy who bubbles with enthusiasm. It is obvious he has a great deal of passion for Obama and his candidacy and would travel to the ends of the earth for Obama. That is why we call him the "Super Volunteer." Obama and Jordan are close personally and have a genuine admiration for each other. They spent many hours together campaigning and developed a lasting special friendship.

Barack Obama would resonate, and his name would seep into voters' consciousness. Some of the people we noticed along the parade route were the same people who attended Obama's "coming out party," in 2000 at the Bethany Union Church.

It took a short time to learn the name, but once you did, you couldn't get it out of your mind. It was easy to match the name with the man. He was talking about the issues at every opportunity, although the media was not tuned in to the Obama campaign at this point. This was a part of the campaign that was not meant for a discussion of the issues. That did not mean the issues should not be discussed. In fact, Obama discussed the issues and answered questions since the day he announced for the Senate. It was just that the media was not interested at that point. It was much too soon.

Most of the media coverage were covering Hull, the multi-millionaire candidate and Hynes, the ultimate Democratic organization man. Obama was polling in the single digits, but nobody surrounding Obama was pushing the panic button. This was the slow period of the campaign, but it was a necessary part of any campaign. This was the period where the relationships were built, and Obama was already building them. We were building an organization too, but we didn't articulate it as such. During the 2000 Congressional campaign against Bobby Rush, we spent two full weeks, eating, sleeping and drinking Barack Obama. Imagine now when we had fourteen months to do this. We were already feeling some impacts of spreading the word.

People would say to us, "I know you guys like that Obama guy, and I like him too, but, he just can't win. He doesn't have money. He doesn't have an organization."

We were persistent and never stopped believing. We just felt it. It was right. Many times in my life I have had moments of doubt and long periods of doubt. Questioning whether a job or a friend was quite right. Questioning whether a business decision was right or not right.

Barack Obama, for Michelle and me, was quite different. We knew it, we felt it, and we were in synch. There wasn't anything anyone could say that could sway Michelle and me against Barack Obama. And we would hear the naysayers. "Stop wasting your time."

Often times in a campaign, rumors and whispers spread about a candidate. Nothing negative came across about Obama either from his friends or from his political opponents. In fact, his political opponents had a great deal of respect for Obama.

Dan Hynes Decides Not to Discuss at This Time

What was obvious was that Dan Hynes was not discussing issues in public. He did not want to get pinned down. It would be months before we knew where Hynes stood on the Iraq War. John Devens, owner of World Folk Music, had called the Hynes campaign to find the candidate's position on issues. Devens was especially interested in the Iraq War and where he was on that issue.

"Issues," he was told by a campaign staffer for Hynes. "Oh no, we are not discussing issues right now. That comes later." John was disappointed by the response.

"Where is Hynes on the Iraq War?" John would insist.

"In due time John." John was deeply disappointed by the response.

Obama was polling poorly and was not known outside the African-American community and outside of Hyde Park. He had high name recognition in our 19th Ward community and the surrounding area, dating back to the 2000 election. Events such as this parade would slowly, surely raise his visibility.

Change comes slowly, gradually, incrementally, and suddenly.

In the African-American community, he had to introduce himself. He started the campaign fourteen months early, and he would need every minute of it. We were so thrilled to be a part of it. We believed in this cause to spread the gospel of Barack Obama. It was an honor and privilege for us, and we gushed with pride.

All the pieces would fall into place. Soon, the "Meetup.com" would come into fruition. The "Obama for Illinois" website was constantly being evaluated and upgraded. It certainly was not the best at that point. There was room for improvement.

Obama had a competitive side to him, and he wanted to be the best at everything he attempted. One of the goals was to turn this "technologically illiterate side" to being "highly literate technologically." As it would turn out, they would have one of the best websites of any campaign by the end of the process. His forming a "Technology Committee" of volunteers showed great leadership in seeing an issue and improving on it. He had a constant desire to improve himself, which in turn improved everyone around him. After all, he is a student at heart.

The First Grassroots Fundraiser at World Folk Music

We had started planning the fundraiser in early February that would be held on July 20, 2003 at World Folk Music Company, and we put every ounce of energy from that point on into promoting Barack Obama for United States Senate.

It was not just about getting people to attend this event and to donate $25.00 to his campaign. It was about recruiting "Pied Pipers" for the campaign. It was the beginning. It was the journey, not the destination. We had sent out nearly three hundred invitations to people who we thought might be interested in attending. We would find that a number of people would donate to the campaign and be unable to attend the event. We needed clones of ourselves out everywhere across our community, across the city, across the county, across the collar counties and across the state.

We were given access to whatever materials we would need from Dan Shomon. We mailed "Friends" cards, informing our friends about Barack Obama. The sign in the window of our bookstore would initiate many conversations about Barack Obama.

We told people about this man, Barack Obama, who would be the next United States Senator from the state of Illinois. We could feel it. We would see Obama three times in July 2003. The first time at the parade in Evergreen Park.

The second time would be at our fundraiser. We had visited the headquarters, located at 310 S. Michigan Avenue, Suite # 1720, shortly after the parade to pick up additional materials for the fundraiser. There was a sign there that tracked the "grassroots fundraising" progress of the campaign: **7/14 $1,021,239**. This was an astounding number this point into the campaign. Throughout the course of the campaign, the sign would be updated often. The campaign had not reached a stage of being overwhelmed by the number of donors, but that was something we expected to happen.

There was precious little publicity and attention being paid to the campaign in the mainstream press, but the African-American owned newspaper, the *Daily Defender*, was keenly interested in the campaign. The headline of the article would have never appeared in the mainstream press at this point of the campaign. It was "Fund-raising success gives Obama momentum." "Banked as of 7/14 '$1,021,239' it reads in black felt pen."[97]

The Barack Obama fundraiser was held on July 20, 2003 at World Folk Music Company.

Here is what Lyn Wozniak, one of our 300 Obama volunteers from the 2000 campaign had to say.

> John then remarked that Obama was planning to run for something else. "Count me in!," said I. "Put my name on the list."
>
> Time marches on. It's now 2003. Michelle said to me, "He's going to run for Senator!" I didn't even ask, who? "Put my name on the list to work for him!" I expostulated. John said, "You're on it, you were the first one to jump in."
>
> The first event was a fundraiser. We assembled in the music shop. A local eatery provided the goodies. It was a nice day, and everybody was in a festive mood. Many of us remarked about the night in 2000.
>
> He arrived (he still looks like my friend Jim). He gave us his background and credentials. By the way, his credentials were the best of the entire field of Senate hopefuls in the 2004 primary.
>
> He talked of legislation that he had written and had passed. The only one of the contenders who had done that. His stand on the issues of the day. Further, he pointed out that he had taken a stand, at a public rally in Federal Plaza, against the war. He did this before the war started.
>
> "Holy Canola," I thought, "This guy is really for real."
>
> The next day I said to John & Michelle. "Where do you want me to go,

---

97 Fund-raising success gives Obama momentum. Joe Ruklick. *Chicago Defender*. Chicago, Ill.: Jul 26, 2003. pg. 5.

what do you want me to do, & when?"

— Lyn Wozniak,
Obama volunteer
2000, 2004, 2008

Lyn started working at campaign headquarters early in the process and would often see Obama. He always made a point to thank the volunteers and Lyn was no exception. Lyn would bring back to the community brochures, buttons, campaign materials and whatever she could reasonably carry on the train.

The fundraiser went off without a hitch. Tricia Alexander, a musician who donated her time, energy, and talents, entertained the crowd while waiting for Obama's arrival. She would play tunes like "This Land is Our Land" and many others. Dyed in the Wool, John Devens' band, also entertained the crowd that afternoon.

Obama, we found, was always running late. It was because he could never leave a room back in those days without being sure to greet and thank everyone there. He must have instinctively known that if you met him, he won you over. And with Obama, it wasn't just one vote he won over. He converted a disciple who would spread the word to the multitudes about the Obama gospel all through the city, county, collar counties and the state. Or a "Pied Pipers" if you will.

Here is what John Devens, the proprietor of the music shop had to say about that day.

There were not a lot of people at our little fundraiser for Barack Obama when he was running for the Illinois Senate in 2004. That did not stop him from coming out. By this time, Barack was getting some notice, but not a lot. I called several people to try to get them to come that day. Many said they would try. Many just said, "Barack Who." They know "who" now.

He was running a little behind, as usual. I was a little worried that we were not going to raise enough money to make it worthwhile for him to make the trip. I had nothing to worry about. This guy was more interested in meeting us and answering questions than how much we could contribute. When he showed up the room changed. He certainly carried himself well. As I sat there listening to his speech I thought he did not have a prayer of winning this election. He was up against an opponent with a very formidable political machine behind him. Hardly anyone knew who Barack was. I have supported so many great candidates who could not break through the barrier that seems to keep great thinkers from attaining political success. Nevertheless, something changed as the speech went along. Suddenly the possibility of his winning the senate seat did not seem like such an unattainable challenge. Toward the end of his speech, I could not help but dream of what a great country this would be if people like him could break through that barrier.

When the speech ended, a small group of people were standing around talking about what a great speech it was. Everyone was very excited, but no one wanted to say it. Then someone said, "This guy is going to be the next President." There was a collective sigh of relief as we began to talk about the possibility. Thankfully, Barack was out of earshot. We realized that Obama's fundraisers were not as much about raising money as grassroots supporters. The money would come, and his organization proved that The People could financially support a great candidate.

Now, when I watch Barack speak in front of thousands of people, I feel a great sense of pride that we helped just a little. I look at the picture on our table of my wife, Julia and me with the next President of the United States and I think, "now millions of people believe."

— John Devens,
World Folk Music, owner

Dave Becker really remembers that day and the everlasting affect it had on him.

Is He (Obama) a Guitar Player?

My name is David Becker, and I have lived in East Beverly for over 30 years. John Presta is a longtime friend of mine. In July of 2003, Presta invited me to World Folk Music to meet Barack Obama, who was running for United States Senate. I had seen Obama's name in the paper, but I didn't really know anything about him. I got there late, and the event was basically over. John introduced me to Barack in the store, and we talked one-on-one for 5 or 10 minutes. I don't really remember anything specific that we discussed, but I vividly remember my "first impression." He seemed very intelligent, reasonable, and calm. He seemed like the kind of politician that I could actually trust and believe. He seemed like the kind of person who could get along and work with people and get things done. I was very impressed, and I became an Obama supporter that night. Unfortunately, I got there too late to have my picture taken with him, or get an autographed book, but I did take a campaign button. When I got home, I called my childhood friend, Steve Weiford, who lives in Madison, Wisconsin. Steve and I are music fans, and we've been to many concerts together. I play the guitar and bass and have played in several bands. We have had many conversations about music. Anyway, I called Steve and asked him if he ever heard of Barack Obama. His response was, "Is he a guitar player?" I said, "Steve, get a pen and write this down......Barack Obama is going to be the first black president!" I told him about my meeting earlier that day. This year during the presidential campaign, Steve reminded me several times about my prediction. My wife and son also became Obama supporters. We contributed to his campaign several times. We all voted for him and so did my friend Steve. Thank you John Presta for giving me a chance to meet Barack Obama!!!

— Dave Becker

~

Nate Tamarin, deputy campaign manager, had been assigned to us to help the fundraiser go smoothly, and it was Nate who came out on the day of the fundraiser. I had asked Nate before the fundraiser about having media come to the event. Nate didn't object, but he added, "If you can get media here, that will be an accomplishment."

We tried to get the media there, but to no avail. They were not interested. And even at this point the presumption was that Dan Hynes would be the next United State Senator from the state of Illinois. We were told by many that we were wasting our time with this Obama fellow.

The words kept coming back to us, "He's a nice guy but... " And it wasn't isolated. So many of our friends and customers would repeat, "He's a nice guy but..."

The media was not focused on Obama or on the campaign. This was not unusual. It was July 2003, after all. This was the quiet time for campaigns to line up the ducks, plan the fundraisers, call the donors, recruit the volunteers, order the materials and hire the staff. Slowly but surely he was building a name and a brand. He was slowly, surely becoming known throughout the city, county and the state. He was starting to recruit "Pied Pipers."

Mainstream media was not focused here because Election Day was nine months into the future. Obama was not one of the favorites to win because he was an unknown. Obama was an underdog and not considered likely to rise above this illustrious field of candidates and experienced politicians. He had not created any excitement, but Nate Tamarin thought that it was not a negative thing either.

"It'll all come in time. It's a process," Tamarin was fond of saying.

Change comes slowly, gradually, incrementally, and suddenly.

The fundraiser was supposed to begin at 1:00 pm. While we did expect Obama to arrive a little bit late, much time had passed. Tamarin was becoming visibly nervous, although he had Obama's cell phone number. Obama could not answer the phone because he was at church and could not answer from the altar. About 1:40 pm, Obama called Tamarin and told him to tell everyone that he was on his way from the West side of Chicago. He would be there as soon as was humanly possible.

We asked Tricia Alexander and Dyed in the Wool to play a little longer to keep everyone occupied. Nearly seventy-five people had come and paid at least $25.00 to hear Obama speak and possibly talk to him.

"Where is he?" would be the question. We were all on edge. Tamarin would go outside to make his phone call and would come back in and tell us how much longer he would be.

Barack Obama Arrives, and I Introduce the Next United States Senator From The State of Illinois

At about ten minutes after two, an hour and ten minutes late, Obama arrived at World Folk Music Company for the big event. We had not lost anyone, and we were pleased. He shook hands with everyone he passed by as Tamarin was leading him to the stage and the microphone. Suzanne O'Shea happened into World Folk Music just to pick up her paycheck just as Barack Obama was coming in. Suzanne is a dedicated music teacher at World Folk Music, teaching Little Folkies Piano and Violin, Infant and Toddler Class, and Creative Music for Special Needs Class.

"What is going on here," Suzanne asked Nate Tamarin as he was leading Obama to the stage. "This is Barack Obama."

"I am running for political office and we are having a fundraiser here," Obama told her.

"Well. Good luck to you," she told Obama. She hadn't thought much about the incident until years later, but realized she had one brief, shining moment in American History that Sunday in July.

The crowd surrounded Obama as Tamarin led him to the stage. The crowd was happy to see him. He had a stunning personal presence. He had "it."

He finally made it near the stage, and I gave a short talk, "Thank you all for coming on this very special day. I want to thank my wife Michelle, Joyce Miller Bean, Kyle Bean, Lauren Bean and to John Devens for agreeing to host this event. And all of you for hanging in there with us."

"I know you didn't come to hear me talk today, so let me introduce to you, the next United States Senator from the state of Illinois, Barack Obama."

He bounced up on the stage and gave me his big hug. He whispered, "Thanks so much for all you and Michelle do." Obama then took the microphone and took over the crowd.

He started out by apologizing for his late arrival, although by now no one cared or seemed to notice. They were just so glad he arrived.

"You know," he would start out saying in explaining his lateness, "some of these preachers get carried away with spirit. And this one was **really** moved by the Holy Spirit." The partisan crowd roared. He had spent this Sunday morning attending church service at one of the African-American churches on the west side of Chicago. He would continue to visit the various churches this Sunday and most Sundays through primary election day.

He then went into the explanation of his name, which was part of his strategy to overcome his "funny name."

"Some people call me yo mama, and others call me Alabama. The name is Obama." The crowd again cheered. They all already knew his name and did not have a problem remembering it.

He then went into a mini-version of his now famous speech at the 2004 Democratic convention. He touched on themes as the powerless being protected from the powerful. Explaining how we are all connected whether we live in Chicago, Cairo, or Peoria. "If one of us is diminished, we are all diminished," and that was another popular theme he often spoke about.

He also commented on "Meetup.com," where he told of enlisting a large number of volunteers. As Tamarin would later tell us, "We don't really understand it ourselves as yet." It was early in the process. While they did not understand it, they had a sense that it was a positive thing.

But as Obama often said, "it is a tool. An important tool, but not the only tool." After the speech, Obama got a standing ovation from the seventy-five people in attendance. I announced that if anyone wanted to take a photo with Obama, I would oblige them. More than a couple dozen people got in line to have their photograph taken with the candidate for Illinois United States Senate. I was always amazed that most Obama photos were spectacular. He was photogenic and those in the photos were also touched by his presence.

This group would be just the beginning of our core group of volunteers that would help elect Obama to the United States Senate. Every person in that room that day believed that he would win this election. Michelle told Robert Davis and his family to come on over and meet the future President of the United States. Obama told Michelle, "Oh, go on, Michelle." Obama downplayed any talk of the Presidency and pointed out that he was running for United States Senate. He never discouraged such talk either. He would talk about achieving the task, but it surely must have stuck with him. That talk of his being President one day was always there, and it was the elephant in the room. Michelle and I openly discussed the possibilities and now Michelle had said it in front of him.

One of the key volunteers for the fundraiser was Joyce Miller Bean, a professor of literature at DePaul University and her two children, Kyle and Lauren . Joyce had donated all of the food for the event. The Beans took the most wonderful photograph with Obama, all four of them smiling broadly. They looked like they were having a good time and, indeed, they were having a good time.

Lauren Bean not only helped with the fundraiser, she became a key volunteer for Obama in this election. Lauren had graduated from DePaul University in June 2003 with a Bachelor of Arts (BA) in Cultural Religious Studies with double Minors in Anthropology and Japanese Studies.

Although to us the growth and commitment of our core group of volunteers, was upbeat and positive, the fact was that Obama was polling in the single digits. His opponents still had the edge of being more prominent in Illinois politics. Hynes was lining up labor union support and was strong with union leaders in Illinois. However, Obama would prove to be a force with the rank-and-file members. The grassroots unions, such as the SEIU and AFSCME, would come out in force for Obama, grassroots organizers and all.

Hynes had a massive fundraising apparatus through the regular Democratic Party. He had access to a political organization that could produce thousands of volunteers for Election Day. The regular Democratic Party in the 2004 campaign knew nothing about the new phenomenon of "grassroots fundraising" or "grassroots organizing" or "netroots organizing." We did not either, but we were learning quickly and could feel the grassroots growing under our feet.

Multi-millionaire Hull was connected to the Governor of Illinois and the Mayor of Chicago. Hull donated massive amounts of dollars and services to the Governor of Illinois. Hull was an enthusiastic supporter of Chicago's Mayor. And yet, the support from the Governor and the Mayor never materialized for Hull for a variety of reasons. Hull was committed to spending millions of dollars of his own money. He was willing to donate to organizations to induce them to support his candidacy. He often made donations to curry support. This was an unusual strategy, this reverse donation. He was spending his money on a professional staff. Hull had originally recruited David Axelrod as his chief strategist, but ultimately Axelrod decided to get on board with Obama, according to David Mendell's book.[98]

The World Folk Music Fundraiser Is a Rousing "Grassroots" Success

The World Folk Music fundraiser was a rousing success. Although we had netted close to $4,000, which is a massive amount of money for a group like ours, this group's worth was priceless in what it would accomplish for the campaign.

We were a group of ordinary, hard-working people. Obama's appeal to ordinary, hard-working people was extraordinary. More important than the amount of money raised, Obama's campaign had recruited at least 75 more "Pied Pipers." All would have different degrees of "Pied Pipered-ness." Some, such as Marilyn Thibeau, would not be able to go door-to-door or work a precinct on Election Day, but she would tell the

---

98 Mendell, *Obama: From Promise to Power.*

world about this man, Barack Obama. She told her circle of friends about him, and her circle of friends would tell their circle of friends. She would donate to Obama on a regular basis. Until the numbers of supporters, donors, volunteers would expand, multiply, and increase exponentially.

Change comes slowly, gradually, incrementally, and suddenly.

There was Robert Davis and his family. His wife, Keeley Binion, would tell all their many friends and family members and neighbors. They would put up signs on their own property, but Davis, before Election Day, would go door-to-door on his block and ask people if they wanted to place a yard sign on the lawn. The campaign would complain they did not have enough money to give us any more yard signs, so Davis would raise the money needed for the campaign so he could accommodate the yard sign demand for his own block.

Davis also gathered signatures for Obama for placement on the ballot. There were dozens and dozens of Robert Davis' on our team and people who worked with us. The signs were stored at our store, Reading on Walden Bookstore on Walden Parkway. We had become a pickup place for signs and materials and a mini-campaign headquarters for Obama for Illinois. We were listed on the Obama for Illinois website. We were listed third on the list, two slots below the campaign headquarters. As an added service, we also delivered yard signs and did sign placement anywhere and everywhere. On many days, we would receive more phone calls related to Obama, the campaign, yard signs, volunteer opportunities, and materials than for bookstore business. And business in 2003 was good.

Help Turn Illinois Obama Blue...

Pick up Obama for Illinois yard signs and window signs at any of the following locations. We will add new locations to the list frequently, so if you don't see a pick-up point near you, check back soon. If you would like to host a pick-up point in your area, please give us a call at 312 427-6300.

You can also download and print your own sign.

You can also request a sign by email: info@obamaforillinois.com

Chicago Downtown
Campaign Headquarters
310 S. Michigan, Chicago | MAP

(312) 427-6300

Chicago South Side
South Side Campaign Office
55th & Dan Ryan, Harold Washington Building
(773) 536-2261

Reading On Walden Bookstore
9913 S. Walden Parkway
(773) 233-7633

Chicago West Side
West Side Campaign Office
15 N. Mayfield, (773) 626-3810

Chicago North Side
U.S. Representative Jan Schakowsky's office
5539 N. Broadway, Chicago | MAP
(847) 424-1998

Alderman Joe Moore's Office, 2049 W. Howard

~

These ordinary people had a lot in common with Obama. Obama and his wife Michelle were still paying on their student loans. Barack sacrificed much in the way of earning power by running for office. They, like many of us, were struggling to pay their bills. They also faced the challenges of raising two young children. We all came up the same way. Michelle and I had a special affinity with him because we were all community organizers.

My wife Michelle's community organizing background was professionally based because of her background and education as a Master of Social Work. Michelle was always interested in community organizing because she saw it as a way to affect change in the community.

Obama Visits the Haunted Castle Up On the Hill to Talk About War and Peace

The third time we would see Obama in July was on July 27, 2003 at Beverly Unitarian church on 103rd & Longwood Drive, also known as the Castle. The structure is said to be haunted, as noted in Ursula Bielski's book, *Chicago Haunts: Ghostlore of the Windy City.*[99] Obama, unbeknownst to Michelle and me, accepted an invitation to speak before a group called the South Siders for Peace. This group opposed the war in Iraq and had demonstrated in front of the Castle the day the war in Iraq had started. Cars would drive past and shout obscenities, but others would show their support against the war. For the most part, the Iraq war was popular then.

This particular day, Obama came to the church on time, and thirty people attended. It was not a fundraiser, but a talk about the Iraq War with a peace group. Obama had been invited as a guest speaker. He took the opportunity to speak out against the Iraq War but also to emphasize he was not against all wars. This was a recurrent campaign theme.

If Obama was disappointed with the size of the crowd, he did not show it. He repeated much of the speech that he gave on October 2, 2002 in Federal Plaza. Here is an excerpt of what he said in the speech:

> I don't oppose all wars.
>
> After September 11th, after witnessing the carnage and destruction, the dust and the tears, I supported this Administration's pledge to hunt down and root out those who would slaughter innocents in the name of intolerance, and I would willingly take up arms myself to prevent such a tragedy from happening again.
>
> I don't oppose all wars. And I know that in this crowd today, there is no shortage of patriots, or of patriotism. What I am opposed to is a dumb war. What I am opposed to is a rash war. What I am opposed to is the cynical attempt by Richard Perle and Paul Wolfowitz and other arm-chair, weekend warriors in this Administration to shove their own ideological agendas down our throats, irrespective of the costs in lives lost and in hardships borne.
>
> What I am opposed to is the attempt by political hacks like Karl Rove to distract us from a rise in the uninsured, a rise in the poverty rate, a drop in the median income – to distract us from corporate scandals and a stock market that has just gone through the worst month since the Great Depression.
>
> That's what I'm opposed to. A dumb war. A rash war. A war based not on reason but on passion, not on principle but on politics.

~

---

99   *Chicago Haunts; Ghostlore of the Windy City.* Ursula Bielski Lake Claremont Press. October 1998.

He then took questions from the audience about the subject. He wanted to discuss the Iraq War. Many of the questions that he was asked were about "not being opposed to all wars."

I do not agree with the assessment that "War is not an option," he would say many times during the talk. "There are times," he explained, "where war is necessary."

Some in attendance there were opposed to all wars. Obama stuck with his view that this Iraq War was a "dumb war." Some wars, he argued, are legitimate. He gave examples of just wars such as the Civil War and World War II. It was at this point that I realized he had one eye on the United States Senate seat, but had another eye on the White House. He may have been downplaying the talk about becoming President of the United States, but he was thinking about one day being President of the United States. I discussed with Michelle later that day that a candidate could not be elected President of the United States unless the candidate had a strong view on the use of military action.

Obama also brought up the fact that his campaign was on this "Meetup.com," after we initiated discussion several weeks earlier at the parade, and was already enlisting hundreds of volunteers. He would have another pipeline here for "pied pipers." He pointed out that in a short time on "Meetup.com," the Obama campaign already had the largest number of people signed up outside of a Presidential campaign. They were the largest group that was running for the United States Senate. These groups were already starting to "meet up" in various places around Chicago and the suburbs.

After a half hour of questions, he said goodbye to everyone and left.

After the talk, Obama had left, but Tamarin stayed behind. Michelle and I talked for an hour about the election and Chicago politics. Tamarin had questions about the Chicago political situation scene and was especially interested in what we knew about Dan Hynes, his political machine, his supporters, strength of their support in the community, and his politics. Hynes was considered the strongest opponent. Tamarin was hungry for our assessment of Hynes. We also discussed with Tamarin in more detail the "Meetup.com" stuff and why we thought that it was important. We lifted Tamarin's spirit since he didn't know what to make of the small crowd at the Castle. It wasn't our event, we pointed out to Tamarin. Had we known about it we certainly would have aggressively promoted the event.

August 2003 Was the Slow, Simmering Summer Month When Obama Gained Steam

During August, we continued our all-out lobbying effort for Obama. We always had window signs available at the store and any campaign materials that volunteers wanted. The intensity was still not there, but it was still very early in the process. We were sending out "friends" cards, working Obama into conversations, discussing the Senate race and advocating for Obama. But slowly, surely, these efforts on behalf of Obama were building awareness.

We also attended our first "Meetup.com" meeting in Hyde Park, and surprisingly, there was a great crowd of Obama-ites in attendance, including Glenn Brown. It was the only time we would meet Brown throughout the campaign. And these meetings were starting to take place all over the city with twenty, thirty in attendance. The importance of these meetings was that these were dedicated volunteers. The grassroots movement was taking hold but it was now being called by a different name: netroots.

Anybody Out There Yet? Anybody Out There Yet?

Michelle and I were known as Mr. and Mrs. Grassroots inside the campaign. Glenn Brown was most certainly known as Mr. Netroots. Glenn moderated the "Meetup.com" web site for the campaign and started the "Obama for Senate Yahoo Group"[100] on Yahoo for the campaign. The first several messages on the "Obama for Senate Yahoo Group" were telling. The first discussions range from talks about the first "Meetup.com" meetings to a brief discussion about Obama's book, *Dreams from My Father*. Someone mentioned that Powell's Bookstore had some copies and they were very cheap. And some talk about a petition drive to place Obama on the ballot. The impact of this site can never be underestimated. Things were happening in the Obama for Illinois campaign rather quickly and in a very short period:

---

100 Later renamed the "Obama Brigade" and which to this day is in existence on the Yahoo Group site.

Anybody out there yet? Anybody out there yet?
Just Checking This transmission may contain information that is privileged, confidential and/or exempt from disclosure under applicable law. If you are not the... glenn_h_brown@...
ghbrown60640

Jul 25, 2003
11:10 am 2 Welcome Welcome
Welcome to the two new (and only other) people on the obama list. And archpundit - I love your blog... ghbrown60640

Jul 26, 2003
6:20 pm 3 meet up meet up
Hi Glenda- I have some concerns about the meet-up. I noticed that the other senatorial candidates also have meet-up times. I have signed up for the... marta_perales

Jul 30, 2003
6:44 pm 4 Re: meet up Re: meet up
Hi Marta, It will be on the 3rd wednesday of the month every month. this months will be on august 20th glenn — In ObamaForSenate@yahoogroups.com,... ghbrown60640

Jul 30, 2003
9:00 pm 5 Obama's book Obama's book
FYI- the title of the book he wrote is Dreams From My Father.

Aug 21, 2003
12:43 pm 6 Re: Obama's book Re: Obama's book
I just got this a couple of days ago from the library! Tracy, I am assuming you were the one I met at the meetup last night talking about that? glenn tracey... glenn_h_brown@...
ghbrown60640
Aug 21, 2003

12:50 pm 7 (No subject) (No subject)
I got my copy of Dreams From My Father at Powell's on Hyde Park for not much money. I'm pretty sure they still have a bunch of copies. Get MSN 8 and help... Gabriel Piemonte
gabrielpiemonte@...

Aug 24, 2003
5:21 pm 8 Obama's book redux Obama's book redux
I just got it from the library too! We should discuss it... JB... Jesse Bacon
baconj_2000

Aug 24, 2003
10:44 pm 9 Hello New Members! Hello New Members!
Welcome to the Yahoo Group for Obama for Senate! This transmission may
contain information that is privileged, confidential and/or exempt from
disclosure under... glenn_h_brown@...
ghbrown60640

Aug 26, 2003
**5:32 pm 10 How To use this discussion list How To use
this discussion list**
If you want to talk to people on this discussion list send an e-mail to
ObamaForSenate@yahoogroups.com. If you want to reply to a message on
this discussion... glenn_h_brown@...
ghbrown60640
Aug 27, 2003
11:46 am 11 Petition Drive? Petition Drive?
What would people think to bringing the petitions into the meetup Barak
needs 5000 signatures to get on the ballot. This transmission may contain
information... glenn_h_brown@...
ghbrown60640

Aug 27, 2003
5:31 pm 12 Re: Petition Drive? Re: Petition Drive?
He's not on yet? Sure, that seems a no-brainer...

Aug 27, 2003
7:11 pm 13 Re: Petition Drive? Re: Petition Drive?
... No one is technically on the ballot yet - there is a deadline (sometime in
november I think) when people need to get their petitions in - this is...
ghbrown60640

~

The Yahoo "Obama for Senate Yahoo Group" website was growing by
the day in the summer 2003. We had to keep in mind Obama's admon-
ishment: that this was a tool and that we should not lose sight of our other
tools.

But what a tool! Volunteers were pouring in from these sites at the rate of dozens a day, and these were volunteers who were having an immediate impact on the campaign.

The Obama campaign would continue to raise modest amounts of money, and Jim Cauley, campaign manager, insisted that cash be held back until the final three weeks of the campaign for the very expensive television commercials. The timing, we were told by campaign aides, had to be right. It was the "sneak attack." We just needed to be patient and trust in the team Obama was assembling.

It was important that volunteers like us continued our grassroots efforts such as telling friends about Obama, sending "friend" cards, attending meetup meetings, and surfing the web with the Yahoo Group and blogging on behalf of our friend, Obama. My wife Michelle was boundless in her energy to promote Barack Obama for United States Senate, sending 'friend' cards all over the world, including her friend, Ted Rothon, who is a retired Social Worker, now living in Amsterdam, Netherlands. Ted enthusiastically told his friends in the Netherlands about this man Obama. And they told their friends. And their friends told their friends. Michelle also sent information to a friend in Israel and a friend in England. And many others did the same. And so on. And so on. And so on. Many volunteers were spending hours at campaign headquarters stuffing envelopes and soliciting contributions. Neil Pomeranke, Lyn Wozniak, and Larry Unruh volunteered at campaign headquarters on a regular basis during summer 2003. Each passing week they reported that the number of volunteers was growing. This early in the campaign, and volunteers were flooding the place. This was the part of the campaign that was the journey. We were on the road to our destination, the United States Senate. And do we dare say it: the White House.

While Obama was slowly building a large grassroots effort, he had a number of well-heeled supporters, people such as Penny Pritzker and other members of the Pritzker family who gave the maximum $12,000 to Obama over a period of months prior to the primary election. George and Jennifer Soros each donated the maximum $12,000, as did some other members of the Soros family. Chicago area attorney Manny Sanchez and his wife Pat Sanchez also donated a considerable sum of money. Manny and Pat were loyal supporters who brought in dozens of others into the campaign. Manny is a name member of the law firm of Sanchez, Daniels

& Hoffman. He is also a prominent leader in the Chicagoland Hispanic business community.

And the list of big donors grew during the course of the campaign. In view of this, the luckiest break the campaign received was the candidacy of Blair Hull. The new campaign finance law was now in effect, which only allowed a maximum contribution of $2,000. If, however, a candidate self-finances, like Hull, then the maximum rises. That new maximum allowed Obama to court some of the people he had met over the years in Chicago and get the maximum contribution. This would add up to a significant total by primary Election Day. That would mean more television commercials in the final stretch of the campaign.

Many things were starting to fall into place, slowly, surely. Obama's name recognition was rising. Small groups similar to ours were starting to spring up everywhere. Howard Dean supporters were gravitating to Obama due in large part of the synergies created by the "Meetup.com" effort, thanks to Glenn Brown's persistence with Tamarin. And Brown's "Obama for Senate Yahoo Group" was instrumental in recruiting volunteers. At this point in August 2003, hundreds had already signed up for "Meetup.com" with the Obama campaign.

More important to the campaign, few had signed up with the opposition. Hynes and Gery Chico had started a "Meetup.com" group, but they didn't have people like Glenn Brown driving it. Even a social network like this "Meetup.com" needed to be worked. It need not be all encompassing, but at least at minimum of maintenance was needed. "This is a tool, but not the only tool," Obama would repeat over and over.

People were meeting on a monthly basis all over the Chicago area from the far South Side, Hyde Park, Ravenswood, Andersonville, Oak Park, and Evanston. In each instance, dozens of people would "meetup" and form little mini-Obama groups and organize on their blocks and in their communities. Little "Pied Pipers" were forming all over the city and suburbs of Chicago. Eventually it would spread to the collar counties and downstate.

During the summer of 2003, Hull spent millions of dollars on television and radio commercials. He began to target the Chicago area and the African-American vote in August 2003. In a page from the Congressional campaign, Bobby Rush did commercials for his friend, Hull. As Bill Clinton helped Rush, Rush was now helping his newfound friend Hull. The gloves were off. *The Chicago Sun Times* reported that one of the first clashes among the Democrats running for U.S. Senate, Obama took a swing Monday at Hull over radio spots that Hull was airing to cut into Obama's African American base.[101] The beauty of this for Obama was that he was getting free air time responding to these commercials, with a big assist from his friend, former Chicago Alderman and radio host Cliff Kelly.[102] Hull paid thousands to the African-American owned airwaves, and Obama would respond to the ads free of charge. And the ratings were excellent. Everybody won except Hull.

This was clearly payback for Obama's audacity to run against Rush in the 1st Congressional race in 2000, however, Hull's commercials featuring Rush proved ineffective. Rush was overestimating his importance and influence in the African-American community, and the image of Barack Obama was slowly, surely starting to take shape. Obama had been visiting churches and attending events non-stop, day and night, since January.[103] His energy was boundless. Hull's energy and drive was no match for Obama's.

Change comes slowly, gradually, incrementally, and suddenly.

Obama and Hynes were fighting for the support of the labor unions. Hynes represented the old guard. His dad would be leaning on the old AFL-CIO people. Obama had the support of the rank-and-file members, and Hynes had the support of the union leaders.

Obama Is a Workhorse and Not Just a Showhorse

In an interview in a downstate Illinois paper, the *Champaign News Gazette*, Obama said, "Nobody in the race is better prepared to be a fighter for working people than I am," said Obama, a senior lecturer at the University of Chicago College of Law. "If you look at the work I've done in the state Legislature, I'm clearly a workhorse, not just a show horse."[104]

---

101 Senate hopefuls vie for black vote - Hull takes heat from Obama for radio ads featuring Rush *Chicago Sun-Times* - August 5, 2003 Author: Scott Fornek.
102 Kelly was convicted of federal charges of bribery in 1987, but has since distinguished himself as a Chicago radio host.
103 Actually, since March 22, 2000, the day after he lost to Bobby Rush, I argue Obama started running again. And that is when this campaign unofficially began.
104 Obama is not your average Chicago Democrat JIM DEY. *News Gazette.* Champaign, Ill.: Aug 23, 2003. pg. A.4.

And we saw it, too. Not only was he in our community at least three times in July 2003, he attended many other events. He attended an event in Bloomington Illinois called the "Illinois Democrat Women in Bloomington" for Obama. He attended Democrats Day in Springfield for the Illinois State Fair in August 2003. He also attended an event sponsored by Congressman Lane Evans. Evans was the first downstate congressman to support Obama, and it was another key endorsement.

It was at this point that Obama was receiving precious little publicity. *The Chicago Defender* was giving the race some coverage when they interviewed both African-American candidates for U.S. Senate. When it was revealed that the federal deficit would be over $500 billion dollars, from budget surpluses not many years earlier under the Clinton Administration, Obama was stunned at the projected deficit. "I think this is a testimony to the destructive and misguided fiscal policy of the Bush administration," he told the newspaper.[105]

Meanwhile, back at Obama headquarters, the intensive money raising efforts were continuing at a steady pace, slowly, surely. Obama was still spending Sundays at African-American churches in Chicago and the suburban areas. And anywhere Obama would be invited to an event, he would attend. "Oh please come out to my place, Barack." He would write it down, hand it to a staff member and he would be there. Anywhere and everywhere.

These were the dog days of the campaign, the time when all the groundwork was being laid, and the foundations were solidified and the frame of the campaign was being built. He was building a solid foundation from the bottom to the top. The campaign had tremendous strength at the base of the foundation and enormous strength at the top.

Change comes slowly, gradually, incrementally and suddenly.

---

105 Davis, Obama: Bush's $500 billion runaway deficit train wrecking economy Strausberg, Chinta. *Chicago Defender.* Chicago, Ill.: Aug 27, 2003. Vol. XCVIII, Iss. 81; pg. 3.

CHAPTER 7

Barack Obama Slowly, Surely Gains Momentum

~

Illinois Comptroller Daniel Hynes formally kicked off his bid for the 2004 Democratic nomination for U.S. Senate on Sunday, September 14th, using the backdrop of an electrical workers hall to portray himself as organized labor's candidate. Hynes spoke to several hundred supporters at Local 134, the International Brotherhood of Electrical Workers.[106] Hynes announced his candidacy a full eight months after Obama. Hynes did not have his infrastructure on the ground. Already at this point, Obama had raised a substantial amount of money from small and large donors, set up a number of small groups like ourselves, was the leading Senate candidate in the country on "Meetup.com," had an above average website in place that was improving by the day thanks to the "Technology committee," and was picking up a handful of endorsements along the way.

It was obvious that Hynes already had thought he had the race won. He was acting like the "entrenched incumbent." Hynes would get the support of the old-time established union leadership, such as the leaders of the AFL-CIO, whereas, Obama's campaign would attract the more grassroots type of unions such as AFSCME and SEIU. Those unions

---

106 Rick Pearson and Brett McNeil, Tribune staff reporters. "Hynes' Senate bid leans on labor: [Chicagoland Final , CN Edition]. " *Chicago Tribune* [Chicago, Ill.] 15 Sep. 2003,2C.1. *Chicago Tribune.*

provided on the ground troops for the candidates. The AFL-CIO provided money. That was the major difference.

Cook County Treasurer Maria Pappas joins the race

And then in late October 2003, Maria Pappas decided to enter the race officially after months of speculation that she would. Pappas was a popular elected official and had high name recognition in Cook County. Steve Neal wrote on October 31, 2003, "Include her in. Cook County Treasurer Maria Pappas." "I'm going to run, and I'm going to win," said Pappas, 54.[107] Maria Pappas' entrée in the race made the field even more competitive because she is a woman and had a chance to attract women voters to her camp.

Hynes' campaign spokesman, Chris Mather, told the *Chicago Tribune* on November 17, 2003 that the story here really is that Dan has the overwhelming support from 62 labor unions.[108] Hynes also had the endorsement of over 600 elected officials around the state. Among Hynes, major supporters in the state were Michael Madigan, John Stroger and John Daley.

Mather was responding to the support Obama had received from the SEIU (Service Employees International Union) and AFSCME (American Federation of State, Municipal and County Employees). There was one clear advantage for Obama to get the endorsement of these two key unions: political organizers and volunteers. Both the SEIU and AFSCME not only support and endorse candidates, but they send paid and unpaid political workers and volunteers to help the candidate of their choice. This was a huge boost for Obama.

The 2004 United States Senate consisted of luck, hard work and enthusiasm.

The unions sent volunteers and paid staff to help Obama's campaign. They sent were enthusiastic about Obama, and it showed in their performance.

An important endorsement for Hynes came on November 18,

---

107 Steve Neal. "EDITORIAL." *Chicago Sun-Times*. October 31, 2003, EDITORIAL: 39.
108 Obama lures some unions from Hynes ; In Senate race, Democrats fight for labor support;
    (Chicagoland Final) David Mendell, Tribune staff reporter. *Chicago Tribune*. Chicago, Ill.: Nov
    17, 2003. pg. 1.

2003, as reported by the *Chicago Tribune's* reporter David Mendell, when Illinois House Speaker Michael Madigan threw his political support and muscle behind Hynes. The Obama campaign accused Madigan of attempting to blunt Obama's growing momentum in the campaign up to that point. In addition to Hynes' union endorsements, he had also received the endorsement of 85 of the state's 102 Democratic county chairs. The party's Central Committee remained neutral in the race, given the talent and the breadth of the field.

Up until November 2003, our group of volunteers was meeting monthly. We were planning on strategy, exchanging ideas, and inviting campaign staff to address our volunteers. We did not know at this point what our specific role would be in the campaign. We just knew we would be involved. By November 2003, the campaign was starting in earnest. The group of volunteers decided we should start meeting weekly. Here is how Lyn Wozniak saw it.

> The primary is in a few months. Michelle says that we'd better get to it. I agree. She says I'm to be at the Luna (our local coffee shop) 7pm Wednesday.
>
> The next Wednesday about ten of my neighbors and me are sipping coffee at the Luna. The discussion is about what we can do to help get the best man for the job on the ballot. We decide on a number of things. Among them to meet every Wednesday there at 7pm.
>
> To that end, I volunteer to pass out Obama literature with a note about the Wednesday meetings. It was cold that following Wednesday when I did it starting with the 536 train.
>
> I called the downtown office to find out where it was. As luck would have it, it's on the way to the train. Since I go downtown each Thursday, I was able to do that, too. Further, the Luna group would give me chores and requests to do and report about.
>
> Our small group was able to blanket the neighborhood with about as many signs as the regular organization did for Hynes. They even knew about us downtown.
>
> We were on the 'official' web site. This was helpful one day. We wanted more signs, but downtown headquarters was running low. They told me that because we were on the web site if I got someone down there 'right now' we could have what we wanted. I made a phone call. Twenty minutes later one of our guys was there. While another of our gang circled the block we

scarfed up everything we could get our hands on and loaded it into the car.
— Lyn Wozniak,
Obama volunteer, 2000, 2004, 2008

Lyn was a fixture at the headquarters. She would often bring back materials that she could carry on the train. Michelle and I would go to pick up yard signs and window signs. We made sure we saw different people at headquarters because the orders were to go easy on the signs. "One per block" please.

We had gotten word from the campaign that they would be opening community offices starting in January 2004. From these locations, there would be intensive door-to-door efforts and get out the vote efforts throughout the communities in Chicago. The campaign decided it could save cash by using satellite offices such as our store to pass out yard signs and materials. An office in our approximate area would not be necessary, saving the campaign tens of thousands of dollars. We were listed on the "Obama for Illinois" website as a pick up place for yard signs and campaign materials.

Another key endorsement came in that month for Obama, the Illinois Federation of Teachers. "Barack Obama will fight for our children and their education," said IFT President James Dougherty. "He understands the needs of public schools, and he has the leadership ability to continue the fight for those schools as a member of the United States Senate."[109]

Money was becoming a key factor in the campaign. Surprisingly, Obama was keeping pace with his main nemesis, Hynes. Obama was getting smaller donations from a large number of people while Hynes was getting large donations from a small group of people.

By the end of the year, December 31, 2003, Obama had raised $3,002,859.17. Of more importance, Obama had $1,789,877.67 in cash on hand. This was the plan. Raise a substantial amount of money and save it for the opportune moment.

But there was one more compelling and important factor. Obama had thousands of small donors. He would have collected donations from

---

109 Obama lures some unions from Hynes ; In Senate race, Democrats fight for labor support; [Chicagoland Final, CN Edition] David Mendell, Tribune staff reporter. *Chicago Tribune*. Chicago, Ill.: Nov 17, 2003. pg. 1

25,000 donors by Election Day in March of 2004.

One thing that did help him get those donors was because Obama's campaign made great use of the different Internet vehicles available at the time, the main one being the "Obama for Senate Yahoo Group. The "Obama for Senate Yahoo Group"[110] would exchange ideas, events, issues and many other things over the Internet, and "Meetup.com" would bring people together.

One key defining moment for Obama came on December 15, 2003 when he received not only the endorsement, but also the full support, from Congresswoman Jan Schakowsky.[111] We read on the website that Congresswoman Schakowsky was supporting Obama for Senate, and we immediately thought of Harvey Mader. We had no idea if Harvey's lobbying on behalf of Obama had an impact, but we were thrilled. We knew this endorsement was huge. The official announcement was made on Dec. 16, 2003 at Women and Children First Bookstore, hosted by our friends and bookstore owners, Linda Bubon and Ann Christopherson.

We called our dear friend Mader, and he was thrilled when Schakowsky endorsed Obama. For Mader, Schakowsky's support authenticated Obama's candidacy for United States Senate. The endorsement was a sign that the Evanston Democratic Party would also be supporting Obama. The endorsement usually meant an overwhelming vote for the candidate supported, in many cases nearly 90% of the vote from Evanston Township.[112]

By January 15, Hull, despite having spent more than $12 million, most of it from his own personal money, had failed to distinguish himself from the crowded field of Democrats. At this point in the race, Hynes and Obama were neck and neck. The thinking among the media was that Hynes would have an advantage because of his access to the party apparatus. It was clear that local party organizations would be

---

110 Later renamed the "Obama Brigade" and which to this day is in existence.
111 Eric Krol *Daily Herald* Political Writer. "Schakowsky endorses Obama: [All Edition]. *"Daily Herald* [Arlington Heights, Ill.] 16 Dec. 2003,7.
112 Obama received 89.38% of the vote in the March 16, 2004 Democratic primary. The next closest area in Cook County (outside of Chicago), was in Oak Park, Illinois. Obama received 87.60% of the vote in Oak Park. The Oak Park group formed in September 2003 as a direct result of the "Meetup.com" meeting. The Oak Park group is an offshoot of the Howard Dean 2004 campaign and later renamed Democracy for America (DFA).

behind Hynes. The only question is the level of enthusiasm they would have for him. We were beginning to sense the level of excitement for Hynes just was not there.

Obama opened two campaign offices that we would visit often for campaign materials. One office, which he shared with Jesse Jackson Jr., was in Matteson, Illinois. Campaign aide to Jesse Jackson Jr., Reverend Lawrence Blackful, was in charge of that office. We would go there often during the campaign when we ran out of signs. By early January, we had already distributed an astounding amount of signs: nearly a thousand. They were spreading everywhere. The word had gotten around quickly that we had the signs. Many days, we would get more inquiries about Obama-type material than we would get about books and book orders.

We had to put the yard signs together and had crews of people help us with this task. The word, by January, was starting to spread about Obama. Our store was being closely associated with Obama. Reading on Walden Bookstore had become campaign headquarters for Obama on our side of town. On a number of occasions, the campaign would need yard signs and call us. We would have passed out 5000 yard signs by the time primary Election Day arrived.

The polls were starting to show dramatic improvements for Obama. The "**to know him is to love him**" factor was coming more into play.

There was a movement developing inside the Obama campaign. The grassroots efforts of the campaign were starting to take hold. Hull was imploding. He had some support in the African-American community because he was campaigning there, but even that was eroding because as Al Kindle pointed out, "As soon as they find out he isn't an African-American, he will be toast."

Hull, it seemed to me, was content on pretending he was African-American. And many voters who we informally polled early in the process certainly thought that he was one of them. Especially with Bobby Rush as his campaign chairman.

But Hull was paying volunteers to put up yard signs. His support was fleeting and would soon disappear. When yard signs are posted on public areas, that is a sure sign of campaign weakness. The strong campaigns have signs on private property because that connotes the permission of the property owner. Obama already had thousands of yard signs all over

Chicago and his other opponents (aside from Hull) had none.

Obama also started resonating with the voters with the Iraq War. Even in early 2004, the war was highly unpopular with many Democratic voters, especially the progressive wing of the party.

On Monday, January 17, 2004, which was the Martin Luther King holiday, our store closed, and we found ourselves with some time. I checked the Obama website and saw that they were opening a new office near 55th & Wentworth. The website posting stated that Obama would attend the ceremony.

It was a significant day for us because we would meet four significant people in our lives and whose friendship remains to this day.

One was Reverend Lawrence Blackful.

Lawrence Blackful was in charge of Obama's Matteson office on Lincoln Highway. The pastor of St. Bethel Baptist Church in Chicago Heights, Reverend Blackful was also a community activist. He is also a leader in the South Suburban Action Conference and is its Executive Director. The group worked on issues: homelessness, education funding, crime, and violence.

The second significant person we met that day was Al Kindle. Kindle had been a long-time veteran of the Chicago political scene. He had served as Alderman Toni Preckwinkle's chief of staff for many years but, at Obama's request, Preckwinkle had loaned him to the campaign for the primary campaign fight on the strength of his ability to "Get out the Vote (GOTV)." It was also the day we met Kevin Watson and Alan V. Manuel. Watson was on leave from the AFSCME labor union. Manuel was a volunteer at the office.

It was in keeping with the spirit of Dr. Martin Luther King. We would meet these four great African-Americans on this holiday and, for the next three months we worked with all four of them to help elect Obama. He would be the third African-American elected to the United States Senate. And not to mention the elephant in the room, a future President of the United States of America.

On this January day, we were again running low on yard signs and demand was growing stronger everyday as a result of our twelve months of preaching the Obama gospel. The excitement was starting to build. We had called Tamarin, and he suggested we call the Matteson office.

The person at the other end said we could have ten yard signs, but no more. We would always take what we could get. We tried to explain who we were to the person on the other end, but to no avail. We would meet on the Dan Ryan Expressway at the 87th Street exit, and we would get the yard signs.

"A little here."

"A little there."

It adds up. Just like a well-run campaign.

"A little here. A little there."

It turned out the person was the Reverend Lawrence Blackful.

Change comes slowly, gradually, incrementally, and suddenly.

What we did not know at the time was that we were both going to the same place, the opening ceremony of the 55th and Wentworth office. Obama would be there. When we arrived, we greeted Tamarin. Reverend Blackful noticed the exchange, saw that we knew Nate, and said, "Oh, the people from the highway." Then Tamarin gave him the run down about us.

"Had I known that, I could have given you more signs," Lawrence told us. Tamarin then told us that there were plenty of signs at the new office and we should help ourselves. The original plan was to have one sign per street, but the demand got so heavy we gathered as many as possible. We were turning our community into "Obama blue."

Many people told us that they could not take a yard sign for Obama, but they were indeed supporting Obama. These were people with Hynes window and yard signs. They would vote for Obama, and that was good enough for us.

At the event, we met hundreds of new people. It was obvious to us the momentum was shifting and shifting quickly. While we were in the African-American community, at least thirty percent of the crowd there was white. A simply amazing number. Unheard of. Even the Harold Washington campaign did not develop this type of coalition.

We were introduced to Obama campaign manager, Jim Cauley. Cauley had a gruff manner. Tamarin told Cauley that we would be working the 19th Ward.

"How are we looking there?" Cauley asked.

"We are going to receive anywhere from 40-50% of the vote in the entire ward and we will win overwhelmingly in the eastern section of the ward," I told him.

Cauley could not believe it. "All I wanted to do is keep from getting creamed there. That is great news. Thank you."

When Obama started speaking, that day, no different than many other times, he pulled his Mike Jordan introduction. "I cannot go on without introducing Mike Jordan," he would sheepishly say. Of course, all eyes would look upward for this six foot six figure and they would see this much shorter, stocky, well-built, and energetic white guy. Obama would call Mike Jordan one of his most valuable players, as Michael Jordan had been to the Chicago Bulls.

Obama then introduced Michelle and me to the crowd. He told the crowd of volunteers that we were his southwest side "powerhouses" and that we had great passion for this campaign, and praised our grassroots efforts. He thanked us and called us his "friends." He was kind in his praise.

We spoke briefly to Obama that day. He personally thanked us again for all of our contributions to the campaign. He asked for our assessment of the 19th Ward and, when we told him, he was not as surprised at all.

Obama wanted to be sure he didn't miss anyone or fail to acknowledge anyone. Hundreds were there. We both got two hugs that day from Obama. He just wanted to be sure he went to everybody.

The campaign was publishing our weekly meetings too and it was having an impact.

Upcoming Events ...
Saturday, February 7, 2004 5 EVENTS
8:30am: Weekly South Side volunteer meeting at the Obama for Illinois South Side Campaign Office. Come out and join your local organization to help Obama win. These meetings are very important, so please plan to attend. The South Side office is located at 5401 S. Wentworth (55th & Dan Ryan) in the Harold Washington Building. For more information please call . . . . .

9:30am: Barack appears on the "Live from the Heartland" Radio Show, listen on WLUW 88.7 FM.

10:00am-11:00am: Barack Brigade Rally in Rogers Park. Join the Senator, campaign staff members, and northside volunteers for a rally and neighborhood blitzing at the Heartland Cafe, 7000 N. Glenwood, Chicago. For more information: Please call . . . . ..

10:00am: Peoria Voter Registration and Visibility Walk. Help build up the support for the Obama campaign in Peoria by meeting with staff members and supporters. Meet at Mt. Zion Church, 305 S. Madison Park Terrace. Refreshments will be served. For more information: Please contact Andrea . **10:30am-12:00pm:** Attend the weekly West Side/West Suburban volunteer meeting at the Obama for Illinois West Campaign Headquarters. Each week receive campaign updates and instructions on how you can personally make sure the west side and western suburbs elect Barack Obama the next United States Senator from Illinois. These meetings are very important, please plan to attend. The West Side/West Suburban office is located at 15 N. Mayfield (5800W) at Madison in Chicago. For more information: Please call LaDerrick Williamsl . . . . ..

2:00pm-4:00pm: Evanston Community Rally. Family Focus Our Place, 2010 Dewey Avenue, Evanston. Join Barack, Evanstonians for Obama, and northside/north shore supporters at a community reception. For more information: Please call . . . . ..

Sunday, February 8, 2004 3 EVENTS

1:00pm-3:00pm: Lincoln Square/Ravenswood Door to Door Canvassing. Meet at the Rockland Cafe, 2601 W. Leland, at the corner of Rockwell and Leland, 1/2 block north of the Rockwell El-stop on the Brown Line. Dress warm and bring friends! Please RSVP to Mary at Marymccar@ . .

2:00pm: New Trier Democratic Endorsement Session. Winnetka Community House, Room 101, 620 Lincoln Avenue, Winnetka. Join Senator Obama and our North Shore supporters at this public event. Voting is limited to paid members of the New Trier Township Democrats. For more information: Please contact…

4:30pm-5:30pm: Winnebago County Democrats US Senate Candidates Forum. Ramada Suites, 200 S. Bell School Road, Rockford. Come hear the Senator and the Democratic candidates for US Senate address the Winnebago County Democrats. For more information: Please contact…

Monday, February 9, 2004

5:30pm-7:30pm: Downstate Campaign Headquarters in Springfield Grand Opening. 627 E. Adams Street, Springfield. Food and refreshments will be served. For more information or to RSVP: Please contact…

Tuesday, February 10, 2004

7:00pm: Obama Reception in Macomb. Sullivan Taylor Coffee House, 119 S. Randolph Street, Macomb. Come meet Barack and his supporters in Macomb, donations are encouraged. For more information: Please contact Andrea at…

Wednesday, February 11, 2004
7:00pm: Beverly Area Volunteer Organizing Meeting. Cafe Luna, 1742
W. 99th Street. We will be discussing volunteer opportunities in the
Beverly/Morgan Park community. For more information, call . . . . . and ask
for Michelle or John Presta. Or e-mail us at readingonwalden@att.net.

Positive news items were appearing in print about Obama. One issue that
Obama was obsessed with overcoming was his name. Michelle and I
consistently said throughout the campaigns that it was not an issue with
voters. It is, in fact, a cool name. One of those names that once you hear it,
you do not forget it. His name, in fact, was an asset. News stories, such as
this story in the *Daily Herald* on February 15, 2004 showed that "By his own
admission, one of the biggest hurdles facing Barack Obama's quest for the
Democratic U.S. Senate nomination is his name." Yet, the story continued,
the unique name — Swahili for "blessed by God" — stands out and may
ultimately help separate him from the other six Democrats running in the
March 16 primary. It added that his challenge is giving voters something to
identify with his unusual name.[113]

The campaign activity at the bookstore was intensifying for this man
Obama. The notation on the website that listed us as a pickup point
made us a popular location on the southwest side of Chicago. The effect
on our business was a mixed bag, however. The great majority of our
customers thought it was wonderful that we introduced this Obama
fellow to the community. There were others who made no comment,
and we knew that we would not bother those with Obama stuff. We
were walking a fine, thin line. We did not want to be pushy about his
candidacy.

"I Don't Know Him," said President George W. Bush.

"You will," said Congresswomen Jan Schakowsky.

A great story making the rounds during this period was one that
Congresswoman Schakowsky loves to tell about Obama. It happened in
February 2004 when she was visiting the White House on behalf of the
Congressional Black Caucus.

---

113 John Patterson *Daily Herald*. State Government Editor. "Betting on name recognition Senate candidate Obama hopes unique moniker will attract voters :[All Edition]. "*Daily Herald* [Arlington
Heights, Ill.] 15 Feb. 2004,15.

Jan Schakowsky told me about a recent visit she had made to the White House with a congressional delegation. On her way out, she said, President Bush noticed her "OBAMA" button. "He jumped back, almost literally," she said. "And I knew what he was thinking. So I reassured him it was Obama, with a 'b.' And I explained who he was. The President said, 'Well, I don't know him.' So I just said, 'You will.'"

We Need More Yard Signs

On Saturday, February 21st we had depleted our supply of yard signs. The demand for yard signs was on the increase, and it challenged us to keep pace. It was our intention to fulfill the requests. Michelle and I already knew and felt that Obama was becoming a phenomenon and that the campaign was catching fire. The grassroots groups were spreading and growing all over the city, county and state. The polling was slowly but surely shifting to Obama's favor now for the first time.

Change comes slowly, gradually, incrementally, and suddenly.

We learned the Matteson office had yard signs. Our friend Reverend Lawrence Blackful said sure, come on down, and did we know that Barack Obama would be there. We always loved talking to Obama and exchanging updates on the campaign.

Reverend Blackful retrieved the yard signs for us. We stepped into Jesse Jackson Jr.'s kitchen and standing nearby was Obama. Blackful started introducing us to Obama, and Obama quickly interrupted Lawrence and said, "Let me tell you about them. These two were there for me early and took the leap of faith. And accomplished so much for me. They are my southwest side powerhouses." It was flattering to hear from Obama.

He started to tell us that he was surprised at this point, that he thought that the real competition would no longer be Hynes, as was thought at the beginning of the campaign. The real competition would be Blair Hull.[114] Obama did not predict victory but did say, "You've got to figure that Hynes is going nowhere now. He peaked. We thought he was the real competition, but it's Hull. But we can take Hull." Hynes had raised a significant amount of money as expected, but the management of the money would be a crucial mistake for Hynes. By the end of the campaign, Hynes would be out of cash, and he could not keep up with Obama's

114 Hull's campaign had not yet unraveled.

onslaught of television commercials. Obama, at the behest of Jim Cauley, had saved his money for the final weeks' commercial blitz.

David Axelrod was aware of the "Blair Hull baggage," but the feeling in the campaign was that Hull could be defeated without any of this leaking out. Axelrod had interviewed with Hull, according to David Mendell's book.[115] Axelrod was aware of the "divorce" controversy with Hull. If it was leaked, it would not come from the Obama campaign. The momentum was starting to move Obama's way. Hull would self-destruct without anyone's help. I called Tamarin and Al Kindle and discussed it with them briefly around that time and they both were on the same page.[116] Obama's not the least worried about it and if it is leaked, it will be from other sources.

Obama asked how our grassroots efforts were coming along, and we had a prediction for him. "We are going to perform very well in the 19th Ward," I told him. "With a little luck we might even squeak it out."

"That is well beyond our expectations," Obama said.

"But I think that maybe we can even take it," I said.

"Let's do it," Obama said.

25,000 Individual Donors to The Obama Campaign

"We have received donations from 25,000 individuals," Obama told us. 25,000 donors: big donors, small donors. None of the other candidates was in that league. Several candidates were raising more total dollars, but had larger donations per donor: 25,000 donors. It was obvious how proud he was of this achievement and the symbolism of this.

Obama told us, "We are going to surprise a lot of people on Election Day. With the grassroots support and the financing to boot."

We didn't bring up the word "netroots" with him, because it wasn't a part of either of our vocabularies at this point, but it would be. He continued, "Oh, and before you go, let me tell you one more thing. I want you to tell me what you think of my new commercials. I think they are awesome, but I want your opinion. Send me word. I am interested in what you think. We have waited a long time to air spots, but we were

---

115 Mendell, p. 163-168.
116 One of the strengths of the Obama campaign, even then, was its unified message. The campaign
   spoke with one voice. In this case Obama made it clear, do not discuss this Blair Hull thing.

waiting for the right time, and now we are going on the air non-stop with them until Election Day. And we have raised enough money to start a week earlier than we originally planned."

We also met Michelle Obama that day for the first time[117] and were both impressed with her. One striking thing that came across to both of us was the attention and love she had for her children. There is no question after several minutes with her that her children are the priority in her life. She thanked us for our help and said she was aware of our work on the southwest side.

"Come-By-Ten" Rally at Liberty Baptist Church

Michelle and I attended an event on March 9th, 2004 called "Come-by-Ten." The event was organized by radio talk show host Cliff Kelley. A rally was held at Liberty Baptist Church located at 4849 S. King Drive.

We knew from the crowd that this campaign was for real. In the middle of an African American community, people of all races were there for this tremendous rally and show of support. Parking along King Drive was challenging. Michelle and I walked several blocks. It was a stunning sight for us. The crowd was hanging from the rafters. The event was called the "Come by Ten," a get out the vote rally. So many of our own volunteers attended to show support for this candidate. John and Lula Gunn were there. Steve Pittman and Candace Baker were also there. And hundreds of others. The media reported that, in the "spirit of Mayor Harold Washington," activists and elected officials say they are holding a "Come by Ten" get out the vote rally today for U.S. Senate hopeful Barack Obama at Liberty Baptist Church to energize voters for a massive turnout on March 16. We got near the stage just before and spoke to Obama and wished him luck. We got a big hug from him, and he thanked us again for our help. The crowd around Obama was getting bigger and bigger.

During his speech, Obama thanked his wife Michelle for her support throughout the campaign, "I don't know why she puts up with me." Michelle interrupted him and said softly into the microphone, "It's because I love you."

You could feel her words. And there was no question in the way

---

117 February 21, 2004.

Michelle Obama said this that it came from her heart. And we all felt the same way about Obama.

The crowd went wild.

March 9th,, in the latest poll, Obama was starting to open up a wide lead on his opponent. This is what Obama was referring to when he spoke to us in Jesse Jr.'s kitchen. The toughest opponent would be Blair Hull and not Dan Hynes. Obama made massive strides in the polls from WGN's own poll. From the week of Feb. 11-17, Obama only had 15% of the vote. During the period from March 3-6, Obama had 33%, a substantial jump in the lead. Obama was now the front-runner.[118]

Michelle and I would not see Obama in person again for a few months, but we would see him on television in the coming days, weeks and months.

The Obama Campaign Starts to Pull It All Together

The time came for us to get to work completing last minute campaign details. We worked on scheduling for Election Day, passing out more yard and window signs, canvassing with literature and the get out the vote effort for primary Election Day.

Mike Jordan was a great resource for campaign materials. He would make several trips to our store dropping off signs and Election Day materials. We would need enough signs for Election Day to man all the precincts in our area of responsibility. Our goal was to place at least two signs per precinct. Where did Mike Jordan get all this energy, I always wondered, even to this day. He was non-stop: if you needed something, anything, Mike Jordan would accommodate your wish. He had boundless energy and passion for Obama.

Michelle and I were the Area Coordinators for the Southwest Side of Chicago and were responsible for nearly 150 precincts. There were dozens and dozens of clones of us all over the city, county, collar counties and downstate. Clones like us. This grassroots effort started back on March 7, 2000. And much was the "Meetup.com" web site. And much was the "Obama for Senate Yahoo Group." And so much was the word we had

---

118 Rick Pearson, Tribune political reporter. "Obama, Ryan out front; With week until Senate primary, Hull staggered by divorce: [Chicago Final Edition]. "*Chicago Tribune* [Chicago, IL] 9 Mar. 2004, 1.1. *Chicago Tribune*.

spread about this man Obama.

The campaign was no longer holding back the yard signs. In fact, they now wanted them out of the offices and warehouses and onto the streets. Campaigns that placed the yards signs on public parkways, such as the Hull campaign, show signs of desperation. Hull only had money. Period. No grassroots efforts. No unpaid volunteers and plenty of paid, passionless volunteers. The joke was that all of his volunteers were paid. He had money to buy thousands of signs, but they were not wanted. The campaign paid staff would place them on public parkways, where they were quickly removed by the individual municipalities. Hull paid his staff well.

Obama Blue Throughout the Community

Yard signs could not be removed on private property. Michelle and I had passed out thousands of signs that were placed on private property. Our community was a "sea of Obama blue." One could not drive anywhere without seeing Obama signs. Communities under our wing were blanketed. A sea of Obama blue.

We had volunteers who would set up signs at polling places for Election Day. The polling places opened at 6:00 am, and we wanted to be sure that the signs were set up well before the polls opened, but not so early as to give the party organization a chance to remove our signs. We instructed all of our precinct workers to make sure the signs were there, and they were to call us if the signs were missing or removed.

We Are Being Cautiously Optimistic: "The Next U.S. Senator from the State of Illinois, Barack Obama."

We had a nervous excitement preparing for Election Day. The polls all now indicated that Obama would receive the Democratic nomination for the United States Senate in Illinois. This usually meant an easy victory over the Republican in the fall. I understood the implications completely. This victory would thrust Obama onto the national stage. We had a job to do here and now. Obama's victory would make history. Twelve years earlier, Carol Mosley Braun also made history when she became the first female African-American elected to the United States Senate, but she was a disappointment. She knew how to get there, but she did not understand how to stay there and move beyond. During her six years in office, Senator

Braun had virtually forgotten the people back home. She rarely made appearances back in Illinois. She didn't build networks or alliances back home where it was needed. And in 1998, she nearly defeated Fitzgerald, which shows that with a little effort and outreach, Braun could have been Senator for life. But she squandered her opportunity.

My great hope was that Obama would be different. That he would "get it." It was important to remind the folks back home often about yourself. It was important to perform constituent services, which meant surrounding yourself with an efficient and competent staff.

March 16, 2004, Primary Election Day

It was primary Election Day, and Michelle and I were ready. All the planning for this day was now complete. We had not planned until late February to be working the streets on Election Day. It was something new for us, but how hard could it be for a couple of experienced community organizers like Michelle and me?

Barack Obama needed us. We needed to see him through to victory. We recalled the pain of losing in 2000. Yes, of course, we were not with the campaign that long. But for this campaign, we had worked fourteen months and had put everything we had into it. We were possessed. I had never believed in anything like I believed in this.

By 5:30 am on Primary Election Day, all of the preparation work was completed. The previous two days we had given assignments to people to put up signs in designated precincts. One volunteer who didn't want to work a precinct out in the open, but wanted to contribute volunteered to put up signs at precincts in the middle of the night. Over a dozen volunteers had taken the assignment of placing the yard signs at the polling places.

Michelle and I had started Election Day by voting at 6:00 am and then breakfast at our local coffee shop, Lumes, located at 116th & Western Avenue. We talked about strategy for the day. We had a truck full of yard signs to put up wherever necessary. We left some signs at the store just in case we had drop-bys. I made sure my newspaper delivery schedule was clear so that I could focus on one goal: electing Barack Obama to the United States Senate.

All of the precincts that we were covering for the campaign already had their share of signs. Since we had plenty of signs to work with, thanks to our constantly visiting three different campaign offices, we were able to put up four to five Obama signs per precinct. Typically, organizations support multiple numbers of candidates. Not us. We focused on one and only one: Illinois State Senator Barack Obama. We would not be working with the regular party organization for this election. And the regular party organization would be focusing on their candidate, Dan Hynes.

Hynes was from our community, so one of the obstacles we had to overcome was the level of support in the community, initially, for Hynes. But the regular party organization never saw us coming. Oh, they were aware of us, but they had no idea of the organization we had built in this community. And we were the model for so many other small groups throughout the city, suburbs, and even the state.

300 volunteers would swarm the area in our community alone. They would be everywhere. Dan Moore would be driving his caravan throughout the community all day until the polls closed at 7:00 pm. Larry Unruh would work the fire station for part of the day and part of the day at the Wentworth office in the get out the vote effort.

Voters would brush past the regular organization workers, toward the Obama volunteers. They would take the Obama materials and palm cards. And the turnout was enormous. There was real excitement in the air. All of our hard work over the past fourteen months was now paying off. The disappointment we felt four years earlier would quickly be forgotten. Back then we only had two weeks to put it together. And look what we accomplished then. We often asked ourselves, what if we had more time. Today, Election Day, we would get our answer.

It wasn't just the 300 volunteers. It involved this entire community. So many people had taken signs for their yards. Thousands of yards had signs that Reading on Walden Bookstore had distributed. That was our plan. We knew where all the Obama offices were and would pick up signs everywhere. We would do it personally or send our volunteers to pick them up. We knew this idea of one sign per block would not be effective.

Many believed, including Obama, that the Primary Election is the General Election. Obama said this on the day he announced his candidacy back in January 2003.

Our 300 volunteers were scattered throughout the 19th Ward and parts of the south side of Chicago. The level of excitement and enthusiasm was at a fever pitch. They all had their roles to play. Some had small roles. Some had bigger roles. Everyone had a role. Some of the 300 volunteers were performing the ultimate. Rise early in the morning, set up the Obama signs before the first voter arrived, waited at the door for the voters, sign up as a precinct watcher, stay with it all day long, and then wait for the official tally at the end of the evening. That was the ultimate warrior this day.

One such ultimate warrior was Ghanim Kassir. We discovered Ghanim from a list that Tamarin supplied. We had asked for names of volunteers from various zip codes such as 60643, 60655, 60805, and 60803. Ghanim was assigned to work the 47th and 48th precincts at the Beverly Woods Restaurant at 11532 S. Western Avenue. Ghanim was a young law student who attended Kent Law School in downtown Chicago. He was living at the time with his in-laws in the community. When I asked Ghanim if he was interested in working mornings or afternoons, he said yes. Wow, another couple of precincts covered for the whole day. Once during the day, he called for a lunch break, and we got relief over to him. We could not have pulled Ghanim away if we wanted to.

These types of enthusiastic people like Ghanim were plentiful. Had we known we were going to work Election Day sooner, maybe we would have spread out some more. The positive aspect of all this was that there were hundreds of people out there like us. All over the city and county. Everywhere. Many had come from the "Meetup.com." Many had come from word-of-mouth. The concept of moving to the next community over if adequate resources were available is something this campaign became very adept at achieving.

Back at the Wentworth field office, the campaign was getting the vans ready with the campaign workers for the GOTV (Get out the Vote) program. Every household that had been identified as a + (plus), would be checked against the voters rolls. This would assure that "our" voters turned out to vote. In the African-American communities, that was nearly ninety-percent of the registered voters. Vans full of paid volunteers (paid fifty dollars for the day) would go up and down each and every street in the African American communities and place door hangers and ring door bells.

Hundreds of volunteers would march door-to-door and physically bring out the vote. Addresses would be checked off. This was Al Kindle's baby.

He also had help from Alan V. Manuel and Kevin Watson. They had confided in us earlier that this would happen and they did not want word of it to leak prior to the election. Anyone who knew Michelle and me knew that the secret was safe with us. The campaign wanted to be sure to get the African American vote and that African-American vote would come out in big numbers. That was Kindle's obsession since January 2003.

Between this office and the west side office, every African American household was reached. A sign would be put on the doors of the voters by the workers coming out of the vans. They would return to find who had not yet voted. It was quite an operation. High voter turnout is sometimes luck. But luck, as those in the campaign like to say, is a residue of design.

This GOTV program/method had been employed twice before successfully. Once in 1983 for Harold Washington who went on to become the first African American Mayor of Chicago. And again, when Carol Mosley Braun defeated Senator Alan Dixon by a slim margin in the 1992 Democratic primary and again in the 1992 general election. The difference in both races was the overwhelming African American vote.

This time with Barack Obama there was a little difference. Well, actually a big difference. Obama also had a presence in other areas outside the African American communities. Like in our own community on the southwest side of Chicago. The grassroots groundswell of support that Michelle, me and our 300 volunteers helped to put in place was starting to take hold and run out of control: in favor of this obscure State Senator from Hyde Park. Obama resonated with many white voters. Like in Hynes' own home ward on the near north side. And many other places like Oak Park and Evanston. And Ravenswood. And Andersonville. And Lincoln Park.

Meanwhile back in our 19th Ward, we could not believe we were pulling it off. We have to credit Kindle for his support and encouragement. Three weeks before Election Day, he said to us, "I'm going to help you build a machine."

"A what?" I said. "Did you say a machine?"

"Yes a machine."

What the hell was Kindle talking about? He went on, "You see, I have always beaten the machine. I know how to beat them. I have never lost to the 'machine.'" Kindle had been there for Harold Washington in 1983 and had been there for Carol Mosely Braun in 1992. I suspect it was the reason Al was on loan from Alderman Toni Preckwinkle's staff. He knew how to beat the "machine" at its own game. He was a strategist extraordinaire.

But without really being aware of what it is called, we had been building a machine all along. It started back on March 7, 2000 when 600 of our neighbors and friends from the community had come to watch a Congressional forum and had come away falling in love with this man named Obama. As incredulous as Michelle and I were about this, by Election Day, we had indeed built a machine. We just did not have a word for it, but Kindle supplied that for us.

Here's how Lyn Wozniak put it:

Count Me in!!

By Lyn Wozniak

While I worked at the downtown office, I rarely did the same thing twice. I have stuffed envelopes, made phone calls, put yard signs together, alphabetized donor slips, and made maps. Because I would show up each week, I got to get those yard signs, scarf up some buttons, get copies of his book for my buddies in Beverly, AND meet and talk to Obama himself!

Meanwhile back in Beverly at the Luna we worked out a plan (by the way it worked). One man organized and ran a motorcade through the neighborhood. Blair Hull paid people $75 to put up his signs, but we had more signs up than he. We were about equal with machine-backed Hynes.

I sent everybody on my Christmas card list a brochure, told them about our regular meetings, and so others did it, too.

Most of us took the training to become voter registrars. We could then register voters right in our neighborhood. We did the train stations again.

Actually, the candidate made it easy to sell him. He simply is the best.

The plan for Election Day was to put someone at the polling places in our area as best we could. We did it. Not as fully as the regular organization, but someone everywhere at some time that day.

Remember I said I was damn cold. I was even though I'd dressed for it. When I got there, I flashed my Obama button, and pointed out that I was the enemy! The regular Democrats smiled indulgently. He who smiles last smiles longer.

They worked in shifts, but they were there for the whole day. They had to push the whole ticket by handing people a list. All I had to do was say, "Punch 26!" At one point someone irritated said, "Get away you Hynes people" but I persevered handed out the card with Obama's picture and said, "Punch

26!" She smiled, took the card, and went in to vote. I didn't gloat.

At another point, I asked where the other guy had gone and how come he didn't get a turn to go in and warm up. He ignored my solicitous inquiry but told me that the other guy had gone in to check the numbers. Well! He came out shortly after that, and he didn't look joyous. I said nothing. I have found that when I gloat, or get smug, I get bit in the butt. Besides, I didn't know the score then. (Had I known then what I found out the next day I'd of had a hard time keeping a straight face. But, of course, they weren't going to tell me that my guy was whomping their guy.)

They started talking about Hull. Now the only thing that worried the Obama people about Hull was that he would drop out and his votes go to Hynes. As it turned out Hynes + Hull wouldn't have been enough to stop Obama.

Obama carried the precincts where I was working. He did well in Mount Greenwood. Everywhere we were, he won or did better than our expectations.

We threw ourselves a party Wednesday. I had thawed out by then.

— Lyn Wozniak, Super Obama volunteer

We had built a "machine" by the time primary Election Day had arrived. We had a coalition of men and women, blacks and whites, mostly progressives and liberals, but also a number of not so progressives and not so liberals: three hundred strong. Even some Republicans. It was the envy of any regular Democratic Ward organization.

Yes, Republicans, too. That was the part that we found a little stunning. Everybody loved Obama. Once you met him and spoke to him and he looked you in the eye and made you feel like the only person in the room, he had won you over.

Dr. Charles Davis, An Inspiration For Our Group

The first person who comes to mind when I think of someone Obama won over was the late Dr. Charles Davis, an African-American doctor with roots in the Harold Washington movement in 1983. Dr. Davis, along with his wife, Patricia McPhearson-Davis, were two of our key volunteers. Dr. Davis was inspiring with his generous contributions to the group. This unlikely group of hundreds of volunteers came together to form a close bond and help send Obama to the United States

Senate. Dr. Davis guided many of the younger people and some of the more seasoned veterans, too. He had great suggestions and fresh ideas for the group. Sadly, Dr. Davis passed away shortly after Obama's General Election victory.

Dr. Charles Davis got the ball rolling on this idea of Al Kindle's of building a machine. Dr. Davis said, "Do you have the poll sheets?"

"Poll sheets? What are poll sheets?" I asked.

Dr. Davis was only going to work the morning shift at his precinct at Sutherland School. He worked the 2nd, 19th, 22nd, and 25th, precincts in the 19th Ward. This precinct was huge for us, and we had the right volunteer there. Dr. Davis stayed the entire day. He worked it and worked it. The regular precinct workers from the Democratic Party were annoyed by his intrusion. We drove by the precinct at Sutherland School several times that day, and each time Dr. Davis said thank you, but he would be ok and did not need any relief. He had his poll sheets with him. Dr. Davis admired Obama for his "energy, inclusiveness, and introduction of fresh new ideas" and wanted to see this to the end.

Poll sheets are the list of eligible voters, with names and addresses, in each precinct. It is what the Democratic Ward Organizations had used to mark off which voters had voted and which ones did not. And which voters were friendly and which were unfriendly. This is where Kindle's question came into play, "You don't want to bring out voters that aren't going to vote your way. Let those voters stay home."

While we did not make widespread use of these sheets as far as tracking voters, they were a huge help in some precincts where we were adequately staffed. Sandra T. Dougherty used the sheets on Election Day to snag the people who had not voted on her block and in her precinct as had many other volunteers that day. At about three in the afternoon on Election Day, Sandra went to her home precinct and marked off all those who voted, and then went door-to-door to knock on the doors of people who did not vote.

Garnet and Eileen Fay greeted us at our polling place. They were assigned the early morning shift at our precinct. They were upbeat and excited. We quickly voted and noticed turnout was already sizable although it was very early in the day.

After Michelle and I voted, we went around to check all the precincts under our care. At one precinct, the House of Pancakes, which was directly across from the 19th Ward headquarters, I recalled placing two yard signs, and I noticed that they were both missing. We did not have a volunteer assigned to this precinct. I pulled over and saw that the signs had been crushed and had dirt footmarks. We replaced the signs thinking nothing out of the ordinary had occurred. It was a garden area and possibly someone deliberately stepped on them and crushed them or perhaps it was a prank.

I thought that if it was deliberate, the person who did it might be observing me and would not crush the signs again. We replaced the signs and went around other locations observing precincts, visiting volunteers, encouraging them. We decided to buy coffee and doughnuts and pass them out to volunteers. It was chilly that day. We made a mental note to check on our crushed signs. After making the rounds again, we checked back and saw from the street that again, the signs were not visible.

Closer inspection again showed they were crushed with dirt footmarks. This time we decided to put up four signs and figured it could not happen again to four signs. We made some more rounds, visited other precincts, and came back and again all the signs were not visible again.

They were crushed and mangled this time: all four of them in a violent manner. I was becoming annoyed. I did not know exactly what to do, but I knew I had to do something. As fate would have it, my cell phone rang and it was Nate Tamarin. "How's it going?" The deputy campaign manager does not call on Election Day to make small talk, so he got to the point. He asked if we needed any more bodies out here. I never turn away help, and I said yes.

All the precincts in Hyde Park, Obama's home district were overcrowded. Tamarin said he had two volunteers looking for someplace to help. John Station & Guidi Weiss had with them over a hundred yard signs. We had just the place for them to work.

I called them both and told them the story about the Pancake House at 10437 S. Western Ave. I thought that the 35th precinct would be the perfect assignment for them. They agreed. John Station said he would know what to do. An hour later Michelle and I returned to find Western

Avenue lined with Obama blue signs for several blocks. Blocks and blocks of Obama blue signs. Since John & Guidi could watch the situation there, no one would dare crush them now. They wouldn't allow it.

Obama easily won this precinct.

It got better. The luck in the campaign was present again: good luck that is.

Neil Pomeranke also was another standout ultimate volunteer who dedicated the entire day to the campaign, including getting the final tally. Neil was a retired high school teacher who spent much of his retired life performing volunteer work for the community. Neil worked the 31st and 40th precincts at Morgan Park Baptist Church at 11024 S. Bell Ave. Our close friends Jim and Birgit Sweeney, who lived in the community, also worked this precinct during the day to help Neil there. Jim is a retired newspaper distributor and Birgit is an MSW (Master of Social Work).

People were coming out of the woodwork on Election Day, and volunteers who we had not scheduled were also working. We did not even know their names. This campaign was a runaway train, and we helped bring it to that fever pitch. Obama was an easy sell once you got to know him. **To know him is to love him**, was at play again. We were getting volunteers the morning of the election. People were stopping by the store. "I heard this is the place to come if we want to help with the campaign."

A young man, Pete Sofiyea, was so excited about the Obama campaign. He had seen the sign in our window and stopped into our store to see what was up with this Obama sign. We told him about our meetings, and he came. Sofiyea was Nigerian-born and quickly became a spark plug for our group. I will never forget his great, and serious intonation, in his deeply rich Nigerian accent; "I want to make history with you!" When he arrived at his assigned precinct that day, he called me on my cell and said in his vocal, rich, Nigerian accent, "John, I am making history with you." His excitement was contagious.

Kevin Lee was a high school math teacher who, at the time, taught at Englewood High School. A PhD in mathematics, Kevin wanted to teach in an underprivileged school because he wanted to help children learn. Kevin also volunteered that day before school started. He also carried his precinct.

Dan Moore, a retiree and a neighbor, had decorated his car with Obama stuff and drove throughout our community in a car caravan the entire day encouraging people to vote for Obama.

Pamela Nunley, a publicist extraordinaire, was out most of the day getting out the vote and working tirelessly for the campaign. She had made several trips to our bookstore picking up yard signs and passing them out to neighbors. She would run out quickly before Election Day and then come back to the store and get more. She was a tireless volunteer.

Steve Pittman, Executive Director of the Illinois Alliance of Retired Americans, helped out. So did Candace Baker. Candace was an assistant professor of Education at St. Xavier University at the time. Shirley Bell-Perine worked the entire day.

Shirley Conley worked a precinct at Bethlehem Lutheran Church. Will and Marsha Cowing, retired Public School teachers, both worked a couple shifts that day. Barbara Duke and Toni Stewart worked a long day together.

Theresa L. Ambuel, who would ride the bus a long distance from her home in the evening to attend our regular meetings, despite the fact she was in her eighties. She insisted that she wanted to be a part of this historic campaign.

Our neighbor, Alfred Barrow, spent the better part of a morning working a precinct. Our friends Carol and Terry Belshaw, both retired, but were dedicated to the cause.

Linda Cooper was the owner of a coffee shop and a dedicated supporter. Obama (and Nate Tamarin) had stopped there after the World Folk Music fundraiser for a late lunch. Linda Cooper was absolutely thrilled to have spent time with Obama at her coffee shop.

Bruce Ellingwood. Joanne and Paul Ginger. Bob Keeley. Kathleen Baggett. Alfred Barrow. Royce and Lorraine Simpson. Carol and Terry Belshaw. Kristen Broady. Susan Burnet. Christina Horde. Debra Smith. Jeff Tangel. Jane Healy. Linda Cooper. Marilyn Burke. Connie Burnet. Kent Busse. Pamela Childs-Laughlin. And hundreds more from our community alone. They poured onto the streets of Chicago and the suburbs and throughout the state of Illinois to spread the word and get out the vote for Barack Obama.

It was breathless. The pace was furious. All the work that had been done for the past fourteen months was now coming to fruition. We had hundreds of volunteers scattered all over the southwest side of Chicago. Amazingly, they were all pulling in the same direction. They were all pulling Barack Obama and pulling him into the United States Senate.

The next Senator from the state of Illinois, we hoped.

Dozens of people whose names we didn't know came by on Election Day just to pick up a yard or window sign either for themselves or for their friends. Some were souvenir hunters. No questions asked. If you wanted it, that was the day to get it.

We passed out over 5000 yard signs since the campaign began, and it showed throughout the community. It gave the look and feel of an Obama stronghold.

Lula and John Gunn. They worked precincts on Election Day and canvassed their community and their block for months before Election Day. John Gunn estimated he knocked on over 700 doors in his precinct. It showed because his precinct voted over 85% for Barack Obama.

It was a glorious day for Barack Obama and the campaign. All of our 300 volunteers were so proud of the accomplishments, but we would have to hear the results for ourselves. Our precinct people were telling us it looked great. We were not expected to win anything in the 19th Ward. In fact, campaign manager Jim Cauley thought we might get "creamed" out here, so we had already exceeded his expectations. We had to beat our own expectations. And Barack Obama said, "Let's do it" to us in Jesse Jackson Jr.'s kitchen.

We would be on the edge of our seats until we got the results later in the evening.

Would things change? Would we vindicate the 2000 loss?

Change comes slowly, gradually, incrementally, and suddenly.

CHAPTER 8

The Most Important Victory of Barack Obama's Life: Primary Election Day, March 16, 2004

~

On the evening of March 16th at 7:00 pm, I was back at the bookstore. The polls were closing. It was a whirlwind day. The time had gone by much too fast, but so much was accomplished. We could feel it. This day was fourteen months in the making. Voter turnout was in our favor, and good turnout favored Obama.

Michelle and I had been rotating all day. We opened at 11:00am that day, so one of us needed to be in the store at all times. When the polls closed, I thought, "Well, it'll be a long night of waiting for poll results. Maybe we should get some popcorn and enjoy watching it on television." I felt Obama would win, based on the polling data we had seen and from word inside the campaign. But seeing is believing.

We received an invitation to the victory party in downtown Chicago and many of our volunteers were going to attend. Steve Pittman and Candace Baker invited us to go to the victory party with them. Larry Unruh mentioned he would be attending. Pete "I Want to Make History with You" Sofiyea would attend. I still had my newspaper distribution duties early the following morning and the pure exhaustion from having put in a full day. We also spent that evening picking up signs from polling places to be used in the general election.

The prospects for victory were everywhere. Earlier in the day, Obama was talking upbeat about his chances. "We didn't have the most money. We didn't have the most connections," Obama said. "But what we had was a committed, energized, impassioned group of people—young people, seniors, black, white, Hispanic. It's because of them that we are in the position to potentially win this thing."[119]

That was the secret of his campaign, and Barack Obama clearly recognized it. He did not have the most money, but he spent it smarter than his opponents. The Obama campaign spent it at the opportune moments. This was by design, and it was the one major accomplishment of campaign manager Jim Cauley. This was what he had brought to the table. Many events of the campaign were by design.

This holding back of the money was by design.

And the grassroots, which was a loosely-knit organization, had been built. It wasn't just that Michelle, the 300 volunteers and I had "built a machine." Barack Obama had built a machine. And then, unexpected factors such as the intelligent use of the Internet. The Internet was still in its infant stages at this point, but the Obama campaign had taken it to its limit in 2004. It would prove useful in later elections.

Other events like the emergence of the "Meetup.com" and the "Obama for Senate Yahoo Group"[120] on Yahoo were unplanned but pleasant surprises. As someone said, "Luck is the residue of design." That was the case here. With so many passionate people out there now for Obama, the momentum was quietly moving in Obama's direction. With all those passionate people working the campaign now, ideas were bound to come to the forefront from unexpected quarters.

Change comes slowly, gradually, incrementally, and suddenly.

Everyone involved in the campaign was pulling in the same direction. I had never seen or felt anything like it. We had worked Obama's 2000 campaign briefly, but it certainly was not anything like this. It was like we had cloned ourselves all over the city, county and state of Illinois.

Grassroots organizing was everywhere. It was the new buzzword in political campaigns.

We did not work any precincts for that Election Day in 2000. It did not occur to us to work the precincts back in 2000. While there were several

---

119 Candidates hopeful to the end ; Last-minute bids in Senate races; [Chicago Final Edition] Rick Pearson and James Janega, Tribune staff reporters. *Chicago Tribune*. Chicago, Ill.: Mar 16, 2004. pg. 1.
120 Later renamed the "Obama Brigade" and which to this day is in existence.

people I would classify as volunteers that day, it was not organized in any fashion. We did everything possible in 2000 that two people who barely knew what they were doing could accomplish. This experience would be of benefit to the campaign in the next election.

After all, how organized could it be? As Will Rogers said, "I don't belong to any organized political party. I am a Democrat." We only had two weeks to pull something together then in 2000. That campaign was based purely on hope. A faint hope. There was no foundation to that campaign. We had hoped people would come out to vote. We had hoped people would donate to the campaign. We had hoped people would put up signs. Hope does not get people out to vote, it does not get people to put up signs, and it does not get people to donate to campaigns.

This 2004 campaign was not like that. We had precinct workers covering 150 precincts. We had areas of Alsip, Merrionette Park, Evergreen Park and Oak Lawn covered. Matt and Rosie Williams finished their newspaper assignments and proceeded to put up hundreds of signs throughout the area. And they passed out palm cards.

In some precincts we had more volunteers than the Democratic Regular Ward organization. We had poll sheets to track whether voters had come out. We were careful to bring out only "our" voters, not the opposition voters. We had learned our lesson.

This campaign took nothing to chance. We did not hope, we knew. We could see it. The ward organization was worried that day and totally caught by surprise. Voter turnout was huge there, and that could only spell trouble for the regular organization. Voters were seeking out our palm cards.

The incident at the House of Pancakes where people stole and destroyed our Obama signs set the tone for us for that day. We refused to get crushed. It made us more determined. The House of Pancakes incident was a catalyst. A catalyst for change. A new style of politics was emerging. We fought back by fighting back cleanly. Not by destroying or crushing their signs. We believe in fairness and in a good, clean fight. We wanted to set the tone for a game of clean politics. Obama had said many times he wanted to "change" the "politics."

We instructed all our volunteers to not tamper with other candidate's yard signs. We do not want it done to us. We can beat them, but we only want to defeat them fairly and on a level playing field. Of course, the opposition would prefer we were not there, that we would go away, but that was not going to happen. If you know us, you know that will not happen. Once we commit to something, we stay with it. We do not turn tail on friends.

The campaign was like a Stealth Airplane: flying under the radar, undetected into enemy territory until it is too late for the enemy to respond. Some was by design. Some was by luck. All was because of the passion of the people working the campaign. It was starting to become a cause and a movement. Many of the volunteers in the campaign told me they worked the Harold Washington campaign in 1983, and they said many of the same feelings they had were re-emerging. The belittling of the campaign in the media and the downplaying of what was accomplished. This campaign was "The Harold Washington coalition on steroids."

The structure of the campaign was purely grassroots. They had begun planting the grass seeds back in January 2003 and by March 16, 2004, grass was growing everywhere. One could argue that the seeds were planted on March 7, 2000, when Barack Obama was the star of the evening. The seeds planted on March 7, 2000 were dropped and spread, and the results were good. The grassroots for the 2004 campaign started back in January of 2003.

An obscure State Senator in a candidates' forum at an obscure little church in an obscure little community organized by an obscure little bookstore's owners.

Grassroots, the Perennial Kind

The seeds were spreading all over. Like with quality seeds, such as 'Royal Yukon', the grass does not take hold immediately and takes time to germinate. The seeds are perennials and not annuals. Annuals come up quickly and then die after the winter frost. Not perennials. They last and last. Much like this campaign. This was the 'Royal Yukon' campaign. The seeds grow slowly, gradually, incrementally, and suddenly.

Grassroots.

Who knows where it will lead?

In places that grass was not supposed to grow. Barack Obama, in the words of Al Kindle, had built a machine. He had identified his voters and then got them out to the polls. Support for Obama at this point was everywhere, thanks to this loosely built but widely spread organization. "Word of mouth." "Meetup.com." The "Obama for Senate Yahoo Group." It was built from the ground up, with a group like ours being part of the foundation and being a model for this type of organizing.

The Democratic Regular Party organizations in Chicago were built on political patronage and jobs as rewards for political favors. The group that Obama had built was much more abstract. It was built on hopes and dreams. It was built on a hope and a dream for change. It was clear now that "change" would be a key issue in upcoming elections. This election was a repudiation of President George W. Bush, something that we would see spread to other states in 2006 when the Congress would change dramatically to the Democrats. Illinois voters were ahead of the curve.

Obama had identified the Iraq War very early as a "dumb war," and that concept was resonating with voters, Democrats and Republicans alike. He did not reject war completely, but he was rejecting the Iraq War. Obama rejected the Bush tax cuts for the rich, and this resonated with the voters. Obama identified issues such as the Patriot Act and global warming as additional issues for future campaigns.

All this added together made for a greatly anticipated victory.

Michelle and her friend Marie Whitney had been working the precincts. I was anxious, of course, about the results. Earlier in the day, around 4:00 pm, I had checked the CBS 2 website, and there was a story by Mike Flannery, the Channel 2 Political reporter and our neighbor, which hinted strongly that it looked good for Obama.

Since the 2000 debacle in Florida, stations were increasingly reluctant to report early results based on exit data. I read between the lines of Flannery's CBS 2 posting, but, of course, I was cautiously optimistic.

It's official: Barack Obama Wins Easily as the Democratic Nominee for the United States Senate and Is Propelled on the National Scene

We had won. WBBM Radio 780 announced at 7:01 pm that they projected Barack Obama as the next Senator from the State of Illinois.

The victory was one of the best feelings we ever had. We had invested fourteen months of intense campaigning. This, I already knew instinctively, was a great leap forward for Obama. This victory catapulted Obama onto the national scene. On the night of the victory party, Obama spent the entire evening lining up for all the interviews that were coming and that would be broadcast across a nation.

They were all there at the victory celebration: CNN. MSNBC. ABC News. NBC News. CBS News. The *New York Times*. And many more.

In addition, international print and broadcasts too. There was even a story in Obama's father's homeland of Kenya. This was the start of something big.

The speech Obama gave that night was again terrific.

In his quest for the Democratic nomination for the United States Senate, Obama was supposed to lose. The deck was stacked against him with many obstacles. One opponent was a multimillionaire pouring his own cash into the race to the tune of over $25 million. Another was a loyal statewide official who was expected to bring the party's ward troops out in force on Election Day and who was reputed to have an awesome organization and money behind his candidacy. Another was a successful President of the Chicago Public School Board who led the schools to greener pastures. Another was a popular county wide candidate, a woman, who was to have detracted votes from Obama.

During his victory speech that March evening, he told his supporters packed into a ballroom, "I think it's fair to say that the conventional wisdom was we could not win. We did not have enough money. We did not have enough organization. There was no way that a skinny guy from the South Side with a funny name as Barack Obama could ever win a statewide race. Sixteen months later we are here, and Democrats from all across Illinois — suburbs, city, down state, upstate, black, white, Hispanic, Asian — have declared: Yes, we can! Yes, we can! Yes, we can!"

That was astounding, but not a surprise. America is hungry for this type of leader. Since the death of the two Kennedy brothers, America had been paralyzed like a deer caught in the headlights. America could not move for a long time. America was dazed and shocked for many years. And then another Bush stole an election from Gore with the help of five individuals on the highest court in the land. Now this new hope had arrived. A great hope for change.

The timing is perfect. Change was coming, and the pace was quickening.

Change comes slowly, gradually, incrementally, and suddenly.

Michelle and I spent the rest of the evening visiting all the precincts. The Obama signs were all strewn into piles at each precinct awaiting pickup from the city of Chicago trucks or from the local suburban disposal units. We drove through our precincts in Chicago, Merrionette Park, Oak Lawn and Evergreen Park.

We decided we would pickup as many Obama signs as possible and then reuse them for the fall General Election. That is our frugal side. We are fiscally conservative. One of the things we liked about Obama is that he had this frugal side, too.

We picked up hundreds of signs that evening with the intention of using them again for the General Election. We also asked our volunteers to save the yard and window signs for the fall. They were in tune to our thinking.

It was a great victory and conventional wisdom was that Obama should breeze past Jack Ryan, the newly elected Republican nominee for the United States Senate. But I thought that Jack Ryan could be a tough opponent for a variety of reasons. He, like Obama, was a Harvard Law Graduate. Jack also had an MBA from Harvard and had spent time teaching in the inner city of Chicago at a Catholic High School, Hales Franciscan High School. Jack was an attractive figure who was married to a "movie star," Jeri Ryan. Jeri is a former Miss Illinois and was crowned in 1989. Jeri ended third in 1990 in the Miss America contest. Jeri had a large role in David E. Kelley's "Boston Public" television show.[121] He has that glamorous side. He was articulate and many of his issues resonated with the voters. He also called himself a moderate Republican, which could help him with the independent voters. We did not believe that Ryan could defeat Obama on his best day, but we preached to everyone who would listen, "Do not take this election to the United States Senate for granted."

Meanwhile, Obama was basking in the media glory. Everybody was getting in on the act. The *St. Louis Post Dispatch* noticed our accomplishments in the 19th Ward. Hynes supporters had expected to lose Chicago's African-American and liberal vote to Obama, but they had banked on countering that with major backing from traditional "machine" voters in the city's labor-heavy wards. In the end, we loved when they said, "Hynes' defeat was so

---

121 http://en.wikipedia.org/wiki/Jeri_Ryan.

complete that even in Chicago's 19th Ward, his father's stronghold, he won by fewer votes than he did in the Metro East area."[122]

And then the *New York Times* authenticated our victory, too. The *New York Times* noted a failure of the ward organizations by saying. "Mr. Hynes's supporters had hoped that the city's traditional Democratic organization and its many ward workers would get out the vote for him. But by Tuesday night, as he addressed his disappointed crowd, Mr. Hynes urged his supporters to back the Democratic nominee."[123]

A Color-Blind Stampede to Victory!

It was not a failure of the ward organizations. It was a stampede by an effective campaign waged by Obama, his staff and the thousands of volunteers enlisted. It was a color-blind stampede to victory. It was an organization that grew based on grassroots organizing techniques, but other factors came into play.

Who would have ever guessed or known what an impact Glenn Brown would make in this campaign? He noticed "Meetup.com," and he noticed the "Obama for Senate Yahoo Group." Brown helped take the Howard Dean model to the next level for Obama.

Who would have ever guessed that a small bookstore, with less than 400 square feet of selling space, could ever have such a huge impact on a community, ever have an impact on a local political campaign, and help propel this man named Obama onto the national scene? It only took four years. And in four more years, we thought, who knows what is possible?

Then the *New York Times* followed up on Thursday, March 18th with a more in-depth analysis that seem to nail it. "In his quest for the Democratic nomination for the United States Senate, Barack Obama was, by many measures, supposed to lose. One opponent was a multimillionaire pouring his own cash into the race. Another was a loyal statewide official who was expected to bring the party's ward troops out in force on Election Day."[124]

---

122 Kevin McDermott Post-Dispatch Springfield Bureau. "OBAMA, RYAN WILL BATTLE IN KEY SEN-ATE CAMPAIGN; MUCH-WATCHED RACE WILL FEATURE TWO YOUNG HARVARD GRADU-ATES :[ILLINOIS FIVE STAR LATE LIFT Edition]." *St. Louis Post - Dispatch* [St. Louis, Mo.] 17 Mar. 2004.

123 Monica Davey. "From Crowded Field, Democrats Choose State Legislator to Seek Senate Seat." *New York Times* [New York, N.Y.] 17 Mar. 2004, Late Edition (East Coast): A.18.

124 Monica Davey. "As Quickly as Overnight, a Democratic Star Is Born. " *New York Times* [New York, N.Y.] 18 Mar. 2004, Late Edition (East Coast): A.20. *New York Times.*

While Michelle and I basked in the glory of victory, we lost Barack Obama that day. Our little group lost him. We lost him to the rest of the state of Illinois and to the rest of the nation. He made history that evening, and he has that special something: charisma. "They like him, they really like him," as Sally Field might say. He validated the "**to know him is to love him**" theory.

We would see so little of him after this night. It is all part of the process and the fact that Obama would be off into orbit. At his victory party, it was reported to us that the television crews were lining up to await the valued interview that night: five minutes with the victorious State Senator from Illinois. He had not won the seat and would not until November. And the swearing-in would be January. But he did get past the most important and most difficult test of the campaign, and that assured his victory in November, many said, but we were not taking anything for granted.

The *New York Times* said in a headline about him, "A Star is Born." Indeed, a star was born. A possible future President, something we had noticed back as early as 2000. I saw that "star" shine on an evening in March 2000. Again, the issue of him being president of the United States was the elephant in the room.

We had requested Obama's presence at our victory party for the night after the election on Wednesday, March 17th, 2004 and thought that his attendance would be a simple matter of him dropping by for ten or fifteen minutes. His attending our event now or later was never to be. Immediately after the election, Obama decided to take a downstate Illinois trip to thank voters. The downstate voters had been neglected over many years, Obama felt, and this political shrewdness was showing again. He wanted to let "downstate Illinoisans" know that they were a part of the state of Illinois. The strategy was to strengthen his areas of weakness, and it would be a long-term strategy that would serve him well.

It would no longer be a simple matter of making a request of Obama and having it granted. Getting Obama to autograph items for ourselves or volunteers would be more difficult. Or getting photographs with Obama would become more challenging. Obama no longer belonged just to the early supporters like us who showed a 'leap of faith.' It took a 'leap of faith' to support him. But now Barack Obama had spread his wings and he was flying. Where he was flying, we did not know. How far could he fly and for how long? It was as if we were proud parents watching a child grow into a beautiful man or a beautiful woman and making their mark on the world. Pride that makes you swell up inside. It is sad because, as a parent, you want to cling forever to your child. But it's a happy day because that was your mission: that your child can go off into the world and become accomplished in the area of his endeavor. Barack Obama wanted to serve the public. The pursuit of wealth was not his goal in life, he often told us publicly and privately. He had accomplished his mission.

Obama would have personal financial issues to deal with despite the fact that he was just elected a United States Senator. His family had gone into debt to get him elected as the Democratic nominee for Senator. He would not collect a salary as a Senator until January 2005. No time to worry about that, now, though.

Well, at least, now we were into "Phase One." We had always talked openly about the elephant in the room, that Obama would someday become President of the United States. It seemed he might have had that on his mind too because he spent much of the spring, summer, and fall of 2004 leading up the general election day campaigning around the country for other candidates in other states, including Senator Russ Feingold (D- WI), who was running in a tough race against Republican candidate and construction magnate Tim Michels.

Obama had traveled down his own road and made a great journey. To get there, he went down *The Road Less Traveled*.[125]

There were rumblings of controversies with the Jack Ryan campaign. Some of the facts of his divorce from Jeri Ryan could haunt Jack who had run a good campaign to win the Republican nomination for United States Senate. But he would need everything he had to defeat Barack Obama, and then some. However, Ryan just did not have what it took to defeat Obama or any candidate who would have emerged from the Democratic primary. Ryan was a political novice who did not "get it." Ryan did not draw the

---

125 Peck, *The Road Less Traveled.*

grassroots effort that Obama drew. He was an attractive candidate, but it takes more than looks to get elected to any office. It takes the entire package. There simply was nothing there. He was not attracting voters in spite of his good looks. He was a Republican in a heavily Democratic state. And he misplayed the entire divorce scandal. With full disclosure, Ryan could have possibly put the scandal behind him and moved on. Instead, Ryan chose to stonewall the divorce issue.

We Interrupt This Book With a Heart Attack for a Brief Moment

On May 27, 2004 my life would change forever. The completely unexpected happened. Obama, the campaign, and our beloved bookstore and my newspaper business would have to take a backseat. At least for one brief moment.

I had a heart attack. The attack was a clogged "widow's artery." In medical terms, it is called the "left anterior descending (anterior interventricular) coronary artery." I would go through therapy and make a rapid recovery, motivated in large part, by wanting to see Obama take his seat in the United States Senate and become President of the United States one day, as I had fully expected since March 13, 2000. As I came out of the stent procedure, I turned to Michelle, "I certainly don't want to leave you, and I want to see this Obama campaign to the end."

During my period of recovery on June 25th, Jack Ryan announced that he would drop out of the race for the United States Senate. Ryan was under pressure from party leaders. The good luck in this campaign just kept pouring in. Obama didn't even have an opponent now.

Late in July 2004, my recovery complete and finding I had no damage to the heart, the campaign continued for us. We were in Phase I of the campaign and getting ready for Phase II, when we got a call from deputy campaign manager, Nate Tamarin at the Obama campaign.

"Did you hear that Barack Obama was going to deliver the keynote speech at the 2004 Democratic convention?" Tamarin asked.

There was tremendous buzz at the time about Obama giving this "speech." Media outlets, such as CNN and many others, wanted to know more about this man Obama. The campaign received requests for copies of the Obama book. And they turned to Brad Jonas, the owner of Powell's Bookstore, to send them out. And he did. Again, a bookstore and a bookstore owner was making a huge impact on the candidacy of Barack Obama. Jonas recalled, "Our supply of books, that started at close to 4000 copies, was running thin. But I had enough to fill the media requests."

Tamarin extended an invitation to attend a special screening of what was to become known as "The Speech." Groups of selected volunteers, about 30 in all including many Shoman-ites, were invited to Trinity United Church, then Obama's church, to view a large screen television setup there. We were excited when we noticed that our friend Mike Jordan was in attendance. James Montgomery Sr. was also in attendance. He was the city's corporation counsel for the first three years of Mayor Washington's term. And Michelle and me. And several other Shomon-ites. The date was Tuesday, July 27, 2004 and we sat with nervous excitement. Obama was already resonating across the country. I told Michelle, many have given this keynote address, Democrats and Republicans and were sentenced forever into political oblivion. In some ways, "The Speech" was a political risk. On this backdrop, the speech began. It was nearly 2400 words and took twelve minutes to deliver:

> Thank you so much. Thank you. Thank you. Thank you so much. Thank you so much. Thank you. Thank you. Thank you, Dick Durbin. You make us all proud.
>
> On behalf of the great state of Illinois, crossroads of a nation, Land of Lincoln, let me express my deepest gratitude for the privilege of addressing this convention.
>
> Tonight is a particular honor for me because, let's face it, my presence on this stage is pretty unlikely. My father was a foreign student, born and raised in a small village in Kenya. He grew up herding goats, went to school in a tin-roof shack. His father — my grandfather — was a cook, a domestic servant to the British.
>
> But my grandfather had larger dreams for his son. Through hard work and perseverance my father got a scholarship to study in a magical place, America, that shone as a beacon of freedom and opportunity to so many who had come before.
>
> While studying here, my father met my mother. She was born in a town on the other side of the world, in Kansas. Her father worked on oil rigs and farms through most of the Depression. The day after Pearl Harbor my

grandfather signed up for duty; joined Patton's army, marched across Europe. Back home, my grandmother raised a baby and went to work on a bomber assembly line. After the war, they studied on the G.I. Bill, bought a house through F.H.A., and later moved west all the way to Hawaii in search of opportunity.

And they, too, had big dreams for their daughter. A common dream, born of two continents.

My parents shared not only an improbable love, they shared an abiding faith in the possibilities of this nation. They would give me an African name, Barack, or "blessed," believing that in a tolerant America your name is no barrier to success. They imagined — They imagined me going to the best schools in the land, even though they weren't rich, because in a generous America you don't have to be rich to achieve your potential.

They're both passed away now. And yet, I know that on this night they look down on me with great pride.

They stand here — And I stand here today, grateful for the diversity of my heritage, aware that my parents' dreams live on in my two precious daughters. I stand here knowing that my story is part of the larger American story, that I owe a debt to all of those who came before me, and that, in no other country on earth, is my story even possible.

Tonight, we gather to affirm the greatness of our Nation — not because of the height of our skyscrapers, or the power of our military, or the size of our economy. Our pride is based on a very simple premise, summed up in a declaration made over two hundred years ago:

We hold these truths to be self-evident, that all men are created equal, that they are endowed by their Creator with certain inalienable rights, that among these are Life, Liberty and the pursuit of Happiness.

That is the true genius of America, a faith — a faith in simple dreams, an insistence on small miracles; that we can tuck in our children at night and know that they are fed and clothed and safe from harm; that we can say what we think, write what we think, without hearing a sudden knock on the door; that we can have an idea and start our own business without paying a bribe; that we can participate in the political process without fear of retribution, and that our votes will be counted — at least most of the time.

This year, in this election we are called to reaffirm our values and our commitments, to hold them against a hard reality and see how we're measuring up to the legacy of our forbearers and the promise of future generations.

And fellow Americans, Democrats, Republicans, Independents, I say to you tonight: We have more work to do — more work to do for the workers I met in Galesburg, Illinois, who are losing their union jobs at the Maytag plant that's moving to Mexico, and now are having to compete with their own children for jobs that pay seven bucks an hour; more to do for the father that I met who was losing his job and choking back the tears, wondering how he would pay 4500 dollars a month for the drugs his son needs without the health benefits that he counted on; more to do for the young woman in East St. Louis, and thousands more like her, who has the grades, has the drive, has the will, but doesn't have the money to go to college.

Now, don't get me wrong. The people I meet — in small towns and big cities, in diners and office parks — they don't expect government to solve all their problems. They know they have to work hard to get ahead, and they want to. Go into the collar counties around Chicago, and people will tell you they don't want their tax money wasted, by a welfare agency or by the Pentagon. Go in — Go into any inner city neighborhood, and folks will tell you that government alone can't teach our kids to learn; they know that parents have to teach, that children can't achieve unless we raise their expectations and turn off the television sets and eradicate the slander that says a black youth with a book is acting white. They know those things.

People don't expect — People don't expect government to solve all their problems. But they sense, deep in their bones, that with just a slight change in priorities, we can make sure that every child in America has a decent shot at life, and that the doors of opportunity remain open to all.

They know we can do better. And they want that choice.

In this election, we offer that choice. Our Party has chosen a man to lead us who embodies the best this country has to offer. And that man is John Kerry.

John Kerry understands the ideals of community, faith, and service because they've defined his life. From his heroic service to Vietnam, to his years as a prosecutor and lieutenant governor, through two decades in the United States Senate, he's devoted himself to this country. Repeatedly, we've seen him make tough choices when easier ones were available.

His values and his record affirm what is best in us. John Kerry believes in an America where hard work is rewarded; so instead of offering tax breaks to companies shipping jobs overseas, he offers them to companies creating jobs here at home.

John Kerry believes in an America where all Americans can afford the same health coverage our politicians in Washington have for themselves.

John Kerry believes in energy independence, so we aren't held hostage to the profits of oil companies, or the sabotage of foreign oil fields.

John Kerry believes in the Constitutional freedoms that have made our country the envy of the world, and he will never sacrifice our basic liberties, nor use faith as a wedge to divide us.

And John Kerry believes that in a dangerous world war must be an option sometimes, but it should never be the first option.

You know, a while back — awhile back I met a young man named Shamus in a V.F.W. Hall in East Moline, Illinois. He was a good-looking kid — six two, six three, clear eyed, with an easy smile. He told me he'd joined the Marines and was heading to Iraq the following week. And as I listened to him explain why he'd enlisted, the absolute faith he had in our country and its leaders, his devotion to duty and service, I thought this young man was all that any of us might ever hope for in a child.

But then I asked myself, "Are we serving Shamus as well as he is serving us?"

I thought of the 900 men and women — sons and daughters, husbands and wives, friends and neighbors, who won't be returning to their own hometowns. I thought of the families I've met who were struggling to get by without a loved one's full income, or whose loved ones had returned with a limb missing or nerves shattered, but still lacked long-term health benefits because they were Reservists.

When we send our young men and women into harm's way, we have a solemn obligation not to fudge the numbers or shade the truth about why they're going, to care for their families while they're gone, to tend to the soldiers upon their return, and to never ever go to war without enough troops to win the war, secure the peace, and earn the respect of the world.

Now — Now let me be clear. Let me be clear. We have real enemies in the world. These enemies must be found. They must be pursued. And they must be defeated. John Kerry knows this. And just as Lieutenant Kerry did not hesitate to risk his life to protect the men who served with him in Vietnam, President Kerry will not hesitate one moment to use our military might to keep America safe and secure.

John Kerry believes in America. And he knows that it's not enough for just some of us to prosper — for alongside our famous individualism, there's another ingredient in the American saga, a belief that we're all connected as one people. If there is a child on the south side of Chicago who can't read, that matters to me, even if it's not my child. If there is a senior citizen somewhere who can't pay for their prescription drugs, and having to choose between medicine and the rent, that makes my life poorer, even if it's not my grandparent. If there's an Arab American family being rounded up without benefit of an attorney or due process that threatens my civil liberties.

It is that fundamental belief — It is that fundamental belief: I am my brother's keeper. I am my sister's keeper that makes this country work. It's what allows us to pursue our individual dreams and yet still come together as one American family.

E pluribus Unum: "Out of many, one."

Now even as we speak, there are those who are preparing to divide us
— the spin masters, the negative ad peddlers who embrace the politics of
"anything goes." Well, I say to them tonight, there is not a liberal America
and a conservative America — there is the United States of America. There
is not a Black America and a White America and Latino America and Asian
America — there's the United States of America.

The pundits, the pundits like to slice-and-dice our country into Red States
and Blue States; Red States for Republicans, Blue States for Democrats. But
I've got news for them, too. We worship an "awesome God" in the Blue
States, and we don't like federal agents poking around in our libraries in the
Red States. We coach Little League in the Blue States and yes; we've got
some gay friends in the Red States. There are patriots who opposed the war
in Iraq and there are patriots who supported the war in Iraq. We are one
people, all of us pledging allegiance to the stars and stripes, all of us
defending the United States of America.

In the end — In the end — In the end, that's what this election is about.
Do we participate in a politics of cynicism or do we participate in a politics
of hope?

John Kerry calls on us to hope. John Edwards calls on us to hope.

I'm not talking about blind optimism here — the almost willful
ignorance that thinks unemployment will go away if we just don't think
about it, or the health care crisis will solve itself if we just ignore it. That's
not what I'm talking about. I'm talking about something more substantial.
It's the hope of slaves sitting around a fire singing freedom songs; the hope
of immigrants setting out for distant shores; the hope of a young naval
lieutenant bravely patrolling the Mekong Delta; the hope of a mill worker's
son who dares to defy the odds; the hope of a skinny kid with a funny name
who believes that America has a place for him, too.

Hope — Hope in the face of difficulty. Hope in the face of uncertainty.
The audacity of hope!

In the end, that is God's greatest gift to us, the bedrock of this nation.
A belief in things not seen. A belief that there are better days ahead.

I believe that we can give our middle class relief and provide working
families with a road to opportunity.

I believe we can provide jobs to the jobless, homes to the homeless, and
reclaim young people in cities across America from violence and despair.

I believe that we have a righteous wind at our backs and that as we
stand on the crossroads of history, we can make the right choices, and meet
the challenges that face us.

America! Tonight, if you feel the same energy that I do, if you feel the
same urgency that I do, if you feel the same passion that I do, if you feel the
same hopefulness that I do — if we do what we must do, then I have no

doubt that all across the country, from Florida to Oregon, from Washington to Maine, the people will rise up in November, and John Kerry will be sworn in as President, and John Edwards will be sworn in as Vice President, and this country will reclaim its promise, and out of this long political darkness a brighter day will come.

Thank you very much everybody. God bless you. Thank you.

— Barack Obama

When he had finished the speech, I jumped up and said, "He hit it out of the park."

We all got to our feet and applauded. We knew he had nailed it. "The Speech" was being televised on C-Span, so we were not getting the commentary you would receive on CNN, MSNBC, CNBC, or Fox News. Nobody had to tell this group. It had elements of many of the stump speeches he had given since we met him, and we had all heard parts of it before. This one, he had put together. We were sitting in the church Obama then attended, Trinity United Church, and it was an honor to be there that evening. We were swelling with pride in this man, Barack Obama. We all knew the different roles we had played. It was not any one person or any one group that catapulted Obama to the national scene. It was everything at once. It was the sum total of all of these events.

My thoughts turned to his book: Would the book be re-released? I knew if it was, it would enjoy the kind of popularity it deserved. I could envision it climbing on the *New York Times* bestseller list: instantly.

The news came within days of "The Speech." The book would be released. The *L.A. Times* reported that the publisher, Crown Books, was immediately reprinting 50,000 copies, with a copy of "The Speech" contained in the new edition. The story of the book — how it came into being and how it came to be republished — has some unexpected twists. It began when literary agent Jane Dystel read a newspaper account in 1990 of how Obama had become the first African American to be elected president of the Harvard Law Review. Sensing a good story, Dystel contacted Obama. But it was years after that first meeting that Obama delivered the manuscript and years more before it was finally published in

---

126 J. Michael Kennedy. "Speech gives a boost to Obama's 'Dreams':[HOME EDITION]. " *Los Angeles Times* [Los Angeles, Calif.] 6 Aug. 2004,E.2. *Los Angeles Times.*

1995.[126] And now in early August 2004, the book would be re-released, and it would be a smash hit. A "hidden gem" was about to emerge. The book and Barack Obama. And Barack Obama would begin to earn royalties from the sale of the book. Money that the Obamas would need to keep up two residences: one in Chicago and one in Washington. The Obamas had already decided to keep the home in Chicago and Barack would commute to Washington on Mondays and return home to Chicago on Thursdays.

The Associated Press was reporting that copies of Obama's book were selling on Ebay.com at a premium.[127] In a word, Obama was hot.

After July 27, 2004, Obama had become one of the most sought after people at the convention after his keynote address, according to a blurb in the July 29, 2004 *New York Times*. There was even talk about one day being President. "As he moved through rooms and hallways, whispers followed: perhaps the man who had just passed would be the first black president of the United States."[128]

Change comes slowly, gradually, incrementally, and suddenly.

We had seen little of Obama that summer and fall. We did see him briefly at his "birthday party" in Matteson, Illinois at the Holiday Inn on August 4, 2004. We received an email invitation. Dan Shomon had inserted a personal note asking us to pass it along to our list.

~

August 4th, 2004 (Wednesday)
Barack's Birthday Bash!
The Obamas are celebrating Barack's 43rd birthday,
and we're inviting our friends!
Holiday Inn Matteson
500 Holiday Plaza Drive
Matteson, Illinois 60443 (at Lincoln Highway and Interstate 57)
VIP Reception (6:30pm - 7:30pm) - $250
General Reception (7:00pm - 9:00pm) - $50
To RSVP (or just join in the celebration!) please contribute via the
internet at: http://www2.obamaforillinois.com/birthdayparty
Or call 312-386-9004. We hope to see you there!

Thousands bought tickets and attended. And incredibly, Obama still

127 THE ASSOCIATED PRESS SPRINGFIELD,. "Obama's memoir enjoys a surge in sales :[Five Star Late Lift Edition]." *St. Louis Post - Dispatch* [St. Louis, Mo.] 3 Aug. 2004,B.2.
128 Randal C. Archibold. "Day After, Keynote Speaker Finds Admirers Everywhere. " *New York Times* 29 Jul 2004, Late Edition (East Coast): *New York Times*.

did not have an opponent and would not until early August. He joked to the crowd that night, "The only opponent I would be afraid of is Michelle Obama." The crowd cheered its approval and wholeheartedly agreed.

Obama had just completed "the speech" at the convention and was now riding high. A thousand people had bought tickets and attended. We paid $50.00 each to get in the door. We waited in line and as Obama came along and spotted me, he asked, "How is your wife Michelle?"

"She's right down the line," I told him.

The Book is Ready to Launch, Too

He also asked about the bookstore, and I told him how pre-sales of his soon to be re-released book were skyrocketing. I told him the phone was ringing off the hook and as he walked away down the line, he gave me a thumbs up. The book would finally receive the attention it deserved. Obama had dreamed of this book one day becoming a bestseller. Never in his wildest dreams could he have envisioned what was happening to him now. "Barack was excited."

He got down to Michelle, and they hugged. He thanked her for all of her help and exchanged a few words, and he moved on down the line.

How Do 300 Volunteers Fit the New Political Order?

One of the items we were uncertain about was our role in the upcoming campaign. It was an awkward position, not only for us personally, but also for our group of 300 volunteers. What would we do for the General Election campaign?

I posed the question to Nate Tamarin. "What is our role in the General Election?"

We did not like Tamarin's answer. "Well, we want to feed you into the 19th Ward." They were the regular Democratic party organization. It was obvious the Obama campaign did not want to offend the original grassroots people who got him there, but Obama also needed the support of the regular party organizations if he had any type of future ambitions.

It was a tough issue. And we discussed it further after the Democratic National Convention speech with other aides in the campaign. We never did come to a resolution. Mayor Richard M. Daley, we suspected and Al Kindle confirmed years later, was deeply concerned about these grassroots groups forming everywhere. With the talk at the time of Congressman Jesse Jackson Jr. seriously considering a run for Mayor of Chicago, these groups could conceivably re-form and get behind a Jesse Jackson Jr. candidacy for mayor of Chicago.

Our grassroots group would always be a wedge between Obama and the regular 19th Ward Democratic organization, and it was uncomfortable for everyone involved. It was not as big a problem for me personally because I had a good relationship with some members of the 19th Ward, such as Alderman Virginia Rugai, State Rep. Kevin Joyce, State Senator Ed Maloney and 19th Ward Committeeman Matt O'Shea.

We did ultimately decide to work the polls on General Election Day and pass out Obama literature and only Obama literature. We would not be denied our wish to finish what we had started. The enthusiasm in our group was already starting to wane because of the general feeling that Obama was a shoo-in to win the election.

In early August, Alan Keyes was nominated by the Republican party to replace Jack Ryan on the ballot. Keyes didn't have much time to organize a campaign and wasn't well-received by the moderate wing of the Republican Party. What made Jack Ryan attractive to many Republican voters was his moderate stand on the issues. He was now being replaced by a true conservative, Alan Keyes. And Keyes had a national following because he had run for President in 2000 on the Republican ticket. We did not want to take this candidacy lightly.

We would have less than one hundred people working on general election day as compared to the 300 plus people for the Primary Election Day.

On October 31, 2004 at about 10:00 am, the Sunday before the General Election Day, we got a call from "Super Volunteer" Neil Pomeranke, who said that Obama was having breakfast at Lumes at 116th & Western. We grabbed some books that we wanted Obama to sign and ran over to the restaurant.

As Obama was coming out of the restaurant, Mike Flannery of Channel 2 News was trailing him, and then Obama spotted Michelle and me. The Channel 2 camera was rolling. We both got a big hug from

Obama, and the moment was captured on the Channel 2 News camera. Obama pointed out to Flannery that we were two of his earliest supporters. He did not have time to sign the books we brought, but he said he would drop by the store later to do that. He was on his way to speak at a church that day and was late as his aide pushed him along.

On Tuesday, November 2, 2004, we had decided that we would have a presence in the precincts on Election Day, in spite of the fact that the ward organizations were now taking over the campaign. We were only able to manage to organize a fraction of the number of people that we got for the Primary Election. There was not a real question whether Obama would win, although Michelle and I never took this for granted.

Now It is Official, The Next United States Senator from the State of Illinois, Barack Obama

At the end of the day, Barack Obama was now officially the junior Senator from the state of Illinois. Winning the general election was anticlimatic. Alan Keyes, who was selected late in the process by the Illinois Republican party, did not mount much of a campaign.

The book, *Dreams from My Father*, was starting to move on the bestseller list. And now Obama was receiving offers from publishers to publish another book. He hired famed Washington, D.C. attorney, Robert Barnett, to sort through the book contract offers he was receiving. Obama said he might write another book, but it would be more about national policy than about him. The money from another book would come in handy, he admitted.[129]

It was our feeling after the General Election victory that we would not work another campaign for Barack Obama again until 2010. He was gaining momentum and networking the national scene. He was in the early stages of forming a national grassroots effort. If he ran in 2008, he most likely would take on Hillary Clinton. Now that would be an accomplishment, I thought, and no easy task. If anyone could successfully challenge Hillary Clinton, it would be Barack Obama. He had what it took.

---

129 Willis, Christopher. "Obama says good-bye to legislative colleagues." *Chicago Defender* [Chicago, Ill.] 9 Nov. 2004, 3. Illinois Newsstand. ProQuest. Chicago Public Library. 18 Jan. 2009.

And Hillary Clinton, I was certain, would never see him coming.

The 2008 election was the first in many years without an incumbent President or a former Vice President in the race. George W. Bush could not run for reelection and Dick Cheney had indicated he would not be challenging for the nomination. It was similar to the United States Senate election in that it was a truly "open race."

So that would mean either running for President in 2012 if another Republican is elected in 2008 or wait until the Democratic incumbent serves two terms and then fight for the nomination in 2016.

Whew.

It was looking like Barack Obama's one and only shot at being President was one year and one year only. 2008.

Although, when asked, he would say that he was only interested in being a United States Senator and finishing out his term. But a guy can change his mind, can't he? Besides, Obama was already making inquiries into organizing in Iowa and would be visiting there often. And Obama was dispatching trusted friends to check out the Iowa landscape. After all, that is what "students" do. Study. Explore. Learn. The minute Obama won the United States Senate primary, my first thought after hearing of the media lining up to interview him was, "He really is going to be President one day."

If I had this thought, he surely did, too. It was not wishful thinking or some type of pipe dream. And people liked him. They really, really liked him. "To Know him is to love him." And it appeared the country was in the early stages of getting to know him.

In December 2004, many Democrats were maneuvering for position for the 2008 race. Obama joked that many folks thought he had an easy time of it in his Senate race in Illinois against a weak opponent. "Nothing could be further from the truth," he said. "You think it's easy signing autographs and saying `not in 2008' a thousand times a day?" That quip was to raise the presidential idea just in case we hadn't already thought of it. Which, of course, we had.[130]

Already a best-selling author, Senator-elect Barack Obama would write three more books in the coming years, including an illustrated

---

130 Marianne Means Syndicated columnist. "THE 2008 CAMPAIGN BEGAN NOV. 3 :[FINAL Edi-
    tion]. " *Seattle Post* - Intelligencer [Seattle, Wash.] 16 Dec. 2004,B6.

children's book with his wife and two daughters. Obama frequently mentioned on the campaign trail that he was a man of modest means. That clearly had changed. He would receive about $1.9 million in advances for the three books, according to a spokesman for the incoming senator.[131]

Change comes slowly, gradually, incrementally, and suddenly.

---

131 Rudolph Bush, Tribune staff reporter. "Obama's $1.9 million, 3-book deal includes 1 children's title :[North Shore Final, NS Edition]." *Chicago Tribune* [Chicago, IL] 18 Dec. 2004, 1NS.18. *Chicago Tribune*.

CHAPTER 9

Debra Shore, Alexi Giannoulias or How Barack Obama Flexes Political Muscle in Illinois

~

Michelle and I thought we would not work another campaign after the great Obama victory for the United States Senate. Never again could we ever re-capture the excitement of that campaign. To be an underdog as Obama was in July 2003, when he polled in single digits and hardly anyone had heard of the man with the funny name, and then win a seat in the United States Senate which propelled him onto the national scene: how could we ever get excited about a candidate again?

Well we could, because in early July of 2005, I received an unexpected telephone call from Debra Shore, the founding editor of *Chicago Wilderness Magazine* and a community activist from Evanston, Illinois. She explained that she was running for Cook County Water Reclamation Commissioner. She wanted my support and the support of our community of volunteers. And Debra Shore said the magic words: Dan Shomon. That gave Debra instant credibility with us.

We would start receiving numerous calls from various candidates because of the reputation we established with the successful Obama effort for United States Senate.

Because I did not want our group of volunteers to blindly jump into every situation that presented itself, I did not give Debra Shore an immediate answer that July 2005 day. We would or would not help, and we would not keep her hanging. When we decided to commit, we would be "all in." Being "all in" was something we had learned from Obama. It was a poker term, a game that Obama enjoyed, but it was also a great analogy for life and for political campaigns. But first, before we got "all in, "we needed to check her out and make sure she was the "real deal." Initially, we knew absolutely nothing about her. So we thought.

As it turned out, several years earlier, Debra Shore had contacted us through the bookstore about her magazine, *The Chicago Wilderness*. She was the founding editor. In addition, judging by her solicitation, she was the Sales Director and the Circulation Director, too.

We sold quite a few copies of *The Chicago Wilderness* magazine over the years, and it got a nice following. The magazine was of very high quality. The magazine sponsored nature trips and walks. And encouraged and organized environmental cleanups. And it kept an eye on the Cook County Forest Preserves. For Debra Shore, vying for Commissioner of the Water Reclamation District Board was indeed a perfect fit.

Michelle and I first discussed this on our July vacation, and it seemed the more I told Michelle about this Debra Shore person, the more excited she got. Debra Shore's politics were in line with ours; she cares about the environment and clean water. "Water matters" was a theme of her campaign. She was the only environmentalist running in the race, although eventually all the candidates started to make the claim once they saw that this resonated with the voters. Debra Shore wanted to protect the forest preserve as evidenced by her work with the Forest Preserve Board. In fact, that was a key mission of *Chicago Wilderness* magazine.

Shortly after returning from our holiday trip and having checked Shore out, we decided we would help her. We would present her to our group. She would need our help because one of her weak areas would be the far Southwest side of Chicago. She was a total unknown in this area.

But that would change. And we would help change that on her behalf.

Change comes slowly, gradually, incrementally and suddenly.

The birth of the Reading on Walden Political Discussion Group

We had decided to come up with a name for the group since "Obama for Illinois" was no longer appropriate. The group decided to adopt the

name of the **Reading on Walden Political Discussion Group**. We had a
small group of 300+ volunteers who knew how to work a successful
political campaign. But what we really loved to do was to get together as
a group and discuss the politics of the day: local politics, national politics,
international politics. We loved it all. And we loved to talk about it. And
discussing books about these things was also exciting for us.

Barack Obama united the **Reading on Walden Political Discussion
Group**. We did not know if we could ever recreate the excitement of
the 2004 Democratic Primary race again. Debra Shore would be the
first candidate we would support under the new name. We were
concerned whether we could get all 300 of our members[132] to work on
a campaign.

Candidates, I have found, set the tone for how they want to run their
campaign. Obama was a prime example. All the campaigns Obama was
involved with were a direct reflection on him. The campaigns typically
had a central message, and Obama was the chief messenger. Through the
Senate campaign, Obama was the press spokesman. Obama set the tone
for integrity, honesty, and lofty ethical standards. It is similar to any other
manager of a retail store, a department head, a CEO, or Chairman of the
Board. It all comes from the top.

Shore's stronghold would be Evanston, Illinois and the immediate areas
surrounding it. Congresswoman Jan Schakowsky was a close friend and
mentor for Shore and strongly encouraged her candidacy. She could count
on surrogates to help her in her back yard while she campaigned in places
like our community. And I also knew from the Obama campaign that
Shore could count on close to 90% of the vote from Evanston Township.
I later mentioned in phone conversations with Shore that she might want
to contact the Oak Park Democrats. Oak Park could deliver 80% of the
vote for a candidate they supported. But Shore was so far ahead of the
game and had by this point already contacted the Oak Park group. And
dozens of other contacts that she received from Shomon and Doug Price.

> In early 2005, someone asked if I would consider running for a seat on
> the board of the Metropolitan Water Reclamation District of Greater Chicago
> (MWRD). Given my interest in conservation — and my belief that water is

---

132 Membership is informal in the Reading on Walden Political Discussion Group.

going to be "the" issue in years to come — I felt that I had something to bring to the board. So I decided to give it a shot.

Running countywide for an obscure office in the second-largest county in the country is hard. So I sought all the help I could get. I needed to build relationships and find supporters wherever I could. I knew I could count on support from the conservation community and the progressive Democrats I had met through the Dean campaign, but I also reached out to the gay and lesbian community, the Jewish community, women, and other constituencies. Someone suggested I should talk to Dan Shomon, who had helped to steer Barack's successful Senate run.

Dan was gracious enough to meet with me, asked me a number of probing questions, and was impressed, I think, by my approach to my campaign. As a result, he was willing to share some tips — principally that I should contact John and Michelle Presta, who "ran a bookstore and a progressive political group" in the 19th Ward of Chicago. He also suggested that I meet with Mike Jordan, the talented field organizer from the far southern suburbs. A few weeks later I ran into Dan and Mike at the July 4th parade in Oak Park.

Other people said I should meet another south suburban veteran politico, Doug Price. Doug was kind enough to trundle up to the north side to meet with me at a coffee shop. He unpacked his bag of skeptical questions and I dutifully answered them. Again, I think I won him over with my preparation and approach to the task of running countywide for the MWRD board.

John and Michelle invited me to come to one of their monthly gatherings at Café Luna, which I did, and had a chance to explain to that dedicated group why I was running for office, what I brought to the campaign, and how I would win. (I was the first person with conservation credentials to run for the MWRD board in 30 years.) They swiftly adopted me, so to speak, and provided substantial help in gathering signatures on petitions, seeking press attention, distributing yard signs, and getting out the vote. I returned to Café Luna a number of times during the campaign and after our victory. This was grassroots organizing at its best.

Through Doug Price and Mike Jordan, I also met another first-time candidate, Alexi Giannoulias, who was then running for State Treasurer in Illinois. In any campaign cycle, candidates tend to see each other quite a bit attending various endorsement sessions and events. And Alexi and I had been adopted by some of the same progressive people. Alexi and I worked a Metra train station in Tinley Park along with Mike Jordan and Alexi's mother Anna early one cold February morning before the primary election. This taught me an invaluable lesson: showing up is the most important thing you can do — as a candidate, as a volunteer. The fact that I was willing to

work hard, in the cold, early in the morning, far from home — that
impressed people.

And the rest, as they say, is history. Alexi won. I won.

— Debra Shore

~

The Water Reclamation Commission had traditionally been used by the
regular Democratic Party as a reward for loyalty. It was never taken
seriously as an agency. The qualifications for being a member of the Board
was directly related to doing political work. Debra Shore, if successful,
would be the first environmentalist elected to the Board. And Shore would
have to work very hard to win a seat. She would have to gain her seat the
old-fashioned way: she would have to earn it.

Her candidacy drew scoffs and giggling on the part of career politicians
who had a hard time believing that this environmentalist could be elected
to the Board. Debra had the audacity to think that she could actually have
an impact on this Board. After all, two of the candidates running were
incumbents, including the President of the Water Reclamation Board,
Terrence O'Brien.

Political jobs as rewards for working political campaigns were
diminishing because of laws passed and court rulings outlawing them as
rewards. This made the value of a group like ours all the more important.
Our group understood that working a campaign with us did not yield a
political reward: monetary, job or otherwise. The jobs no longer existed,
and prosecutors like Patrick J. Fitzgerald, who began serving as the United
States Attorney for the Northern District of Illinois on September 1, 2001,
were clamping down on the system of rewards. Fitzgerald has prosecuted
Republicans as vigorously as he has prosecuted Democrats who violated
the public trust.

The established political organizations in Chicago were tied to the
patronage system. The 19th Ward, where we lived, was a stronghold for
that type of organization. The 19th Ward typically had one of the highest
voter turnouts in the city for most elections.

Shore mentioned Dan Shomon's name, and I knew this phone call was
Obama connected since Shomon at the time was Obama's Political
Director. The phone call caught me by surprise, since I believed that our
political activism was now over. What else was there to accomplish? We

had given Obama a big boost, and he obviously was not in need of our help. Even when the day arrived that Obama announces for President of the United States, our political group would just be one of many.

So we thought.

Shore had officially announced her candidacy on June 21st, 2005. There was little fanfare or media overage. After all, who was Debra Shore? She was not an incumbent, and she had not previously run for or held political office. Many candidates who announce for office, especially Water Reclamation, do not make it to the ballot because of insufficient signatures or signatures thrown out or challenged by incumbents. The system is stacked against challengers and outsiders.

It was too early for a candidate to get attention at this stage. For an unknown candidate, such as Shore, the odds were very long. Most candidates fizzle out before they reach the petition stage. There are issues of raising funds, recruiting staff, volunteers (and coordinating volunteers) and collecting ballot signatures. Later comes the marketing and name recognition aspect. One step at a time.

I told Shore that while I had heard of the MWRD,[133] I knew little about the responsibilities of a Commissioner and that I really did not know what the function of the MWRD was, thinking that is was something about dirty sewers and human waste and contaminated water. MWRD has a large budget with a large number of employees and is a government agency. One of our local 19th Ward politicos, Kathleen Meany, was a member of the MWRD for many years. I also knew the office holders held six-year terms.

Since Shore had gotten my name and telephone number from Shomon, Obama's campaign manager in 2000 and campaign manager at the start of the 2004 campaign, this gave Shore, at least with me, immediate credibility. Shomon would not have given her our number if she were not a quality person.

I was curious about the Shomon connection and wanted to know more, still knowing that Shomon would not refer her to us without a good reason or knowing that we would like her immediately. We thought our days of campaign organizing were over. We never discussed with Shomon that we were in the political activism business or that we wanted to continue

---

133 Was once called the Metropolitan Sanitary District.

political work. We had kept our list of volunteers and occasionally met as group. And Shomon would be one of the recipients of our emails.

We were physically and emotionally spent from the Obama campaign for the United States Senate, with the primary election being the climax and the general election being anti-climatic. We were just recovering from all that excitement. It was occasionally stirring up again because Obama's name was rarely out of the news. Obama had become larger than life. His name was known throughout the country now, and he even had a large following in many countries around the world, including places like Kenya. The expectation was that he would one day run for President of the United States. The question came up during interviews on national television and Obama gave the pat answer of "I was elected to the United States Senate and will serve the people of Illinois."

I was more and more convinced it would be 2008.

All indications were that he was certainly exploring a run for the Presidency of the United States. Shortly after being elected to the United States Senate, Obama started the Hopefund and appointed two trusted aides to work with it, Nate Tamarin, as the executive director, and Jordan Kaplan.

Obama was everywhere. He was Tim Russert's guest on Meet the Press. He flew to Omaha to have lunch with Warren Buffett. He was on stage with Willie Nelson. And then he was on stage with Barbra Streisand. I had never met a politician quite like him, and America didn't either. He was a regular guy who talked about regular things. There was not a subject he couldn't or wouldn't discuss. He could discuss baseball, basketball, the proliferation of nuclear armaments. No subject was taboo or out of bounds. And he was interested in everything. He was interested in life. His curiosity knew no bounds. He would be great company at Thanksgiving dinner at home, at a baseball game, or just going to the movies and discussing it afterward.

Senators Peter Fitzgerald and Carol Mosely Braun were nearly invisible for twelve years. They had forgotten where they came from. They were into the Washington scene and not into the Illinois scene which was, after all, where they came from.

Obama, who succeeded both of them, had not forgotten where he came from, and he constantly reminded us. I knew from this flurry of activity that Obama was running for President, and it would be sooner rather than later. After all, opportunity knocks once. Do you answer? That is the choice one makes.

This Debra Shore phone call certainly was connected to Barack Obama, if not directly, then certainly indirectly. If we liked her, we are certain Shomon knew by now. It would be difficult for us to walk away and not help her. How could we say no?

I asked Shore during that first conversation, "Does that mean Dan Shomon is endorsing your candidacy or working on your campaign?" I received an honest answer from her. That was indicative of her integrity, and that set the tone for our relationship.

"No." she said. "I sought out Dan Shomon, and he agreed to meet with me and informally give me some advice. He was nice enough to give me the names of some people I could contact that might be helpful."

She had also gotten other "Shomon-ite" names from Shomon such as Mike Jordan and Doug Price. Shomon must have taken a liking to Debra, or why would he be helping her? Although Debra sought out Shomon, he could certainly have blown her off.

Shomon, she said, was not sure whom he would endorse for the Water Reclamation Board. She said that there was a possibility that one of the candidates in the race might hire him as a consultant, so he did not want to commit to her initially, although he was happy to advise her.

I called Dan to check out the story, and he confirmed it exactly as she stated. He also added that he thought that Shore was my kind of candidate. She was a progressive. It was not unusual for Obama, whether through Shomon or on his own, to endorse and support candidates after his 2004 Democratic primary victory. In March 2005, Obama got involved in a local race in Aurora Illinois.[135]

The Obama "machine" would actively support and endorse candidates. Michelle, the 300 volunteers and I were part of this machine. Obama certainly knew who Debra Shore was and was aware that she was an early supporter, so at the very least, Obama was aware of Shomon's activities. Shore was also rooted in the important Democratic Party Organization of Evanston. It was important to support this group. Shomon was also

---

135 Scott Fornek. "Obama backs suburbs' Dems, but says he's no 'kingmaker'." Chicago Sun-Times (IL) March 30, 2005, News: 28.

Obama's "Illinois Political Director," a position he held until December 2005.

Shore's integrity, I found early in the process, was without question. She had integrity written all over her.

When we initially talked, Shore let me know that she was gay. She would mention it in her stump speeches during those days and then move on to the issues that she cared about. She did not want to ignore the issue, and she did not want to run away from it.

If elected to the Water Reclamation District, she would be the first openly gay person to serve on the Board. She handled the issue with grace, and she never avoided the issue. I did not flinch because I do not believe that a person's sexual orientation qualifies a candidate, and more importantly, it does not disqualify a candidate from office.

Since I already was aware of *Chicago Wilderness* magazine, it was obvious to me that Shore was a great fit for this office. It was one of those "ah hah" moments.

We finally settled on a date for her to attend one of our monthly meetings. I also suggested to her several other groups[136] that would likely welcome her warmly. The groups had also popped up during the 2004 Democratic primary, were for Obama, and managed to stay together. Some of the groups were outgrowths of Howard Dean's unsuccessful bid for the Presidential nomination.

After exchanging of some dates, Shore agreed to appear before the Reading on Walden Bookstore Political Discussion Group on October 5th, 2005. We promised to promote the event. Michelle and I had not yet met Shore personally, but we decided to support her candidacy.

The notice that I wrote went out:

> Debra Shore, founding editor of Chicago Wilderness Magazine and a Democratic candidate for Commissioner of the Metropolitan Water Reclamation District in 2006, will be appearing at Cafe Luna located at 1742 W 99th Street on Wednesday, October 5th at 7:00 pm. Ms. Shore will be explaining the function of the Metropolitan Water Reclamation District and the role played by Commissioners. In addition, she will also be seeking support for her candidacy as a Metropolitan Water Reclamation District

---

136 One such group was the Oak Park Democratic organization, Democracy for America group.

Commissioner.

The Metropolitan Water Reclamation District is a government agency created in 1889 to protect the water quality of Lake Michigan, the major drinking water supply for the Chicago area. The MWRD is charged with preserving and enhancing the health of our water systems.

The public is invited to attend. This gathering serves as a great venue to personally meet candidates for public office, so that the voter can make an informed decision when going to the polls.[137]

We knew little about this county agency and its function. I certainly had no idea what the duties of a Commissioner involved.

Our meeting was for 7:00 pm, but Michelle and I, as is our practice, were there early for the meeting. When we arrived, we noticed someone who we thought might be Shore, and it was. We were able to spend a little time with her.

Michelle and I chatted with her, and she gave us a background on herself. Besides being the founding editor of *Chicago Wilderness magazine*, she was a community activist, a community leader.

She also told us she attended a select training for women candidates running for political office in Illinois called The Illinois Women's Institute for Leadership (IWIL). Only the best are accepted at IWIL, and it was obvious that Shore learned much at the Institute.

IWIL is an educational (501[C][4]) organization that exists to encourage and train women to become effective leaders in Illinois government and politics. The organization grew out of discussions about the need for more women in politics. Many of the founding members of the Board of Directors have worked diligently to build the organization and raise the funds needed to conduct the training programs. The first class was selected in 2002.

The program is open to all Illinois women who have a commitment to serve in public office and a willingness to commit the time necessary to participate fully. The application process begins in January with a mid-March deadline. IWIL's Delegate Selection Committee reviews candidate applications, and the Committee interviews finalists personally. Class Delegates are announced in early April, and the first session is held in June.

137 September 14th, 2005.

Delegates must obtain permission from their employers in order to participate fully, and attendance at all sessions is mandatory. The program includes an extensive session on fundraising and their final assignment is to put that training to work in organizing the annual Fundraiser/Graduation event.[138]

We developed a personal friendship with Debra Shore and got to know her in the months leading to Primary Election Day. In the process, we shared in her joy. We would have shared in her sorrow, too, but there was little sorrow in this campaign. I told her once that a great book title for her campaign would be "All the Right Moves." There were few low points in this campaign because Shore poured all of her being into this campaign.

She ran one of the best local campaigns. Her strategy was to meet everybody and anybody. The idea is to "show up." Even if she knew that she could not possibly get the support of a Ward Committeeman or an elected official, she would still meet with that person. She did not avoid people who she knew would not or could not support her.

On the evening of October 5th 2005, Debra Shore gave her stump speech to the Reading on Walden Political Discussion group. That evening we were only able to garner a dozen people, but she blew all of them away. She touched on issues like water, the environment and conservation. She said she was the only environmentalist running for the board.

On October 15th, 2005, we learned that one of the sitting Commissioners, Bus Yourell, was planning to resign, and not run for reelection. Shore thought this boded well for her candidacy. Voters typically voted for candidates in this field that they were familiar with, and Bus Yourell certainly was a familiar name in Cook County Illinois politics. Things were slowly falling into place for Shore. The petition drive was going to start shortly with Shore's self-imposed goal of 16,000 signatures to bulletproof her from being knocked off the ballot if her petitions were challenged.

Change comes slowly, gradually, incrementally, and suddenly.

I always admired Shore's "tenacity" and "audacity." One time during

---

138 http://www.iwil.org

the campaign, she was attending a party that a Township Committeeman was sponsoring. This Committeeman was not one of her fans. She needed a ride there, but we could not help that evening. I expressed surprise to one of her campaign people that she would even be attending this event because I was aware of that Committeeman's strong feelings toward Shore. She went anyway, and I'm sure she wowed him.

That is what I admired most about Shore. She always kept doors open even a crack. She was in constant touch with a recognized, high-profile Ward Committeeman, and he liked her very much although publicly he did not support her. But they developed a great relationship. It paid long-term dividends for her and the Committeeman. Though, as she told me more than once, at least they won't work that hard against you if they have some type of relationship with you. This attitude carried her a long way personally and politically.

Shore was featured in the *Chicago Reader*. The article said that Shore thinks the Metropolitan Water Reclamation District could be key to the future of the region and the environment and that's why she's raising real money to win an office most candidates barely campaign for. "Candidates for Commissioner of the Metropolitan Water Reclamation District usually don't have Web sites, don't march in the Gay Pride Parade, and don't receive endorsements from Democracy for America "meetups." The board of commissioners is typically filled by Democratic organization veterans and longtime district employees, and campaigning typically means buttering up the committeemen who do the slating, passing out yard signs, and hoping your name comes first on the ballot."

"But Debra Shore isn't typical. A 53-year-old conservationist, she's the Howard Dean of this year's race, a dark horse outsider who's lining up heavyweight endorsements (including Congresswoman Jan Schakowsky, State Representative Julie Hamos, and Cook County Board commissioner Larry Suffredin), firing up young progressives, and raising some serious cash, over $80,000 in the last four months."[139]

This is what Debra Shore had posted on her website on November 9, 2005. She was genuinely excited about the rapid progress of the campaign.

---

139 Hayes, Christopher. "Running on Water." *Chicago Reader* [Chicago] 28 Oct. 2005, 1.

I hope you are as excited as I am about the momentum our campaign is building.

The October 28 cover story in *The Chicago Reader* about my run for the Metropolitan Water Reclamation District has produced many new volunteers eager to help elect someone with genuine conservation credentials to the board (go figure!).

The campaign was gaining momentum, volunteers, money and energy were pouring into the campaign just through the tenacity of this outstanding candidate.

Change comes slowly, gradually, incrementally, and suddenly.

NOVEMBER 12, 2005

We announced a petition drive on Saturday, November 12 and asked for volunteers. We didn't get a huge response from people. The Debra Shore candidacy was still slow in resonating. Neil Pomeranke, Shore and I went out for several hours that day and collected a large number of signatures. What was most important, though, was that we were able to talk to dozens of voters, and many later became volunteers for the campaign, especially for Election Day.

It was a great time for the three of us to get to know each other, and it was an investment in time in our community that would pay off dividends on primary Election Day for Shore. While the turnout was not what we had hoped for the petition drive, I never once heard Shore grumble or complain about that day.

The odds were clearly stacked against her because she was not a "regular Democrat." She would have to raise money the hard way, one donation at a time. She could not count on the big money contributors to come her way, at least not until she was the incumbent. She could not count on the main party stalwarts, although she did make a presentation to the Cook County Democratic Party for their endorsement of her candidacy. It was unlikely that the regular Democratic Party would endorse Debra Shore. Her political affiliation was with the Evanston Democratic Party, and it was her base and meant that she could count on a big vote plurality from Evanston. She was aware of how many votes she needed to win and was constantly moving toward that goal.

As of November 20, 2005, the campaign had collected 11,000 of the

16,000 signatures that she wanted.[140] Debra Shore also mentioned in an email that she would be appearing the next day, Monday, November 21st, before the Democratic party slate makers. Although she did not expect to get the endorsement, she did expect to make an impact. And she always thought it was important to "show up." Then she posted this on her website about the Democratic slate making process.

> Party leaders will meet on Monday, November 21 to hear candidates present their credentials and make their bids for the party's endorsement. In truth, they care about two things: money and organizational support.
> Can you help us show Debra's broad-based grassroots support by raising an additional $5,000 before Monday and by reporting the number of signatures you have collected on petitions so far?[141]

The party endorsed the two incumbents in the race and another candidate, Barrett Pedersen. The party endorsed Pedersen for the open seat. He was the Leyden Township committeeman and suburban chair of the Cook County Democratic Party. Barrett wanted to run two years earlier, but the party closed ranks around one of their own, according to sources inside the Democratic Party.

Our reputation as community activists was spreading. Now, our reputation as political organizers was getting around rather quickly. The Obama victory for United States Senate had established our reputation of being relentless organizers with an ability to bring divergent groups of people together for a common goal. Our group of volunteers was 50% African-American and 50% white.

For the most part, our group's political point of view was left leaning and progressive. The uniqueness of our group is that the volunteers expected nothing in return, except good government. Make us proud, I always liked to say to the candidates we are supporting. The Shakman decree, which outlawed politically-based hiring and was being enforced by United States Attorney Patrick J. Fitzgerald, was making life difficult for regular party organizations.

---

140 November 21, 2005 email from Debra Shore.
141 http://www.debrashore.org.

DECEMBER 2005

One of Debra Shore's goals for the campaign was to get the top spot on the ticket. It was drawn by lottery. If not the top spot, then the top woman on the ballot would suffice. She did end up the top woman on the ballot, albeit the second ballot position. She was pleased. Here is the *Chicago Sun Times* report on her petition filing on December 12, 2005. Debra Shore collected **20,194** signatures to bulletproof placement on the ballot. She had exceeded the goal of 16,000.

Then we received this personal email from Debra Shore on December 14th in which she told us she received 20,194 signatures circulated by 274 individuals. It was becoming obvious to us this was becoming a real grassroots campaign. She didn't have "powerful friends" and didn't have "big-time donors." She just had lots of little things slowly.

DEBRA SHORE FILES FOR CANDIDACY

I am excited to announce that this morning I filed my petitions as a candidate for the board of the Metropolitan Water Reclamation District of Greater Chicago. We had more than 20,000 signatures gathered by hundreds of volunteers from all reaches of Cook County.

I was the 21st candidate to file for office, which is auspicious because we will be celebrating victory on March 21! As far as we know, the other candidates filing for Water Reclamation District today were Dean Nichols, Dean Maragos, Jack Hagerty, Patricia Horton and the party-endorsed slate of Terry O'Brien, James Harris and Barrett Pedersen.

And we BEAT THE SLATE, which came in with 4,000 fewer signatures than we did!

This is a remarkable achievement, and I am humbled by the faith in me and in the democratic process that this effort represents. Manifold thanks go to all, but especially to Larry Wier who single-handedly collected more than 1,000 signatures to Justin Smith and Mark Perez of the League of Conservation Voters, to Adelaide Rowe and Bob Johnson, to Ben Helphand and Paul Smith of the Logan Square Neighborhood, to volunteers from the 44th and 49th wards, from the Human Rights Campaign and the Sierra Club and to many, many others.

20,000 signatures sends a powerful message, but it's not about me. It's about you, and the thousands more in our county who believe that government can and should be of the people, by the people and for the people. It,s about protecting our precious natural resources, about bringing fresh ideas to the Water Reclamation District, about integrity and

accountability in government. And it's about our collective vision of
supporting a sound economy and a sound ecology.

With your help and continued effort, we can work together toward a
healthy, sustainable future for all.[142]

~

Change comes slowly, gradually, incrementally, and suddenly.

And on December 22nd, Shore announced that they had raised
$150,000 and had $100,000 cash on hand. Quite a feat for an insurgent
candidate. "Sign on to the Winning Ticket. It's a Shore Thing! Hokey?
Yes. But today we learned that I will be second on the ballot and the first
woman listed for the March primary. This is excellent news because in
these down ballot races, such as for the Metropolitan Water Reclamation
District, ballot position is key. Since people can vote for three
candidates, being in the second position is very favorable. We're excited
indeed![143]

In early January 2006, I mentioned to Shore that I had a conversation
with State Representative Kevin Joyce, and that he thought the surest
thing in the Water Reclamation race was that Shore would win. He
wasn't supporting or endorsing Shore, but just making an observation.
Shore was delighted that she was on "Kevin's radar." She knew this
meant she was having an impact.

And along comes Alexi Giannoulias

On November 22nd I received a telephone call from Alexi
Giannoulias. He said, "My name is Alexi Giannoulias and Barack Obama
gave me your telephone number. I'm running for Illinois State Treasurer
and Barack thought you might be willing to help."

I was taken aback. If true, I was honored that Obama thought so
highly of Michelle and me. I had to find out. I was not sure about the
Obama connection, so I had to check Giannoulias out with Shomon. I
told him I would get back to him. He left his phone number.

I sent Shomon an e-mail:

Hi Dan:
Got a call from Alexi and he mentioned your name. Good guy?

---

142 http://www.debrashore.org.
143 Id.

Thanks

Shomon replied and said simply, yes, good guy!!! friend of Barack's.

Alexi Giannoulias gave me his cell phone number and said to please call anytime. I learned to spell his name that day, have not forgotten since, and have yet to misspell G-I-A-N-N-O-U-L-I-A-S.

Had I read Michael Sneed on the 20th of November, I would have seen her blurb. The information, as usual was good. "Buzzville . . . Is Sen. Barack Obama (D-Ill.) using his ever-growing political clout in the state treasurer's race? -Translation: Buzz among politicos is that Alexi Giannoulias, the son of a prominent banking family and a veteran of Obama's senate campaign, will throw his hat into the treasurer's race as a liberal Democrat."[144]

And then on the 25th shortly after my call, Shomon had the publicity machine for Giannoulias on a roll as this appeared in the *Chicago Sun Times*. Dan was the chief strategic architect of this campaign and had a plan in place that would catapult Giannoulias to victory. Shomon is a master political strategist having devised the plan for Obama's United States Senate victory. It was important to Obama's national standing that Giannoulias show his political muscle. It had to be proved that the United States Senate victory was not a fluke and that Obama was the most powerful political figure in Illinois politics. Much like in 2000, when Bill Clinton was the most powerful figure in Illinois politics, Obama had to stand on his own, and he would prove that through Giannoulias. Since Shore had been campaigning for months and was starting to resonate with voters too, it was clear that this strategy would work.

"Alexi Giannoulias, a 29-year-old Chicago banker, was once a professional basketball player in Greece. Now Giannoulias wants to try out life in the political court by running in the Democratic primary for state treasurer."[145]

Giannoulias got into the race very late because he waited to see whether the sitting Illinois State Treasurer, Judy Baar Topinka, would run for reelection or announce for Governor. When Topinka announced her run

---

144 "Michael Sneed." *Chicago Sun-Times* (IL) November 20, 2005, Final, News: A04.
145 Mary Wisniewski. "Chicago banker seeking Democratic nomination for state treasurer." *Chicago Sun-Times* (IL) November 25, 2005, Final, Financial.

for Governor, Giannoulias immediately jumped. He knew better than to take on an "entrenched incumbent."

Giannoulias was a young twenty-nine year old banker, a former college basketball player, and a professional basketball player in Europe. I asked Giannoulias what experience he has that would qualify him to be Illinois State Treasurer. He told me about his family banking experience and his educational background. I said, "How unique an idea, a State Treasurer that understands managing money through education and experience."

We didn't know it at the time, but Giannoulias would be managed by our friend and fellow Shomon-ite, Doug Price. Shomon had drawn the political blueprint for this campaign, and Doug Price[146] would carry it out. Price was one of the original Shomon-ites and worked some early campaigns with Shomon, Mike Jordan and Obama.

We already had our hands full trying to help Shore in her run for Water Reclamation. We were fully committed to helping her.

One of the first projects for Giannoulias was gathering petitions for placement on the ballot.

Since we had been through this process before, we knew that we had to be careful. We were running against the party this time. Giannoulias jumped in the race at the last minute, therefore we had a short window of time to collect signatures for him. We wanted to make sure that we did the job correctly and could fight against any challenges. The odds were stacked against us because of the time. Organizational skills and experience had come into play. We called everyone we knew who would help.

We had long completed our petition work for Shore and so the field was clear for us to help Giannoulias.

One great help in collecting signatures was Robert Davis who was able to gather hundreds of signatures for Giannoulias.

Meanwhile, many obstacles were placed in front of Giannoulias every step of the way. But he overcame them, we gathered signatures, and he filed his petitions. Then comes Illinois Speaker of the House Michael Madigan and his cohorts. Madigan argued that the integrity of the party endorsement process had to be protected, therefore they were challenging

---

146 Doug Price had a heart attack and was briefly hospitalized during this period. He was able to return and continue to successfully manage the campaign.

Giannoulias' petitions.

But Madigan had a double standard, failing to challenge the petitions of a sitting governor who would surely receive party support, Gov. Rod Blagojevich. Former Chicago alderman Edwin Eisendrath was challenging the governor, and the bad blood between Madigan and Blagojevich was becoming legendary. The Illinois' Democratic Party will not try to remove former Chicago alderman Edwin Eisendrath from the March primary ballot for governor, we found to our astonishment, however, the party was supporting an effort to have Giannoulias removed as Democratic candidate for state treasurer.[147]

Many of the challenged petitions were gathered by the **Reading on Walden Political Discussion Group** volunteers, and we knew them to be valid.

On January 4, 2006, Giannoulias attended the regular meeting of the Reading on Walden Political Discussion Group and spoke to us. He stayed and listened to the band play. We discussed the petition challenges he was receiving and how we could help since it was many of our petitions that were being challenged. The Illinois Board of Elections had contacted us and some of our members. We were confident about beating back the challenge and knew that since we played by the rules, we would not have a problem. We were able to successfully defend the challenge.

Al Kindle would be proud. We beat the machine and upheld Giannoulias' signatures.[148] It proved again that doing the right thing, not taking shortcuts, pays off dividends. While he was distracted from his campaign for a short time, Giannoulias would remain on the ballot.

We all knew of the political motivations behind the challenge. Madigan was threatened by Obama, and now he would have to worry about the additional threat from Giannoulias. This did not sit well with those of us involved in the campaign.

My observation of this event was that it catapulted Giannoulias from being an untested young man to a battle-tested veteran. And it happened almost that fast.

---

147 DOUG FINKE STATE CAPITOL BUREAU. "Eisendrath escapes objection; But Democrats want Giannoulias removed from treasurer ballot. "*State Journal Register* [Springfield, Ill.] 28 Dec. 2005.
148 Al Kindle was a paid political consultant for the Giannoulias campaign.

Later in the campaign, Giannoulias was the victim of a smear campaign and false rumors from Madigan, alleging that Giannoulias had mob ties, which Giannoulias successfully overcame. Madigan was very threatened by this candidate as a threat to his power and his plans for his daughter Lisa's future as either governor or to succeed Obama in the US Senate (should Obama become President). We watched as Giannoulias turned from a raw 29 year-old untested young man to a 30 year-old polished politician.

Giannoulias, who was eventually elected as Illinois State Treasurer, was given no chance to win the Democratic nomination. However, Obama, through his political director and confidant Shomon, quickly reassembled his grassroots team from 2004 to help Giannoulias win. Others speculated that should Obama become President of the United States, Giannoulias could very well succeed him in the United States Senate.

It was a show of power and strength for Barack Obama and another great victory that proved that his elevation on the national scene was not a fluke. These victories may very well have led to his presidential campaign.

On December 5, 2005, several weeks after my conversation with Giannoulias, this appeared in the *Chicago Tribune*: U.S. Sen. Barack Obama (D-Ill.) said his endorsement of Alexi Giannoulias, 29, vice president of the Giannoulias family's Broadway Bank in Chicago, was not a challenge to the slating process of the state Democratic Party. Instead, he said it was a reflection of his friendship with Giannoulias, who was an early supporter and financial backer of Obama's 2004 candidacy for the Senate. "I've got a very personal relationship with Alexi," Obama said. "He was critical for me in terms of reaching out to the Greek community, other ethnic communities in the city. He was there from the start, when people didn't give me a shot."[149]

We attended a fundraiser on Thursday evening, December 29th for Giannoulias at the Funky Buddha Lounge at 728 West Grand Chicago. Shomon mentioned to Giannoulias that we were working with Shore, and Alexi said that Shore is a terrific candidate. Edwin Eisendrath attended the reception and was lobbying for support among the crowd for his challenge to the sitting governor, Blagojevich. Also in attendance was State

---

149 Rick Pearson, Tribune political reporter Tribune staff reporter Ray Long contributed to this report. "Parties get set for busy primary; GOP, Democrats have rifts in ranks:" [Chicagoland Final,
CN Edition]. *Chicago Tribune* [Chicago, IL] 5 Dec. 2005, 2C.1. *Chicago Tribune*.

Representative Kevin Joyce.

Giannoulias told us that night that he felt tremendous pressure to win the race because of the Obama endorsement. He also was highly honored that Obama chose to support him. He talked about the enormous physical energy of Obama and of his great admiration for the man.

Finally, the petition challenges ended officially on January 24, 2006 when the Election Board decided that the petitions were valid. The state Democratic Party gave up on its attempt to try to have Giannoulias tossed from the March 21 ballot, setting up a Democratic primary battle with Paul Mangieri, Madigan's handpicked candidate from downstate Knox County.

And this is what Kristen McQueary reported in late January, shortly after the Madigan crowd gave up on the petition challenges. "Pressure's on, folks. . . He's got a spur up his rear end on this one," one source said of Madigan.[150]

Many of the early supporters of Alexi Giannoulias, who stood at a press conference with Giannoulias and Obama, had now abandoned him due to enormous pressure from Illinois House Speaker Michael Madigan. And Madigan also suggested to other state party leaders that they encourage the endorsement of Paul Mangieri. Madigan pressured all state representatives who supported Giannoulias and strongly suggested that they change their allegiances to Paul Mangeri. State House Representatives John Fritchey, Robin Kelly, Harry Osterman, David Miller and Will Davis refused Madigan's suggestion. State Senators Reverend James T. Meeks and Kwame Raoul also stood by Giannoulias' side, when many Democrats were abandoning him.

Congresswoman Jan Schakowsky announced in February her support for Giannoulias. Joining Schakowsky at the press conference was North Side Democrats state Rep. Harry Osterman and Cook County Commissioner Larry Suffredin.[151]

Debra Shore's Campaign is Smooth Sailing

Debra Shore's campaign continued its streak of great luck. On March

---

150 Kristen McQueary. "Kristen McQueary: Ding! Election season under way." *Daily Southtown* (Chicago, IL). January 29, 2006.

151 John Chase, Tribune staff reporter. "Race for treasurer splits Democrats ; GOP governor hopeful has tax-relief proposal: [North Final Edition]." *Chicago Tribune* 3 Feb. 2006.

10, 2006, the *Chicago Tribune* endorsed Shore for Cook County Commissioner of the Water Reclamation District. This was just the beginning of the slew of endorsements for her. While it was luck, this luck did not come by accident, but by design. She was prepared when she talked to the Editorial Boards.

"Priority One this year is the nomination of Debra Shore, a founding director of Friends of the Forest Preserves and editor of *Chicago Wilderness* magazine." the *Chicago Tribune* editorial stated. "Shore is a deeply respected and powerful voice in Chicago-area conservation circles, and her concern for the environmental quality of the district's land holdings—many of which citizens use just as they do forest preserves—would make her a welcome addition to a board that now devotes most of its energy to engineering issues. Shore has excellent ideas for policy changes to reduce the worsening impact of rainwater runoff as more and more of the Chicago area is covered by buildings and pavement."[152]

Then on March 13th, Shore received two more endorsements: The first was a ringing endorsement from the *Daily Southtown*. They cited Shore's commitment to the environment and safe water. There's usually not much interest in the Metropolitan Water Reclamation District, but there should be. The huge government agency has 2,100 workers and a budget of $800 million.[153] On the same date the *Chicago Sun Times* headline was "Add Shore to Water"[154] On March 15th, The *Daily Herald* did an excellent analysis of the race and pointed out the strengths and weakness of all the Democratic candidates.[155]

By March 19th, Shore's grassroots efforts were paying dividends. The *Chicago Sun Times* was writing stories acknowledging she had high name recognition. This, in spite of the fact that Board President Terrence O'Brien was also on the ballot.

Early election results from March 21, 2006 for Shore and Giannoulias

---

152 "Our choices for clean water: [Chicago Final Edition]. " *Chicago Tribune* [Chicago, IL] 10 Mar. 2006, 1.20. *Chicago Tribune*.
153 "Editorials : Our choices for water district." Daily Southtown (Chicago, IL) March 13, 2006.
154 "Add Shore to water district board." Chicago Sun-Times (IL) March 13, 2006, Final, Editorials: 39.
155 "Metropolitan Water Reclamation District: [Cook,D7,L4 Edition]." *Daily Herald* [Arlington Heights, IL] 15 Mar. 2006, 3.

as reported by the *Chicago Sun Times* had them both as the victors. In spite of the fact that 19th Ward politicians had stood with Alexi on the day of his announcement with Obama, Giannoulias' name was not on the 19th Ward palm card that was passed out to voters, much to our surprise. The name of Paul Mangeri was. The pressure from Speaker Madigan was that the ward organization was to follow the party line. Madigan had also sent precinct workers to the Ward as a show of strength.

Our group had placed Giannoulias the signs in the precincts, but many of them were crushed or stolen. We had our crews out passing palm cards that simply said, "Shore and Giannoulias."

The final vote total in the 19th Ward for Giannoulias was that he lost by 230 votes out of over 15000 votes cast. This was a great showing for Giannoulias and once again proved that Obama was not a fluke.

Shore's final tally was equally impressive. She received nearly 12% of the vote in the 19th Ward and 14% of the vote citywide. In a crowded field of nine candidates, Shore was the top vote-getter. Shore received a thousand more votes in the city of Chicago than the President of the Board, Terrence O'Brien. This, in spite of the fact that the party organizations were out in full force on behalf of O'Brien.

The vote results were certified for Shore, and here is how her website reported those results.

> Yesterday election officials in both the city and county certified the results of the March 21 primary election. I am absolutely thrilled to report that out of a field of nine candidates vying for three seats, I came in first. First in the city and first in the county. In Chicago, I placed in the top three vote-getters in 39 out of 50 wards; in the suburban townships, I placed in the top three in 27 out of 30. (When the precinct data become available, we will analyze the results in more detail. If you're interested in seeing this analysis, let us know.)
>
> . . .
>
> In the final result, more than 224,000 people voted for me.
>
> Let me thank you again. This was a Big Win. Clearly it's the result of hard work, a smart campaign, great direct mail pieces (thank you Pete Giangreco), a snappy web site (thank you Joe Grossmann and Phyllis Wier), and a fierce team of warriors (Adam, David, and Scott). I think it's also because people responded to our message – that water matters, that a

vision for the future of this region matters, that stewardship of the precious natural resources that sustain life on earth matters most of all.

Perhaps the most gratifying part of this win is that so many people had a hand in it and can rightly share in the excitement and reward. That's by far the most wonderful element of a genuine grassroots campaign and I am so proud and honored to have been a part of it.

— Debra Shore

~

Giannoulias and Shore Breeze to Victory, With the Obama Grassroots Movement the Real Victor

Alexi Giannoulias becomes Illinois State Treasurer and Debra Shore was elected. "I'm not running to be something, I'm running to do something," Giannoulias said.[156]

As in the 2004 Democratic Primary, the primary race essentially was the general election. Both Shore and Giannoulias breezed to victory in the general election. Amazingly, Shore again got the most votes in the General Election in spite of the fact that the President of the Board, Terrence O'Brien, was in the race. She was a political force.[157]

While Giannoulias had the tightest victory margin of all the statewide candidates, the outcome of his victory was never in doubt. For Giannoulias, who had never run for public office before, the victory was particularly sweet. It was not a sure thing that because Obama was supporting and endorsing Giannoulias, that it would be an automatic victory. That could have resulted in a voter backlash. In the final analysis, the victory or defeat in this race was in Giannoulias' hands. He proved up to the task and was widely touted to have a bright future in Illinois. He had everything thrown at him, and he withstood the onslaught from the big guns in the Democratic Party. Like Obama, Giannoulias signs were crushed and mangled and he still survived and thrived. That was the real test for Alexi.

Michelle and I attended his victory party on election night and watched how this green, inexperienced young man had turned into a

156 Tara Malone *Daily Herald* Staff Writer. "Giannoulias victory mirrors trend for state offices: [All Edition]." *Daily Herald* [Arlington Heights, IL] 8 Nov. 2006, 19.
157 Chris Fusco, Kate Grossman and Janet Rausa Fuller. "Democrats sweep statewide offices: Giannoulias to be one of state's youngest elected officials ever." Chicago Sun-Times (IL) November 8, 2006, Final, 2006 Election Extra: A9.

seasoned political veteran.

He said in his victory speech, "I'm not running to be something, I'm running to do something."

I believe him.

Giannoulias did not receive official party endorsement because of Madigan's influence and the fear on many regular Democrats and Ward organizations to stand up to Madigan. Giannoulias turned out to be a worthy adversary.

Giannoulias could have easily folded when his petitions were challenged, but he did not. Giannoulias could have folded when he failed to receive regular party support, including support from people who originally stood by him, and he could have backed off, but he didn't. He could have folded when Madigan spread false charges against him and his family bank business that had no basis in reality, only the reality that Madigan wanted him out of the way, but he didn't give up or fold.

Alexi never stopped believing in himself and the group of Shomon-ites around him stood by his side and never gave up.

Giannoulias has a bright future in politics, whether it is for another statewide office, including being Governor of Illinois. A member of the House of Representatives is also in the cards for him, or possibly a member of the exclusive club, the United States Senate. He has plenty of time to pursue any of those endeavors and will choose wisely.

He will always be Alexi Giannoulias to us, a talented, fine, caring human being. We are proud to call him friend.

Giannoulias' victory was not against the Republican Party and his Republican challenger, Sen. Christine Radogno (R-Lemont), but against the Democratic-endorsed candidate, Knox County State's Attorney Paul Mangieri, who had the full weight of Madigan and the Democratic Party machinery behind him. The deck was stacked against Giannoulias, and he fought back with the help of lots of people.

Madigan is not accustomed to losing, and he always gets what he wants, however, this time Madigan had faced something he had not seen before. Barack Obama had built a "machine," as Al Kindle had put it. He was fighting Kindle, who was a part of the Giannoulias campaign, who is a force unto himself. He was fighting the Shomon-ites, who learned how to win. The genius behind the Obama machine in Illinois was Shomon, and the large and growing cast of Shomon-ites. There is no question that many Democratic Party regulars supported Giannoulias out of fear that some of these grassroots, loosely-based organizations would support Giannoulias anyway and embarrass them once again by defeating the party apparatus. That was certainly the reason for Giannoulias' support from the 19th Ward.

When the final histories of these campaigns are written many years from now, historians will come to one conclusion: Barack Obama would be nowhere without the friendship he developed with one Dan Shomon. It was Dan Shomon who begat Mike Jordan and Doug Price and Michelle Presta and John Presta. And, as Andy Griffin once said on his show, "That is a lot of begetting."

The only thing left after the Giannoulias victory for Barack Obama to accomplish was becoming the President of the United States. That was my first reaction when I spent some time with him many moons ago in March 2000. "He's going to be President of the United States one day." I was certain. The timing I could not predict.

Sooner rather than later.

Congressman Jesse Jackson Jr. Opts Out of the Mayoral Race, Reads the Tea Leaves

The Mayoral race in February 2007 involved Barack Obama.

Bobby Rush had learned his lesson against Daley. Jesse Jackson Jr., would later learn a valuable lesson from Congressman Bobby Rush. The damage caused by a defeat to Mayor Richard M. Daley could be damaging to a politician's career. That is the reason in 2007, Jesse Jackson Jr. made a decision to opt out of the mayoral race. He cited a new majority in the Congress and his having a higher influence and visibility on the House Appropriations Committee.

The truth was, according to the political insiders we talked to, Jesse could read the writing on the wall. Daley was strong politically, and Jesse Jr. could not attract enough of the white vote or the lakefront liberal voters that was needed to win. He would also need another white candidate to split the vote with Daley, and that was now unlikely. Jesse Jr.'s negatives were much too high to defeat Daley, and while he could get close, being close does not elect you Mayor of Chicago.

Jesse Jr. became convinced he could not defeat Daley in 2007, but kept his name alive in case a serious indictment came down and then he would run. The indictment of Mayor Daley never happened. Had it happened, Jesse would step in. The only chance that Jesse had was an indictment, or a decision on Daley's part that he would step down.

Another failure for Jesse Jr. was his attempt to recruit Aldermanic candidates in every ward. He was able to only muster a handful, and those were lukewarm. Jesse Jr. could not find the right people to run on his ticket, and he was receiving a cool reception. He just did not have the direct contacts or the network outside of his turf in place to pull off something like that. Many of the Obama people who helped in 2004 were not enthusiastic about a Jackson candidacy. During the 2004 campaign, one of our volunteers, John Gunn, an African-American, picked up some brochures with Obama's and Jesse Jr.'s picture on the front. The next day John brought back all the brochures to us and said, "I can't sell this. The people I talk to don't like Jr. and frankly, I don't like Jr. either." John was honest enough to speak to us that way. So we stopped passing those brochures out to volunteers and returned them to headquarters.

Our group of 300 volunteers established a foothold for Obama outside of the African-American community. The ensuing snowballing effect that he helped to create led Obama to the next group and the next group.

Change comes slowly, gradually, incrementally, and suddenly.

CHAPTER 10

Barack Obama Decides to Run for President of the United States

~

It is true that in Barack Obama's quest for United States Senator of Illinois, it took "A Book, Two Bookstore Owners, 300 Volunteers and A Community to propel Barack Obama onto the national scene." But to compete for the ultimate prize, President of the United States, I'll freely admit it takes more than that.

A great book title for the United States Senate campaign of 2004, ironically, would be *It Takes a Village*[158] by Hillary Clinton. For Obama to defeat his multiple opponents in Illinois, it took a village. A very large village.

To be elected President of the United States, it takes much more than just a village. It takes many villages. It takes many towns. It takes many cities. It takes many states.

It takes *A Good Beginning*[159] in Iowa, New Hampshire, and South Carolina.

Those states alone would not be enough. Not with such formidable opposition as Hillary Rodham Clinton. It takes luck, and it takes skill. It takes organizational ability, and it takes money. These are all things that the Barack Obama of 2007/2008 had plenty of. It took one more

---

158 Clinton, Hillary Rodham. *It Takes a Village: And Other Lessons Children Teach Us*. New York: Simon & Schuster, 1996.
159 Contrast with Snicket, Lemony, and Brett Helquist. *The Bad Beginning*. New York: HarperCollins Publishers, 1999.

thing to obtain the Democratic nomination for President in 2008.

Oprah Winfrey. Again, a book lover is at center stage in playing a role in an Obama campaign, this time in the form of Oprah Winfrey.

Oprah was one of the keys to the Democratic nomination for Obama. She has been the key to success for many independent bookstores and many mega bookstores, too. She has revived the thirst and hunger again for reading and for books. Oprah, brought the "Book Discussion Group" to a new level and she brought a Presidential campaign to a new level.

It takes Oprah.

During Oprah Winfrey's twenty-plus years as a talk show host, there never was question that when an author appeared on her show to promote a book, the book would automatically have built-in sales. Oprah has influence because the viewing public trusts her judgment.

At our bookstore, the telephone would ring quite often immediately after The Oprah show announced the "Book Club" selection at 10:00 am. And the caller would ask, "Got that Oprah book?"

The more enthusiastic that Oprah was, the bigger the sales of the book would be and the more frantic the caller. And the earlier they would call, probably between commercials to be sure not to miss it, the caller would be even more frantic. Sales sharply increase when Oprah talks and gets behind a book.

It takes Oprah.

One complaint bookstores would have at the beginning of the Oprah Book Club was that "We never know what book Oprah will be featuring until it is too late. Often the book would be out-of-stock, the customer would have to order it, and sometimes you would lose the sale."

The Oprah Book Club fixed all that. Here is how it worked.

Two weeks prior to Oprah announcing her selection on the air, the particular publisher's rep that was carrying the book would always call and say, "We have the next Oprah book. It is $24.95 and how many would you like?" They wouldn't reveal the name because they didn't know or were sworn to secrecy. Bookstores could then order the book, sight unseen, book unknown because the bookstores trusted Oprah.

Then if a bookstore owner didn't have enough copies of the Oprah Book, you could only blame yourself.

Oprah has single-handedly created a "buzz" about reading with her Oprah Book Club selections. It was Oprah Winfrey who made the words "Book Discussion Group" a common part of our language. She has taken some unknown, obscure authors and made them into household names.

When Oprah started her Oprah Book Club, the sky was the limit in book sales. She always had influence on book sales, but the "Oprah Book Club" just took her influence to another level: the stratosphere.

Oprah's Book Club even inspired books written about the "Oprah Book Club." One such book is *Reading with Oprah: The Bookclub that Changed America by Kathleen Rooney*.[160] Here are some publishers' comments about this book and about Oprah from Kathleen Rooney.

> Adored by its fans and deplored by critics, Oprah's Book Club has been at the center of cultural authority and literary taste. This book explores the club's revolutionary fusion of books, television, and commerce. The author demonstrates how the club that Barbara Kingsolver calls "one of the best possible uses of a television set" has, according to Wally Lamb, "gotten people of all ages to read, to read more, and to read widely."

That is the essence of the Oprah Book Club. It has "gotten people to read," who otherwise would not have. What special attribute does Oprah possess that makes America trust her? She has that way about her. She exposes her personal vulnerabilities in her show, and she is not afraid to confront them. She has dieted all these years. We have watched her gain weight, lose weight, gain weight, and lose weight. The common thread throughout the process is that we always love Oprah with her vulnerabilities and all.

Before the introduction of Oprah's Book Club, she was a powerhouse for the publishing industry. The only requirement for the publisher: Oprah must love the book. Publishers lobbied heavily to get a book in the Oprah Winfrey door.

Oprah was instrumental in introducing another weight loss/health

---

160 Rooney, Kathleen. *Reading with Oprah: The Book Club That Changed America.* Fayetteville: University of Arkansas Press, 2005.

guru-Bob Greene. His latest book, *The Best Life Diet*,[161] is a necessary read for anyone serious about weight loss and maintaining good health. This book, coupled with an earlier publication, *Get With the Program!*[162] are must haves for the health conscious library.

She introduced a medical doctor, Dr. Andrew Weil, who is a visionary doctor when it comes to your health and well-being. Weil is more in the alternative medicine area, but that by no means takes anything away from his legitimacy as a health guru.

His first book, *Spontaneous Healing*,[163] is a passionate and convincing book about alternative medicine. He makes use of components of recognized systems of the body, and reveals how the body can heal itself and how those who are inflicted can enhance that healing. Some of his other worthwhile books are *8 Weeks to Optimum Health*[164] and *Natural Health, Natural Medicine*.[165]

These books influenced our own lives because of the issues addressed in the books. One of the best books on the subject of health and weight loss is *You on a Diet: The Owners Manual*[166] by Drs. Mehmet Oz and Dr. Michael Roizen. They have become celebrities in their own right and deservedly so. Oprah features these two unique and talented personalities on her show on a regular basis.

Dr. Oz is an alternative-medicine maverick and a cardiologist known to implement acupuncture during open-heart surgery. Dr. Michael Roizen developed the Real Age concept of calculating one's biological age, as opposed to chronological age. With a few modifications in diet and exercise, you can suddenly become younger in Real Age.

They use analogies such as comparing the adrenals to the shape of Mr. Potato Head's hat. They give anatomical guided tours of the body. What they do is make health fun.

161 Greene, Bob. *The Best Life Diet*. New York: Simon & Schuster, 2006.
162 Greene, Bob. *Get with the Program!: Getting Real About Your Health, Weight, and Emotional Well-Being*. New York: Simon & Schuster, 2002.
163 Weil, Andrew. *Spontaneous Healing: How to Discover and Enhance Your Body's Natural Ability to Maintain and Heal Itself*. New York: Knopf, 1995.
164 Weil, Andrew. *Eight Weeks to Optimum Health: A Proven Program for Taking Full Advantage of Your Body's Natural Healing Power*. New York: A.A. Knopf, 1997.
165 Weil, Andrew. *Natural Health, Natural Medicine: A Comprehensive Manual for Wellness and Self-Care*. Boston: Houghton Mifflin, 1995.
166 Roizen, Michael F., and Mehmet Oz. *You--the Owner's Manual: An Insider's Guide to the Body That Will Make You Healthier and Younger*. New York: Harper Resource, 2005.

I was struck by their comparisons of the body to things, like saying if you eat red meat, the meat rots in your intestines. Why would you want to eat something that rots there? This was unhealthy, they would point out.

How often should you get your thyroid level checked?

How much gas does the average person produce in a day?

Some of their other books are great too. *You: On a Diet: You, on a Diet: The Owner's Manual for Waist Management.*[167] The team behind "*You: The Owner's Manual An Insider's Guide to the Body That Will Make You Healthier and Younger*"[168] applies its signature wit and wisdom to food metabolism and nutrition. Roizen and Oz pack in a lot of material - quizzes, 'factoids', and 'myth busters' along with diet and exercise plans, recipes, and a two-week 'rebooting' program.

The following list is the 65 selections to date of the Oprah Winfrey Book Club.

1   September 1996: *The Deep End of the Ocean* by Jacquelyn Mitchard

2   October 1996: *Song of Solomon* by Toni Morrison

3   November 1996: *The Book of Ruth* by Jane Hamilton

4   December 1996: *She's Come Undone* by Wally Lamb

5   February 1997: *Stones from the River* by Ursula Hegi

6   April 1997: *The Rapture of Canaan* by Sheri Reynolds

7   May 1997: *The Heart of a Woman* by Maya Angelou

8   June 1997: *Songs In Ordinary Time* by Mary McGarry Morris

9   September 1997: *The Meanest Thing To Say* by Bill Cosby

#10   September 1997: *A Lesson Before Dying* by Ernest J. Gaines

#11   October 1997: *A Virtuous Woman* by Kaye Gibbons

#12   October 1997: *Ellen Foster* by Kaye Gibbons

#13   December 1997: *The Treasure Hunt* by Bill Cosby

---

167 Roizen, Michael F., Mehmet Oz, Ted Spiker, Lisa Oz, and Craig Wynett. *You, on a Diet: The Owner's Manual for Waist Management*. New York: Free Press, 2006.

168 Roizen, Michael F., and Mehmet Oz. *You, the Owner's Manual: An Insider's Guide to the Body That Will Make You Healthier and Younger.* New York: Harper Resource, 2005.

#14   December 1997: *The Best Way to Play* by Bill Cosby

#15   January 1998: *Paradise* by Toni Morrison

#16   March 1998: *Here on Earth* by Alice Hoffman

#17   April 1998: *Black and Blue* by Anna Quindlen

#18   May 1998: *Breath, Eyes, Memory* by Edwidge Danticat

#19   September 1998: *What Looks Like Crazy on an Ordinary Day* by Pearl Cleage

#20   October 1998: *Midwives* by Chris Bohjalian

#21   December 1998: *Where the Heart Is* by Billie Letts

#22   January 1999: *Jewel* by Bret Lott

#23   February 1999: *The Reader* by Bernhard Schlink

#24   March 1999: *The Pilot's Wife* by Anita Shreve

#25   April 1999: *I Know This Much Is True* by Wally Lamb

#26   May 1999: *White Oleander* by Janet Fitch

#27   June 1999: *Mother of Pearl* by Melinda Haynes

#28   September 1999: *Tara Road* by Maeve Binchy

#29   October 1999: *The Poisonwood Bible* by Barbara Kingsolver

#30   November 1999: *Vinegar Hill* by A. Manette Ansay

#31   December 1999: *A Map of the World* by Jane Hamilton

#32   January 2000: *Gap Creek* by Robert Morgan

#33   February 2000: *Daughter of Fortune* by Isabel Allende

#34   March 2000: Back Roads by Tawni O'Dell

#35   April 2000: *The Bluest Eye* by Toni Morrison

#36   May 2000: *While I Was Gone* by Sue Miller

#37   June 2000: *River, Cross My Heart* by Breena Clarke

#38   August 2000: *Open House* by Elizabeth Berg

#39   September 2000: *Drowning Ruth* by Christina Schwarz

#40   November 2000: *House of Sand and Fog* by Andre Dubus III

#41   January 2001: *We Were the Mulvaneys* by Joyce Carol Oates

#42 March 2001: *Icy Sparks* by Gwyn Hyman Rubio

#43 May 2001: *Stolen Lives: Twenty Years in a Desert Jail* by
Malika Oufkir

#44 June 2001: *Cane River* by Lalita Tademy

#45 September 2001: *The Corrections* by Jonathan Franzen

#46 November 2001: *A Fine Balance* by Rohinton Mistry

#47 January 2002: *Fall on Your Knees* by Ann-Marie
MacDonald

#48 April 2002: *Sula* by Toni Morrison

#49 June 2003: *East of Eden* by John Steinbeck

#50 September 2003: *Cry, The Beloved Country* by Alan Paton

#51   January 2004: *One Hundred Years of Solitude* by Gabriel
García Marquez

#52 April 2004: *The Heart Is a Lonely Hunter* by Carson
McCullers

#53 May 2004: *Anna Karenina* by Leo Tolstoy

#54 September 2004: *The Good Earth* by Pearl S. Buck

#55 June 2005: *The Sound and the Fury, As I Lay Dying, and
Light in August* by William Faulkner

#56 September 2005: *A Million Little Pieces* by James Frey

#57 January 2006: *Night* by Elie Wiesel

#58 January 2007: *The Measure of a Man: A Spiritual
Autobiography* by Sidney Poitier

#59 March 2007: *The Road* by Cormac McCarthy

#60 June 2007: *Middlesex* by Jeffrey Eugenides

#61 October 2007: *Love in the Time of Cholera* by Gabriel
García Márquez

#62 November 2007: *The Pillars of the Earth* by Ken Follett

#63 January 2008: *A New Earth* by Eckhart Tolle

#64 September 2008: *The Story of Edgar Sawtelle* by David
Wroblewski

#65 September 2009: *Say You're One* of Them by Uwem
Akpan

Thus, the impact of Oprah in the publishing world is tremendous. She had endorsed many books, but she had not previously endorsed any political candidate for office.

Not until Obama came along. What a title, *Along Came Obama* by Oprah Winfrey. The impact she had on Obama's obtaining the Democratic nomination is significant. Oprah Winfrey has parlayed her love of books and her wish to see real change come into this world by supporting Obama.

Yes, Oprah has been a large part of our life as bookstore owners, and now she had a big impact on the ultimate prize, President of the United States. Oprah, Michelle, and I were involved in both books and Barack Obama.

It takes Oprah.

You Were Born in the United States, You Can Be President

My papa, Giovanni Presta, was fond of telling me that I could be President of the United States because I was born in this country. You needed to be a natural-born citizen to become President of the United States. He told me this countless times, and each time he told me, it was like his first time.

The subject of United States Presidency came up often for discussion in our household. My papa loved to tell me the story of his own papa. His father, my grandfather, Serafino Presta, was an American citizen. My grandfather became an American citizen in 1894 and was in America for a second tour starting in 1901, the same year that Theodore Roosevelt was the Vice President of the United States and the President of the United States in 1901. He had succeeded William McKinley, who was assassinated that year.

My grandpapa was born in Italy in 1869. He had come to America to find work and support his family. He worked on the railroads in Summit, Illinois and made a decent, living wage.

What people do not realize, my father would state, is that the depression was all over Europe too. In many ways it was much worse there, and it set the stage for Adolph Hitler to come to power and World War II.

In late 1932, Franklin Roosevelt became President of the United States. In addition, papa would proudly recall what his papa (my grandpapa) told him, "America is going to be all right. They just elected another Roosevelt."

My dad repeated that to me a number of times over the years.

"America is going to be all right. They just elected another Roosevelt."

My grandpapa was in America during the first Roosevelt Administration and admired Teddy Roosevelt, a Republican, greatly. He had many unkind things to say about Herbert Hoover, who grandpapa said did not care about common people, he only cared about the wealthy and the privileged class.

Franklin Roosevelt was a Democrat, and my grandpapa called himself a Democrat. My father also called himself a Democrat. The Democrats, my grandpa and papa would say, care about the common people. Democrats tended to increase the number of immigrants allowed into America every year, papa would say. My papa was able to come and bring my mama and two siblings because Harry Truman lightened up on the requirement for entry into the country in the late 1940's.

My dad was a Democrat. He voted for Stevenson: twice. He voted for Kennedy. Lyndon Baines Johnson. Hubert Humphrey. George McGovern. Jimmy Carter, well Jimmy Carter just once and then he voted for Ronald Reagan. That is a story for another time, but it is certainly a reflection of America in 1980.

Anyway, the Presidency has been a passion of mine passed down from my papa to me and from his papa to him.

Barack Obama.

Never did I dream that I would ever meet, much less get to know, a future President of the United States. It is an unlikely story that can only happen in America. What is wonderful about America is that a common, decent human being, such as Barack Obama, can rise up and become President of the United States.

It was not that many years ago that Obama walked among us. He is Everyman. He worked side by side in the "Gardens," known as Altgeld Gardens, one of Chicago's toughest communities on the far Southside of Chicago. It takes personal toughness to survive an environment like "The Gardens."

When Obama decided to run for the Presidency is unknown outside his political circle, but it was obvious to me that there was movement around May of 2006. Many of the media types were smelling it. The plan was already in place and, the decision was made. It was likely that after "The Speech," the talk of his political future intensified. Obama started to help others campaign and was already starting to collect favors from other politicians.

I was walking down historic Longwood Drive in my Chicago community, when I saw Mike Flannery at the Memorial Day Parade in 2006. Mike was not working that day as a reporter but was enjoying the parade with his family. Mike is the Political Editor of CBS Channel 2 News in Chicago, who was aware that I had a special personal relationship with Obama. He suddenly stopped and pointed at me and said in his unique style that I had seen many times on television, "Barack Obama: Running for president or not?"

I was a bit startled at first, but I regained my composure and simply looked him in the eye and said, "Yes, of course he is."

The time was May 2006, and it was obvious to me.

Striking when the iron is hot is a worn cliché, but in this case descriptive of what Obama was up against. He had to run.

Now. 2008.

There was no waiting if he ever had a chance to reside on Pennsylvania Avenue. 2012 wouldn't do it. 2016 wouldn't do it. Nor 2020.

Now.

Now is Barack Obama's time. In this year, 2008. Hillary Clinton will be formidable, but it is worth the risk. She could be beaten. It would not be easy to defeat her, but it could be done.

Hillary Clinton would be running as the "entrenched incumbent." The entitled one to the Presidency. Obama had some experience running against an "entrenched incumbent" who was really the incumbent. It was the only chance one of our own would have to get to the White House and make a difference in this country. A country that President George W. Bush has run into the ground.

We need to put all that behind us now and get behind Barack Obama for President.

I did not have any inside information and did not discuss it with people close to Obama. Not that anyone inside the Obama inner circle would say to me, "Hey John, Barack's running for President. Don't say anything."

No, that was not it at all. Obama's words and actions on April 12, 2006, showed he was making a run for the nation's highest office. The information was my observation based on my experiences around Obama. On April 12, 2006, I received an email from Nate Tamarin, who was Obama's deputy campaign manager in 2004. The email read to the effect that he was leaving the Hopefund and would be moving back to Chicago. I read this as a signal that Obama was in the early stages of a Presidential bid and would be setting up his campaign headquarters here in Chicago.

To me this was "prima facie evidence" that things were changing. After Obama's election to the United States Senate, he appointed Tamarin to be the Executive Director of the Hopefund. These Political PACs are set-up by Senators who are ambitious and running for higher office, and Obama did this shortly after taking office. He could only entrust this position to Tamarin.

Tamarin said he was leaving the Hopefund and was going to do some traveling with his wife. My thought was, "Some well-deserved time off before the really big campaign begins."

How else can they knock off the incumbent, well, not quite the incumbent, but she will certainly act that way.

Hillary Clinton.

Tamarin's email said he was coming to Chicago to look for a job. Hmm. I thought. I then called Tamarin, and he told me that, yes, he had found a job with The Strategy Group, a political consulting group that specializes in political mailings. The evidence continues to mount. The Strategy Group is a national campaign group powerhouse headed by Pete Giangreco and company, specializing in political mailings. Tamarin would not leave the "hottest political prospect of the century" to go work for a nationally known political consultant, unless it was directly related to the "hottest political prospect of the century."

The focus of the first meetings with the Obama campaign in late 2006 and early 2007, was about the Iowa caucus and only the Iowa caucus.

Iowa would be the battleground. There was talk that Hillary Clinton would bypass Iowa, much like Bill Clinton in 1992. But Obama would not be bypassing Iowa. John Edwards, the 2004 candidate for Vice-President, was already campaigning in Iowa, and he was viewed by the Obama campaign as the chief rival. Iowa would be the major battleground. Iowa would be the focal point. Obama's small group of trusted friends had already laid out the path to victory in Iowa.

Obama was convinced he could win it with the grassroots groups organized from his 2004 United State Senate bid, the Debra Shore campaign, and the Alexi Giannoulias campaign. Many of the groups were still in place. Like the Reading on Walden Political Discussion Group. The geographical proximity to Iowa was a clear advantage for Obama.

The Obama campaign recruited the old-timers, many were Shomonites, to make telephone calls on behalf of Barack Obama to assure that crowds would be at events for Barack Obama. Nothing was being taken to chance.

All of this was geared toward the official announcement on February 11, 2007. It had become bigger than all of us. Yes, we helped give Barack Obama a jump-start in politics. If he didn't accomplish it with our help, he would have eventually accomplished it with someone else's help. Maybe then would have been too late. There was a reason Dan Shomon walked into our bookstore and our life when he did. There was a reason that Barack Obama lost that Congressional race but had so many victories to declare that night. He just didn't know it yet.

The Presidential campaign started in Iowa. The organizing portion was twelve months in the making. Obama spent a lot of time in Iowa. I was at the campaign headquarters once in Cedar Rapids and once in Dubuque. Many of our 300 volunteers from the United States Senate race volunteered in Iowa and did great work. But now for the Presidential election, this number would jump exponentially. Alexi Giannoulias worked the streets in Iowa on behalf of Barack Obama. So did Debra Shore. And even his former political opponents such as Dan Hynes did too. Many Illinois politicians made their way to Iowa.

The Obama campaign had already done its preparation for Iowa. Finding out why others won and, more importantly, why others lost.

They found, for example, that the Howard Dean people seemed to talk down to the Iowans. At least that was the perception of the Iowa people, according to Tamarin. Didn't know the price of wheat. Couldn't relate to farmers or had much empathy for them. Were overdressed for campaign sessions.

Yes, the Obama campaign learned from those mistakes by the Dean campaign. They related to Iowans in ways no one else has ever before and probably ever will again. They got it right. Scary in a way. So many mistakes in 2000 and so few since. How is that possible?

The announcement day of February 11, 2007 was a long day. First the announcement in Springfield, then to Iowa, back to Illinois at the University of Illinois Pavilion, and then for an evening fundraiser at the Hyatt.

Here is what one of our 300 said about that day's ride to Springfield.

Feb 11, 2007 - I took the Amtrak train to Springfield this weekend. I arrived at 10pm and rather sleepily checked into my hotel room. When I awoke, I saw streams of people getting off buses and flocking to the Old Capitol building where our 16th President often spoke. When I arrived there, I was met by a crowd of 15,000 white farmers, black mothers, businessmen, university students, children, and all people from all occupations, who had come from all over the Midwest. On such short notice, I was surprised to see such a huge and diverse crowd. I saw 15,000 people who had cancelled their plans for the weekend to meet in a small town in IL to stand out in subzero temperature. I saw 15,000 people who are fed up with the decisions that have been made for this country. I saw 15,000 voices begging for change. They chanted: Obama.

He stepped up the podium to "City of Blinding Lights." He spoke of bringing the soldiers home. He spoke of a universal healthcare plan. He spoke of more government support of higher education. He spoke of combating global warming and the energy crisis. He criticized the "smallness of our politics" and our current governments' avoidance of the big decisions. He spoke of transforming this nation. He spoke with unbelievable audacity and conviction. It was a low-key speech, anything but simple, with deeper undertones than most politicians can manage. What's more, he did it without a teleprompter.

"It was here, in Springfield, where North, South, East and West come together that I was reminded of the essential decency of the American people - where I came to believe that through this decency, we can build a more hopeful America.

"And that is why, in the shadow of the Old State Capitol, where Lincoln once called on a divided house to stand together, where common hopes and common dreams still, I stand before you today to announce my candidacy for President of the United States."

When he spoke, in his eyes we saw truth. Our toes were frozen, but his words warmed our hearts, and we became hopeful. I believe this man can and will change our country.

This man, as the Amtrak conductor suggested later that night on the way back to Chicago, is "the real deal."

By Kathleen Murphy (Brian Murphy's daughter)

⁓

Shomon had emailed me to invite me to volunteer that evening at the Hyatt for the finale to the "Announcement." It was a thrill for me. I was the ticket-taker at the door, and I saw people like Bill Daley, Bruce Sagan, Manny Sanchez, Pat Sanchez, Penny Pritzker, Alexi Giannoulias, Lisa Madigan, Dan Hynes and hundreds of others.

During the speech Obama gave that night at the Hyatt, he talked about his girls and how they asked him, "Are you still doing that President thing?" That night he brought up the idea of getting his kids a puppy once they got to the White House. "Now they are really on board." And the crowd laughed. He talked about passing up wealth for public service. Michelle Obama also spoke to the crowd that night and talked about public service.

Mike Jordan was there with his wife. Jordan re-introduced me to Michelle Obama, who was just stunning and glowing. I just thought what a great first lady she will make.

I was able to talk to Obama after his talk to the crowd and wished him luck. He asked how Michelle and the bookstore were and in that order. In front of me was Powell's Bookstore owner Brad Jonas. He was the man who once owned nearly 4000 copies of Obama's book, *Dreams from My Father: A Story of Race and Inheritance*.

It was exhilarating to have been part of this opening day celebration. A decision was made early in the campaign that a major emphasis would be made on the Iowa caucus, not so much for the number of delegates it could produce, but the psychological advantage it could give the Obama campaign.

> Sweet column: Obama's Illinois operation. Campaign to launch "Camp Obama"
>
> CHICAGO—Democratic White House hopeful Barack Obama has state directors and paid staff in the early primary and caucus states of Iowa, New Hampshire, South Carolina and Nevada. Based in his national campaign headquarters on Michigan Avenue in Chicago — the home office for Camp Obama — Obama is building a separate political operation in Illinois.
>
> The point is not just to win the Feb. 5 Illinois primary — Obama has a lock on that election — but to tap into his tremendous strength in Illinois and train people on his behalf.
>
> The Illinois Obama operation has already started to train workers to send to the other states to help.[169]

During the month of April 2007, the campaign held trainings in Illinois all over the state with the many grassroots groups formed in 2004. The regular party organizations were also involved. And the groups that were instrumental in helping Alexi Giannoulias and Debra Shore in 2006, were also involved.

Seminars were conducted by campaign staff in Illinois: Rockford, Rock Island, Peoria, Skokie, Woodstock, Joliet, Highland Park, Carbondale, Lake Zurich, Macomb, Quincy, Winnetka, Collinsville, St. Charles, Arlington Hts., Oak Park, Evanston, Schaumburg, Naperville, Lombard, Homewood and all parts of the Chicago area: north northwest, southeast, southwest and south side.

Our meeting was held April 29th at World Folk Music Company in the evening. A good crowd came and many in attendance did indeed work in Iowa and most were assigned to Cedar Rapids, Iowa. The geographical proximity of Iowa made this a perfect fit. The drive from Chicago and different parts of Iowa varied, from three to five hours, and usually required a weekend of work.

Thousands of volunteers were recruited in Illinois to work the Iowa caucus. It just made sense to recruit a group of people who were seasoned campaign veterans. The focus of the group was to identify voters and caucus goers and then figure out a strategy to assure that they arrived at the caucus sites on time.

---

169 Lynn Sweet. "Getting ready to roll - Obama's Illinois workers train to help campaign elsewhere." *Chicago Sun-Times* (IL) May 3, 2007, Final, Editorials: 37.

It was a much different campaign than the Illinois Senate race and the statewide Giannoulias race. It was more complex.

Meanwhile, much groundwork was being done in future caucus and primary states. The Obama campaign made sure that a presence was felt in all of the early states and developed contingency plans for the later states in case the primary went past those few early states.

Another Grassroots Victory, This Time in Iowa

Illinois volunteers helped to carry the day in Iowa. Obama came in first in the Iowa caucus held on January 3, 2008. Obama received 37.6% of the vote, John Edwards 29.7% of the vote and Hillary Clinton 29.5% of the vote. Barack Obama had beat the expectations game and was considered a huge winner in Iowa. And it was all due to the strength in having Illinois volunteers helping there and the early training starting in late 2006.

All this was done under the radar again and out of the Clinton campaign's view. There was some talk that Hillary Clinton would ignore Iowa and focus on the future primaries, but the feeling became that if she ignored it, Obama and Edwards would blow her out of the campaign. They would have.

This forced the Clinton campaign to commit resources it hadn't planned on, according to sources inside the Obama campaign. The Obama camp did extremely well in the areas nearest Illinois on the eastern part of Iowa. Cedar Rapids, Davenport and Dubuque were strongholds that were flooded with volunteers from Illinois. Des Moines also was a great strength for Obama, as was the area on the west near Sioux City.

Our friend Mike Jordan worked the Iowa caucus and was noticed by an AP reporter. He was featured in an AP story. Mike always says publicly and privately, "Barack is the same man I met in 1998 as he is today," Mike said. "Isn't that incredible? Possibly will be the most powerful man in America."

It was the Iowa caucus that set the tone for the campaign. Throughout the primary, Obama showed his organizational skills, which are great, and Obama breezed to victory in every single caucus state.

Many events occurred between January 3, 2008 and the evening

Obama declared himself the presumptive nominee. Grassroots and Netroots carried the day all across the country. The Illinois experiences had taught the campaign so much, and much of the knowledge and skill was applied on a national level.

Meetup on Steroids

The Obama campaign had also taken the internet fundraising and volunteer recruiting to a new level never before seen in political history. Fundraising would not be a problem as it was in 2000. The campaign had received up to this point, donations from 1.5 million distinct donors. An amazing feat. And to think not many years ago, in a kitchen in Jesse Jackson Jr.'s campaign headquarters, Obama told Michelle and me how he was so proud of receiving donations from 25,000 individuals who donated to his United States Senate campaign. But what a drop in the bucket 25,000 is compared to 1.5 million donors and climbing.

Changes come slowly, gradually, incrementally and suddenly.

To think, it can be traced back to our friend Glenn Brown many years earlier who said "You gotta try this "Meetup.com" thing and this "Obama for Senate Yahoo Group" thing.

Glenn Brown will be remembered as a significant footnote in the Obama campaign history, and the campaign will be forever grateful to him.

We can all be proud of the achievements made in this campaign. Indeed, a small group can change the world.

"Never doubt that a small group of committed citizens can change the world; indeed, it's the only thing that ever has!"
— Margaret Mead

In early June 2008 Barack Obama declared himself the Democratic nominee in St. Paul, Minnesota, which would be the home of the Republican National Convention.

> "Tonight I can stand here and say that I will be the Democratic nominee for President of the United States," Obama declared in a speech to a raucous crowd at the Xcel Center in St. Paul, Minn.
>
> Obama went on to praise his Democratic opponents as "the most talented, qualified field of individuals ever to run for this office" and saved

special plaudits for Hillary Rodham Clinton.

He referred to Clinton as "a leader who inspires millions of Americans with her strength, her courage and her commitment to the causes that brought us here tonight."[170]

~

I believe he will change things and change them for the better. He is one of us and always will be. It was not many years earlier he walked among us, soliciting votes for his State Senate campaign, campaigning for Pamela Woodward for State Senate (although she lost), Debbie Halvorson for State Senate (and she won and is now a Congresswoman succeeding Congressman Jerry Weller), his own campaign for Congress (that he lost), and his historical United States Senate victory.

It was not long ago that he knocked on Linda Kozloski and Tom Bohn's door, thanking them for her displaying an Obama sign in their window. Barack Obama is like Michael Jordan hitting the jumper at the buzzer and, for us old-timers, Johnny Unitas, hitting his receiver in the final two minutes. John Elway and Bret Farve would fit too. He is Bill Russell denying Wilt Chamberlain yet another championship.

A winner.

That is the essence of Barack Obama. He learned to win from losing.

And my own life.

As we approached the General Election, we were invited to an old-timer's party in Hyde Park. And as fate would have it, we ran into Al Kindle.

Yes, Al Kindle again.

Al was with Alderwoman Preckwinkle that day, and when we spotted her, Michelle and I said, "Is Al here?"

"He's out on the porch," she said.

When we saw Al he said, "Michelle and John, I need you again. I've been hired to deliver Indiana for Obama, and I would like your help."

I said sheepishly, "I don't suppose you want us to build another 'machine' in Indiana."

"Yes, as a matter of fact, a 'machine.' One more time for Obama."

And that is just what we helped to do. Kindle explained that the Indiana strategy was to deliver big in northwest Indiana, for one thing.

---

170 http://blog.washingtonpost.com/thefix/2008/06/obama_presumptive_nominee.html

He specifically wanted us to go there and recruit people in the most Republican part of northwest Indiana: Schererville, Lowell, St. John's, Merrillville.

How Kindle explained it, "We want to make white people comfortable about voting for Barack Obama. That is where you and Michelle come in. We need you to organize hundreds of people throughout northwest Indiana. We need you to come out of northwest Indiana with a large plurality."

And so we recruited the people who helped Obama in 2004, Shore in 2006, Giannoulias in 2006. People like Brian Murphy, who was the heart and soul of the group. It was Murphy that helped "fire 'em up." Murphy is an engineer for the Chicago Fire Department and poured all of his being into the campaign in Indiana. There was Tom Barber, who Michelle and I met in the early 1990's and he served on the BAPA Safety Committee with us.

We met Mary Baker during this campaign. Mary Baker and her husband, Jeff Brown, bought a house from a previous supporter and volunteer, Meg Lewis-Sidime. Meg is employed by the labor union AFSCME. And Mary is a fine lawyer, moved into the house so we lost one supporter and gained another. Mary had signed on as a volunteer for "Lawyers for Obama," a group that was a watchdog for voter fraud at the precinct level. Mary later volunteered her time and service to the successful Al Franken recount in Minnesota.

There was a feeling in the campaign that many of the leaders and volunteers just did not have enough experience to help deliver Indiana. We fit the bill and put word out about help in northwest Indiana.

And that was just what we did. We made white people comfortable about voting for Barack Obama. To not be afraid. We loved to tell people our Obama stories and the voters, even those who that were undecided, loved to hear the personal stories about Barack Obama. They absolutely loved the Linda Kozlowki story. And how during the 2003 parade he would not bypass anyone in a wheel chair and would spend a couple minutes exchanging pleasantries.

We connected in Schererville with Chief Field Organizer David Campbell (Campbell just like the soup, he would gleefully say), and brought dozens of volunteers there that put in hundreds of hours after

Labor Day. The main job was to identify our voters and then bring them out on Election Day.

And once again, it worked. One last time for Obama. And all of the old-timers in the campaign. We decided not to attend the celebration at Grant Park on Election Night but opted to celebrate our great victory with our new-found friends in northwest Indiana. A Democrat had not won Indiana in 44 years and he was from the south: Lyndon Baines Johnson. And President-elect Obama would become the 44th President of the United States.

My own life was transformed by a book. *Dreams from My Father: A Story of Race and Inheritance.* It was transformed by a bookstore: Reading on Walden Bookstore. A bookstore owner: my wife Michelle, who transformed my life and made my community and my nation a better place to live. 300+plus volunteers and friends who changed our life and the life of a nation. And changed my beloved community. This community transformed my life in a way I can never calculate or can ever measure. And Michelle and I will never forget where we sat through all of this. We had ringside seats to American History.

As my papa might say were he with us now, with a nod from his papa, "America is going to be all right, they just elected Barack Obama." And if he didn't, I will say it, too.

Touché.

Change comes slowly, gradually, incrementally, and suddenly.

Acknowledgments

A special thanks to the entire **Beverly Hills/Morgan Park community** for making our eighteen years as booksellers special.

~

Special thanks to **President Barack Obama**. Our store will be forever identified as "Barack Obama's Bookstore." We were there when the Senator lost in the spring of 2000 and we were there when he won the Democratic primary in the spring of 2004. Winning is better.

~

Ronald Carter who kept us connected to Barack Obama during those dark years, after March 21, 2000 to January 22, 2003.

Dan Shomon for introducing us to **Barack Obama**. And without Dan Shomon, President Barack Obama would not be President Barack Obama today.

Greg Richmond for telling **Dan Shomon** about us, which led to **Barack Obama**.

Dr. Charles Davis – who passed away just after Obama's election to the United States Senate and his wife **Patricia McPhearson-Davis**, who both inspired this group of volunteers.

Jean Holling – our next door neighbor and friend, who owned and operated Floral Designs on 99th Street. Jean helped nurture our love for flowers, plants, and other growing things

Marge Crema - former Mount Greenwood Branch Librarian who was so generous to us.

Joyce Colander - Beverly Branch Librarian, whose generosity and support made us feel special

Eda Shrimple – who helped us find the location for our Walden Parkway Bookstore.

Augie Aleksy, owner of Centuries & Sleuths Bookstore, whose friendship we will always treasure.

Barbara D'Amato, whose love of literature and her generosity with other authors knows no bounds.

Special thanks to **Harvey Mader** who was born in 1916 and still has the passion for life and politics. Harvey was an early endorser and supporter of Senator Paul Wellstone, Congressman Jan Schkowsky and President Barack Obama. Not bad company. Support the best candidate, he always said, providing the candidate is a Democrat, which was Harvey's mantra.

~

The entire **Reading on Walden Book Discussion Group**. We love every one of them.

~

And to some of the members of our group of 300 :

To the **Reading on Walden** "Obama for Illinois" volunteers that later became the **Reading on Walden Political Discussion Group**. Here are some of the 300 volunteers and I apologize to those we missed. These are the people who were part of our grassroots efforts that put up yard and window signs, sent out 'friend cards,' attended meetup meetings, surfed the web on the Yahoo Group for Obama, canvassed door-to-door, passed out brochures, circulated and collected petitions to place Obama on the ballot, made a donation, solicited a donation, worked a polling place, passed out a palm card, and all on behalf of advancing the candidacy of our friend, **President Barack Obama**. Evangelina Allen, Theresa L. Ambuel, Gloria Andrews, Kathleen Baggett, Donald Baird, Candace Baker, Mary Baker, Tom Barber, Ellen Barr, Alfred Barrow, Stephanie Barrow, Nan Barsotti, Joyce Miller Bean, Kyle Bean, Lauren Bean, Cheryl Becker, Dave Becker, Norine Beirne, Chuck Beirne, Barbara Bell, Shirley Bell-Perine, Carol Belshaw, Terence Belshaw, Dave Bieschke, Cheryl Bonner, Bennie Bonner, Deborah P. Bonner, Alana Broady, Kristen Broady, Lisa Brock, Lizzie Brown, Patricia M. Brown, Bob Bruno, Kevin Bryant, Paula Bukacek, Richard F. Bukacek, Marilyn Burke, Connie Burnet, Susan Burnet, Kent Busse, Delores Butler, Danny Butler, Ken Catalanotte, Mary Ellen Channon, Bruce Chenoweth, Pamela Childs-Laughlin, Kelley Clute, Carolyn Collins, Amber Commodore, Shirley Conley, Sheila Conlon, Linda Cooper, Will Cowing, Marcia Cowing, Dawn Dalton, Dr. Charles Davis, Patricia McPhearson-Davis, Keeley Binion, Robert Davis, Benjamin DeBerry, Patricia Deiters, Bill Deiters, John Devens, Julia Devens, Danielle

DeVito, Marco DeVito, Saundra T. Doughery, Roland Dougherty, Ann Duggan, Barbara Duke, Kate Eaton, Carolyn Edmonds, Ensign Ellinger, Bruce Ellinwood, Suzanne Engle, Eileen Fay, Garnet Fay, Samantha Fields, Dorothy Flott, Kay Flynn, Gary Foster, Virginia Foster, Mark Freeman, Capers Funnye, Michael V. Garvey, Joanne Ginger, Paul Ginger, Maurice Givens, William Goddard, Lisa Griffin, Robert Gronko, John Gunn, Lola Gunn, Rashid Halloway, Johnny D. Hampton, Mosea Harris, Becky Healy, Dan Healy, Jane Healy, Christina M. Horde, Mike Horner, Nathan Houston Sr., Janet Howard, Margaret Howard, Shirley Hudson, John H. Lewis III, Lisa Jaburek, Scott Jaburek, Cathey M. Johnson, Joseph Johnson, Linda Johnson, Murray Johnson, Rachel Johnston, Derek Jones, Michelle Jones, Monic Jones, Foster Garvin, Jr., Ed Juillard, Ghanim Kassir, Mary Kassir, Bob Keeley, Kathleen Kennedy, Mary King, Robert Kolkebeck, Mike Kominarek, Trish Kominarek, Kathy Konopasek, Linda Kozloski, Kimberly Lacey, Kevin Lee, La Vern Little, Peggy Love, Georgianne Lucas, Jay Luchsinger, Deborah A. Mabery, Harvey Mader, Pamela Martin, Barbara McBride, Steve McBride, Kelly McCarthy, John McGivney, Terry McMillan, Patricia McNicholas, Sheila McNicholas, Debra Mitchem, Darryl Mollison, Mary Mollison, Caroline Mooney, Timothy Mooney, Dan Moore, Harold Moore, Selles G. Morris, Brian Murphy, Kathleen Murphy, Stephen Nelson, Phil Nieman, Nancy North, Pamela Sims Nunley, Doris Odem, Jerome Oswald, Kathy Fredricks Oswald, Alicia Perla, Betsy Perrine, Joanne Petkus, Leo Petkus, Carole Piller, Simon Piller, Steve Pittman, Neil Pomerenke, Diane Powell, Gertrude Preyar, Robert Raddatz, Lloyd Rice, Laura Richardson, Dorothy Riley, Robert Roehm, Ted Rothon, Brenda Rowland-Redd, Rita Ryan, Joan Sheehy, Meg Lewis Sidime, Lorraine Simpson, Royce Simpson, Nathaniel Smiley, Carol Smith, David Smith, Debra Smith, JoAnne Smith, Pete Sofiyea, Jeri Sparks, Mary Sparks, Bill Spizzirri, Laura Spizzirri, Anna Stange, John Station, Ruby Stevenson, Toni Stewart, Diana Strong, Donald Strong, Sean Sullivan, Roland Swanson, William Swanson, Jim Sweeney, Birgit Sweeney, Marshall Taggart, Jeff Tangel, Kathleen Tangel, Steve Teschner, Marilyn Thibeau, Jeanette Thomas, Steve Thomas, Adrianne Topic, Anna Tuccoli, Larry Unruh, Jim Vaclavik, Barbara Valerious, Robert Vinson, Don Wantanbe, Emma Washington, Evalina Washington, Guidi Weiss, Patricia Wells, Joshua Westbrook, Ronald Wheeler, Judy Wherley,

George White, Marie Whitney, Ellen Wiggins, Gail Williams, Kathleen Williams, Matt Williams, Roger Williams, Rosie Williams, Lenore Wolfe, Lyn Wozniak, Karen Yates, Darryl Young, Andrea Zopp, and a cast of thousands and thousands of dedicated volunteers all across this nation and world.

Our deceased friends:

Neil Pomerenke: A "super" volunteer and a very special friend to Michelle and me, who worked hundreds of hours toward the goal of electing Barack Obama. Obama would often greet Neil at headquarters and every time, Obama would thank Neil for volunteering.

Sheila Doherty McDonald: Who inspired reading in the classroom by purchasing hundreds books from our store and donating them to the St. Barnabas school library.

Jerry Rom: Who inspired students to read in the classroom and was always a joy when he entered our bookstore.

Joseph Meegan: Who inspired me into "Community Organizing."

Gerry Hayes: Who taught at the St. Xavier Class Renaissance Center and promoted literature.

Julia Martin: The author of "What's Julia Reading?"

Nancy Lyons Byrne: former Beverly Branch Librarian, who passed away in November of 2006. It was Nancy who connected the library with the community and made it one.

Obama for Congress, 2000 campaign:
The Agony of Defeat

Sunday, March 12, 2000, Southside Irish parade. Then Illinois State Senator Barack Obama marching in the 2000 Southside Irish parade. Barack Obama immediately recognized us both although
we had just met. He has a great memory for names and faces. He shouted out our names and then
pointed at us just as I was shooting this photo. Obama is wearing a green hat and a green 'Obama
sticker' in honor of the Southside Irish St. Patrick's Day parade. He will likely be known as the
'green' President.

Our first Obama event: The Meet and Greet Fundraiser
at Café Luna, March 13, 2000

A small crowd had gathered here but the majority
were elected officials. This was our first photo with
Obama. It was on this night Michelle and I became
convinced he would one day become President of
the United States. It was the second time we heard
him speak, and he was electrifying. He was terrific
one-on-one. Still is. The concept of TKHITLH (to
know him is to love him) came about that evening
for me. Left to right, John Presta, Barack Obama
and Michelle Presta.

Barack Obama is talking to a small group,
including Jeff Dixon (standing to the left of
Obama). Jeff's father is former Illinois Senator Alan Dixon. Senator Alan Dixon was defeated in the 1992 Democratic primary by
Carol Mosley Braun, who was elected as the
second African-American Senator (the first
Democrat) since Reconstruction.

Obama campaign manager Dan Shomon and Jim Sweeney.

Barack Obama addressing the small gathering at Café Luna.

From left to right, Dan Shomon (standing), Robert "Bob" Bruno and Barack Obama. You will notice that Dan and Bob have the Obama for Congress buttons and to the bottom right is an "Obama for Congress" sign. I placed the sign in Bob's yard that evening, and he was one of the first on his block to get one. After the defeat Bob told me, "Whatever he runs for, I want to be the first to get a yard sign." And Bob told me repeatedly over the years, "That guy's going places" and several times told me, "He's gonna be President one day."

Obama concedes the 2000 Congressional election to Incumbent Congressman Bobby Rush with Michelle and Malia, March 21, 2000. (ASSOCIATED PRESS PHOTO/FRANK POLICH).

We put up our Obama for Congress sign in our yard. A lonely sign for the Obama for Congress race. The typical reaction was "Who?"

Obama for Senate: The beginning, the summer and fall of 2003, getting ready for launch

State Senator Barack Obama, D-Chicago, announced his candidacy for U.S. Senate on Tuesday, January 21, 2003. Among those attending: State Senator and Lake County Democrat Chairman Terry Link, former Chicago Bears star Chris Zorich, Obama, Congressman Danny Davis, State Senator Jacquelyn Collins, and Senate President Emil Jones.

Our July 2003 World Folk Music Fundraiser

In June 2003, John Presta holding up the invitation to the July 2003 World Folk Music Fundraiser.

July 2003 parade in Evergreen Park, IL. Dan Shomon (second from left) with other parade marchers. We were all instructed to return the Obama shirts after the parade so they could be re-used. Michelle and I still have ours.

July 2003 parade in Evergreen Park. This is me showing the Obama for Senate sign and behind me is the Obama parade car that followed us along the route.

July 2003 parade in Evergreen Park.Michelle Presta, Barack Obama, and John Presta (me.)

John Devens preparing the stage for musician Tricia Alexander. Devens' band, *Dyed in the Wool*, played prior to Obama's arrival.

Lauren Bean adjusting the balloons in last-minute preparations for the arrival of Barack Obama. Lauren designed all the balloon bouquets and decorations for the event.

The balloons were decorated with brochures and buttons from the campaign of Obama for Senate.

Joyce Miller Bean in last-minute preparations for the arrival of Barack Obama.

Barack Obama addressing the crowd with his famous stump speech.

I had just introduced Barack Obama as the next United States Senator from Illinois. And he was.

Michelle Presta, Judy Wherley, and Robert Roehm, all wearing their Obama for Senator buttons.

Barack Obama and Robert Roehm. Roehm later used this photo on his 2008 Christmas card.

Robert Gronko getting his book autographed by Barack Obama. In the background are Robert Roehm and Garnet Fay.

Tony Stewart and Barack Obama.

Mary Sparks and Barack Obama.

Garnet Fay posing with Barack Obama.

This is one of my favorites: I call it "Meet the Beans." Barack Obama, Lauren Bean, Joyce Miller Bean, and Kyle Bean.

Left to right: Barack Obama, Birgit Sweeney, and Jim Sweeney.

Robert Davis and Barack Obama.

Barack Obama and Shirley Conley.

Left to right: Dawn Dalton, Barack Obama, and Rita Ryan.

Barack Obama and Laura Richardson.

Barack Obama and Mary Elen Channon. Mary Ellen learned about this event because she was our book rep for St. Martin's Press. And, of course, she is one of our favorite reps.

Barack Obama and Linda Cooper. Linda owned Café Luna at the time, and, after the fundraiser, Obama and campaign staffer Nate Tamarin had an early dinner at Linda's place.

Barack Obama was surprised to see Ronald Carter at this event, and Obama had no idea that Ron and I were close friends. Ron is the publisher of the *South Street Journal*.

And this is Barack Obama, Michelle Presta, and John Presta (me).

Left to right: Barack Obama, Julia Devens and John Devens. John owned and operated World Folk Music at the time and quickly agreed to hold the fundraiser there.

Left to right: John Gunn, Lula Gunn, and Barack Obama. John and Lula are tireless community activists and have made our great community a better place to live.

Team Obama Democrat Day 2003. In this photo: Juleigh Nowinski, Jim Cauley, Nate Tamarin, Dave Feller, Dan Shomon, Liz Drew, Lauren Kidwell.

Larry Unruh, a bicycle enthusiast, during the primary campaign. Some more great marketing. Larry was relentless in his work and support of Obama.

Larry Unruh, a bicycle enthusiast, during the primary campaign.

Some more great marketing. Kathy Konopasek's house that could be seen everyday for a year from the Metra train by thousands of people.

Obama for Senate, Spring 2004:
Ready for Launch on the Launch Pad

Another Obama for Illinois meeting on Wednesday, February 11, 2004. Left to right; Garnet Fay and Larry Unruh.

On Monday, February 23, 2004, just a short time to election day, we are passing out Obama brochures at the 111th Street Metra station. Left to right; Michelle Presta, Joanne Petkus and Neil Pomerenke.

Reading on Walden Political Group
Obama for Illinois meeting, February 25, 2004

That is me holding up an Obama sign. The demand for yard signs at this point was growing stronger by the day.

Left to right: Reverend Lawrence Blackful Jr., and John Devens.

That is left to right; Caroline Mooney, Rebecca Mooney and John Presta (me).

Rebecca Mooney sitting next to the Obama sign.

Michelle and I attended an event at Liberty Baptist Church on Tuesday, March 9th, 2004 called "Come by Ten," where Obama spoke. It was a rally that was held at Liberty Baptist Church located at 4849 S. King Drive. By the time it started, it was SRO (Standing Room Only).

Obama for Illinois meeting, March 10, 2004

Another Obama for Illinois meeting on Wednesday, March 10, 2004. Left to right; Steve Pittman and Dr. Charles Davis.

At our Obama for Illinois meeting on Wednesday, March 10, 2004. Left to right; Patricia McPhearson-Davis, Will Cowing, and Candace Baker.

At our March 10, 2004 meeting. Left to right; Neil Pomerenke, Linda Cooper and Susan Burnet. Susan had been instrumental in helping organize the "candidates' forum" in 2000.

Primary Election Victory Party, March 17, 2004

Leo and Joanne Petkus. Two dear friends and passionate activists.

Joanne Petkus and Gloria Andrews.

David Mader and his father, Harvey Mader. It is difficult to read, but Harvey is wearing a button of his friend, Senator Paul Wellstone. And it is a "Wellstone for President" button.

Left to right, Toni Stewart, Neil Pomerenke and Garnet Fay.

The Obama victory party, March 17, 2004. Toni Stewart, Pete 'I Want to Make History with You' Sofiyea, and Neil Pomerenke.

Susan Burnet, Toni Stewart, and Larry Unruh.

The Obama victory party, March 17, 2004. Left to right; John Presta (me), Ghanim Kassir, Mary Kassir and Lyn Wozniak.

Alfred Barrow and Toni Stewart.

Saundra and Roland Dougherty.

Roland Swanson and John Presta (me).

Pete 'I Want to Make History with You' Sofiyea, Darryl Young, and Steve Pittman.

Left to right, Dr. Charles Davis, Patricia McPhearson-Davis, Saundra Dougherty and Roland Dougherty.

John Presta announcing the election precinct
results.

Alana and Kristen Broady.

Carol Smith and David Smith.

Garnet Fay, Harvey Mader, and John Presta (me).

Left to right, Larry Unruh, Robert Davis and Susan Burnet.

John Presta, Larry Unruh and Robert Davis.

We were thrilled when Reverend Lawrence Blackful brought his family to our victory party. Come and meet the Blackfuls: from left to right, Keisha Blackful, Lavonte Blackful, Lawrence Blackful Jr., Keila Blackful, and Lawrence Blackful III.

Left to right, Robert Davis, Susan Burnet and Harvey Mader. Sitting with his back to the camera is Maurice Givens.

The display window of Reading on Walden, the day after Barack Obama won the 2004 Democratic primary, March 18, 2004. Balloons were by Jean Holling of 'Floral Designs on 99th Street,' our neighbor and friend. Barack Obama was now on his way.

Two of our favorite volunteers, Ghanim and Mary Kassir, attended the opening of the Matteson office on Saturday, January 3, 2004. Here they pose with Barack Obama and Jesse Jackson Jr. We didn't meet the Kassirs until March of 2004, but what an impact these two dedicated people had on the campaign. (PHOTO COURTESY OF GHANIM AND MARY KASSIR)

Obama for Senate, Summer 2004:
Launched into Space

In early August of 2004, the "book" was re-released. The book, *Dreams from My Father*, had been out-of-print for many years. Now the book was brought back to life and immediately climbed the bestseller list. Oh, and so did Barack Obama, the political candidate.

Nate Tamarin posing at Trinity
United prior to 'The Speech.'

The CSPAN production man on the left and behind him seated
is Mike Jordan.

This is the group personally invited to view what is now known as 'The Speech.' Prior to the
speech we had no way of knowing that he would hit it out of the park. Far left, first row is Michael
Jordan. Michelle and I are in the middle. We were welcomed by the Trinity United Church con-
gregation with open arms.

Our store sold many political titles. This is June 23, 2004. The Obama book was still out-of-print
at this point, but several months later was re-released and zoomed up the *New York Times* bestseller list.

The Obama Birthday Party

It's a birthday party for Barack Obama. On August 4th, 2004 Obama celebrated his 43rd birthday at the Holiday Inn in Matteson, Illinois. Over a thousand of his closest friends came that evening. Toni Stewart and Barbara Duke.

Toni Stewart and Michelle Presta.

Michelle Presta and Shirley Bell-Perine.

The Obama family blowing out the candles.

Obama is flanked by some of his friends. State Senate President Emil Jones (left of Obama) and Larry Walsh (right of Obama). On the far left is Congressman Jesse Jackson Jr., State Senator Maggie Crotty is on the left holding the small Obama sign.

The crowd is going wild here as he thanks supporters for taking that "leap of faith" as he called it.

Left to right, Jesse Jackson Jr. at the microphone, State Senate President Emil Jones, Michelle Obama and Barack Obama.

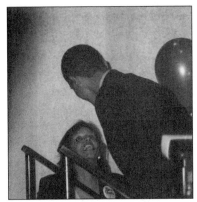

Here is Barack climbing onto the stage and greeting his friend, State Representative Robin Kelly. Robin is chief of staff to Alexi Giannoulias as of the pub date and is now a candidate for Illinois State Treasurer.

Barack Obama clapping, with his daughter, Malia Obama.

Jesse Jackson Jr. introducing the elected officials on the stage.

Left to right, Jesse Jackson Jr., Emil Jones, Michelle Obama, Malia Obama (hidden) and Barack Obama.

Michelle Obama, Malia Obama and Barack Obama.

Michelle Obama and Barack Obama.

The Fall 2004 Campaign

This photo is the staff in the Fall 2004 of the Will County Obama/Coordinated Campaign. In the front row left to right is Scott Ickis (field coordinator), Dianne Waller-Nyman (office manager), Chris Lunningham (assistant office manager), Rebecca (Price) Piper (GOTV coordinator), and Dan Shomon. Doug Price and Barack Obama in the top row.

In this Nov. 2, 2004 file photo, Illinois Senator-elect Barack Obama, holds Malia, and his wife Michelle, holds Sasha, and are covered in confetti after Obama delivered his acceptance speech in Chicago. Obama was only the fifth black U.S. Senator to be elected in history.
(ASSOCIATED PRESS/M. SPENCER GREEN)

Senate Election Victory Party

Left to right, Toni Stewart, Michelle Presta and Barbara Duke.

Two of the volunteers helping us celebrate his victory in the General Election. Tyler Hewitt, left, and Kevin Lee, right.

Some of our committed volunters.

Michelle is holding the "Election Results" for the precincts we worked.

The aftermath.

Here is Michelle holding up the election results for the 19th Ward

Here is one of our favorite volunteers, Lyn Wozniak, who wrote the wonderful diaries that brought life to this book. Lyn was wearing a hat from the Obama campaign that said, "A Job is Homeland Security."

2005, 2006 and 2007: Well into Orbit
2008: into His Own Orbit

Vice President Dick Cheney, right, administers the Senate oath to Sen. Barack Obama, D-Ill., left, during a mock swearing-in on Capitol Hill Tuesday, Jan. 5, 2005 as his wife Michelle, center and children, Malia, front left, and Sasha look on. (ASSOCIATED PRESS/LAWRENCE JACKSON)

The Debra Shore/Alexi Giannoulias Campaigns

Our friend Debra Shore.

(Photo courtesy of Debra Shore)
Debra Shore, Barack Obama and Nancy Segal.

Debra Shore visited the Reading on Walden Political Discussion Group for the first time on October 5, 2005. She was a big hit that evening. Steve Thomas heads a band called the Beverly All-Stars and plays jazz in the community every Wednesday.

Lyn Wozniak, Neil Pomerenke and Larry Unruh.

Debra Shore addressing the Reading on Walden Political Discussion Group.

Kathy Fredricks and Michelle Presta.

We had a great time and gathered a lot of petitions on November 12, 2005. Here is Neil Pomerenke and Debra Shore.

Petition Filing Day

Kathleen Kennedy and Michelle Presta in Springfield filing petitions.

Michelle meets Alexi in Springfield on "petition day."

Alexi Giannoulias' Fundraiser at the Funky Buddha

Dan Shomon invited us to a Giannoulias fundraiser at Funky Buddha's on December 29, 2005. John Presta (me), Dan Shomon, and Michelle Presta.

He is speaking to the crowd gathered. That is James Seaberry on the left, Alexi in the middle and Steven Thomas on the right.

Alexi Giannoulias and Larry Unruh no doubt debating an issue.

Alderman Manny Flores (1st Ward) is introducing his friend, Alexi Giannoulias.

Alexi Giannoulias and Debra Shore Visit the Reading on Walden Political Discussion Group, February 1, 2006

Wednesday, February 1, 2006 all the candidates we were supporting came to this meeting. Left to right, Alexi Giannoulias, Debra Shore, John Sullivan and Circuit Court Judge Kathleen Kennedy. Judge Kathleen Kennedy, a candidate for the Illinois Appellate Court in Cook County, in 2006 ran a highly ethical campaign, raising money only from family and friends in order to avoid the appearance of impropriety. Judge Kennedy can hold her head up high, and so can we for supporting her, and I hope one day she will sit on the Appellate Court. I support the Judicial Campaign Reform Act, which was introduced in the Illinois legislature would create a voluntary program of public financing of election campaigns for the offices of judges of the Illinois Supreme and Appellate Courts and set mandatory contribution limits on all judicial election campaigns.

Alexi Giannoulias addressing the crowd. Circuit Court Judge Kathleen Kennedy is in the background.

Debra Shore addressing the group. Circuit Court Judge Kathleen Kennedy is in the background.

Anna Giannoulias and Michelle Presta on the day of Alexi Giannoulias' announcement for U.S. Senate.

From left to right: Newly elected Commissioners of the MWRD in 2006 are Patricia Horton and Debra Shore. In the middle is Metropolitan Water Reclamation District (MWRD) President Terrence J. O'Brien.

Senator Obama attending Book Expo to promote his new book, *Audacity of Hope*. May, 2006.

The Presidential Campaign
The Iowa Caucuses

We took a trip through Iowa at the end of October, 2007 and persuaded these two staffers to pose for us. Photo in Cedar Rapids Iowa.

And they took a photo of us.

The last time we saw him in person. Highland, Indiana on October 31, 2008, Halloween. We were only 100 feet from him but we might as well have been 100 miles away. The place was jammed and rocking that night as 40,000 of his closest friends attended.

Winning Indiana for Obama

Prior to the Presidential election, we got together to strategize about how we can win Indiana. Illinois was a given, but Indiana would be uphill and next to impossible. We nudged it out by a handful of votes and northwest Indiana (where we and thousands of volunteers worked) was the difference. Left to right, Will Cowing, Donald Baird, Larry Unruh, Sheena Patton, Mike Jordan (the real one), Daniel Moore, Michelle Presta, John Presta (me), Caroline Mooney, Robert Davis, Tom Barber and Carol Belshaw. Caroline Mooney is the owner of the Blue Moon Coffeehouse where we hold our monthly meetings for the Reading on Walden Political Discussion Group.

Obama addressing the crowd in Highland Indiana on October 31, 2008.

Our own Brian Murphy, a retired Chicago fireman and dedicated community volunteer, "firing 'em up." He kept the group inspired throughout the hard-fought campaign and has always been an inspiration to Michelle and me.

As Obama is leaving the stage in Highland Indiana, the joy is written all over his face. If Obama can carry Indiana, with a big boost from northwest Indiana and a big boost once again from Illinois volunteers, Obama would be the first Democrat to win Indiana since LBJ won it in 1964.

Brian Murphy, Michelle Presta and John Presta awaiting election results.

David Campbell jumps for joy as he learns of the hard-earned victory in Indiana, the first time in 44 years a Democrat won Indiana. And Campbell was a key.

Sherry Stewart, Office Manager and Chief Inspirer at the Schererville Indiana office, tells it all. Complete joy at the victory of our next President of the United States.

The group of dedicated volunteers in Indiana are doing a victory dance.

Illinois State Treasurer Alexi Giannoulias being interviewed by the media on the day of his announcement
for U.S. Senate.

Illinois State Treasurer Alexi Giannoulias announcing for US Senate.

Mike Jordan discussing Indiana strategy with members of the Reading on Walden Political Discussion Group.

Tom Barber next to, ah, oh a cardboard
cutout of Obama. That is the best we can
do these days.

Mike Jordan (the real one), Holly Davis and her dad
Robert Davis.

Health care reform rally.

Robert Roehm and Judy Wherley's 2008 Christmas card, showing photo of Robert and Obama from the 2003 World Folk Music Fundraiser.

Michelle is forever the activist. Health care is a burning issue for Michelle and me. And we hope for the country.

President Barack Obama and First Lady Michelle Obama dancing at the Biden Home States Delaware/Pennsylvania Inaugural Ball, 1/20/09, in Washington, DC. (Photo taken by the publisher who had the vision to publish this book--Sheilah Vance, President & CEO of The Elevator Group.)

INDEX

Appendix

1ˢᵗ Congressional District Democratic Candidate Forum
Tuesday, March 7, 2000
7 p.m. – 8:30 p.m.
Candidate Questions

1. What plans do you have to reduce vehicular emissions and vehicular traffic and at the same time would you support a massive mass transit construction program that benefit Chicago and its surrounding suburbs and lessen the dependency on our highways?

2. Are the gun control laws now in place adequate and are they being enforced to your satisfaction? What kind of legislation are you proposing or would you propose for more effective gun control?

3. Do you believe it is important for the community-at-large to have accessibility to the 1st District Congressman from Illinois and how would you work to maintain and improve accessibility of the community to the Congressional Office?

4. HUD was started to encourage home ownership. That goal has not always been achieved. What solution would you propose that would fix HUD and place it back on track with its true mission?

5. An attempt was made during the first years of the Clinton Administration to get consensus on some kind of health care reform. That attempt failed, and the number of people uninsured in the U.S. has now grown to an estimated 44 million. What kind of health care reform plan would you support?

6. What role do you think the federal government can and should play in the funding of domestic violence and sexual assault victim services?

7. During the last few years, cost-saving measures by the U.S. Postal Service resulted in the removal of a large number of mailboxes in our area. We are concerned that rounds of service cuts may become a routine, leading eventually to justification for privatizing the postal service. Would you support a larger Federal subsidy for the postal service, or do you think privatization may be a solution?

8. In general, do you think that economic sanctions are an effective foreign policy tool? Specifically, do you think that the economic sanctions now in place against Iraq and the Cuban embargo are serving a purpose and should stand, or should they be lifted?

9. What do you think have been the positive and negative effects of the North American Free Trade Agreement (NAFTA) on large businesses; small businesses; U.S. workers; foreign workers? In view of this, would you vote for or against NAFTA if it were proposed today?

10. How do you propose to lessen the time that railroad trains block grade crossings and how you deal with the inherent conflict of requiring "whistle blowing" versus "safety concerns?"

11. Will you please tell us something about how your campaign is financed: What do you expect this campaign to cost? What proportion of your campaign funds are from private donations? From corporations and businesses? From public sources? What are the relative proportions of funds that come from inside vs. outside the district?

12. What kind of campaign finance reform would you support? Please say whether you would restrict or prohibit contributions from any particular source.

13. Would you advocate any changes to the current income tax structure? Please include in your answer personal and corporate income taxes as well as social security taxes on wages.

14. Would you favor privatization of social security?

15. Should sales and other transactions conducted on the internet be taxed? What do you see as the impact of tax-free internet sales on state and local governments to maintain current levels of service?

16. What do you think is the proper role of the federal government in public education today?

17. Under what conditions would you approve sending troops to foreign lands?

18. Would you favor raising the "minimum wage" to a level closer to a "living wage?"

19. Do you think that Federal spending on drug enforcement should be increased, decreased, or reallocated? Where should the emphasis on efforts be?

20. What federal money or programs would you access to reinvigorating the 95th Street Shopping District (from Western to Ashland), the so-called "Quality Mile."

21. Would you support federal funding for the construction of a bike path along the Rock Island/Metra line serving the south side and the south suburbs?

1st Congressional District Democratic Candidate Forum
Sponsored by
East Beverly Association, League of Women Voters of Chicago, Citizens Information Service

Tuesday, March 7, 2000, 7 p.m. – 8:30 p.m.
Bethany Union Church

Rules and Format

Format

1. <u>Races</u>: The 1st Congressional District Democratic Party position will be part of the Forum. All Democratic Candidates properly filing their candidacy with the Illinois State Board of Elections were invited.
2. <u>Moderator</u>: Carol Maier, President, Board of Directors, League of Women Voters of Chicago (LWV).
3. <u>Timekeeping</u>: EBA will conduct timekeeping. A sign will be raised to notify candidates when their time limit has been reached.
4. <u>Announcements and Introductions</u>: EBA will have one-minute to thank people for attending, introduce attending public officials and offer gratitude for the various persons assisting with the forum planning. CIS will have one-minute to educate the audience about their voter services. CIS will introduce the moderator. The LWV moderator will outline the format and rules for the forum. The LWV moderator will introduce the candidates.
5. <u>Forum Order</u>: The doors open at 6:30 p.m. The forum will begin promptly at 7 p.m.
6. <u>Time</u>: One hour and fifteen minutes (1:15) will be provided for the race.
7. <u>Opening Statements</u>: Two minutes per candidates selected randomly by the moderator prior to the start of the forum. Opening statements should focus on biographical information.
8. <u>Questions</u>: Questions were compiled by East Beverly Association in cooperation with local community groups. These questions will be circulated to the candidates by March 1, 2000. Candidate responses will be on a rotating first response basis. Responses can be no longer than one-minute in length.
9. <u>Questions from the Audience</u>: There will be no questions selected from the audience.
10. <u>Closing Statements</u>: Two minutes per candidates selected randomly by the moderator prior to the start of the forum.
11. <u>Total length of candidate statement/questions</u>: 2 minute opening,1 minute response per question, and 3 minute closing.

Rules

1. <u>Candidates' promotional materials</u>: A table will be provided outside the auditorium for candidate materials. Candidate banners cannot be hung in the building or the auditorium. Candidates' signs cannot be displayed within the auditorium nor may candidate materials be passed out inside the auditorium.

2. <u>Community organization promotion materials</u>: A table will be provided outside the auditorium for community organization materials. Community organization signs or banners may be displayed on the stage as agreed by LWV, EBA and CIS. Community organizational materials may not be passed out inside the auditorium. LWV, EBA and CIS will make a joint statement that any protestors are not from either organization.

3. <u>Audience seating</u>: There will be no assigned seating for candidate staffers, LWV, EBA, or CIS board members or the press.

Checklist

1. <u>Length of Forum/Questions</u>:

   → EBA/CIS President – 1 minute each – <u>total 2 minutes</u>
   → LWV Moderator – <u>total 5 minutes</u>
   → Candidate Opening Statement – 2 minutes each – <u>total 6-8 minutes</u>
   → Candidate Question/Answer – 30 seconds per question, 1 minute per response – <u>total 3.5 to 4.5 minutes each</u>
      • With 3 candidates there will be time for 20 questions – <u>total 70 minutes</u>
      • With 4 candidates there will be time for 14 questions – <u>total 63 minutes</u>
   → Candidate Closing Statement – 2 minutes each – <u>total 6-8 minutes</u>
   → Length of forum for 3 candidates is 89 minutes; for 4 candidates is 86 minutes

2. <u>Moderator</u>: Carol Maier, President, League of Women Voters of Chicago.
3. <u>Timekeeping</u>: EBA will keep time. LWV will provide a stop watch and time signs.
4. <u>Welcome Tables</u>: Tables will provided at the entrance to the auditorium for candidate and community organization materials.
5. <u>Security</u>: The local police will be present at the event.
6. <u>Signage</u>: CIS and LWV will place signage on the stage.
7. <u>Miscellaneous</u>: Candidates will be provided water.

COMING IN 2010 FROM THE ELEVATOR GROUP

Dining with the Dollar Diva by Elizabeth Fisher (March)

Treasures of the Museum (a children's book) by Deborra Richardson, Chair, Archives Center, Smithsonian Institute Museum of American History (June)

Cousin Myrtle, a novel, by P.J. McCalla (August)

Five Keys to Navigating the Land Mines of Divorce by Sheilah Vance (August)

ALSO AVAILABLE FROM THE ELEVATOR GROUP

Land Mines, a novel, by Sheilah Vance

Journaling Through the Land Mines by Sheilah Vance

Chasing the 400, a novel, by Sheilah Vance

Soul Poems: Life as Fertile Ground by Melodye Micëre Van Putten

Obamatyme: Election Poetry by Melodye Micëre Van Putten

A Student's Guide to Being Happy in Argentina by Hope Lewis

Heads Deacon, Tails Devil, a novel, by P.J. McCalla

AND FROM THE ELEVATOR GROUP FAITH

A Christian Woman's Journal to Weight Loss:
A 52 Week Guide to Losing Weight With the Word
by Patricia Thomas

Creativity for Christians: How to Tell Your Story and Stories of
Overcoming by the Members of One Special Church
by Sheilah Vance with Rev. Felicia Howard (June 2010)

For more information about the books above,
see www.TheElevatorGroup.com or contact us at:

ELEVATOR GROUP
• PUBLISHING •

Helping People Rise Above™

The Elevator Group,
PO Box 207 • Paoli, PA 19301
610-296-4966 (p)610-644-4436 (f)
info@TheElevatorGroup.com